T0132646

FLUID ENGINE DEVELOPMENT

FLUID ENGINE DEVELOPMENT

DOYUB KIM

CRC Press
Taylor & Francis Group
Boca Raton London New York

CRC Press is an imprint of the
Taylor & Francis Group, an **informa** business

AN A K PETERS BOOK

CRC Press
Taylor & Francis Group
6000 Broken Sound Parkway NW, Suite 300
Boca Raton, FL 33487-2742

Printed on acid-free paper
Version Date: 20161019

International Standard Book Number-13: 978-1-4987-1992-6 (Pack - Book and Ebook)

Library of Congress Cataloging-in-Publication Data

Names: Kim, Doyub, author.
Title: Fluid engine development / Doyub Kim.
Description: Boca Raton : Taylor & Francis, a CRC title, part of the Taylor & Francis imprint, a member of the Taylor & Francis Group, the academic division of T&F Informa, plc, [2017] | Includes bibliographical references and index.
Identifiers: LCCN 2016028981 | ISBN 9781498719926 (hardback : acid-free paper)
Subjects: LCSH: Hydrodynamics--Data processing. | Fluids--Computer simulation.
Classification: LCC QA911 .K485 2017 | DDC 532.00285/66--dc23
LC record available at https://lccn.loc.gov/2016028981

Visit the Taylor & Francis Web site at
http://www.taylorandfrancis.com

and the CRC Press Web site at
http://www.crcpress.com

To my wife.

Contents

Preface

Fluid animation is a complex problem. Solving fluid dynamics is considered to be one of the most challenging problems in mathematics [58], but at the same time, the beauty of its complexity has influenced many developers and researchers in a variety of domains including visual effects in feature films [22], interactive games, AR/VR applications, and even media arts. However, the complexity of fluid dynamics often overwhelms new learners; even a person with great programming skills and mathematical knowledge often gets lost in the equations and struggles to find where to begin.

The goal of this book is to provide a headfirst starting point for a novice to build a fluid simulation engine. The main audiences for this book are visual effects engineers, game developers, media artists, and any curious students/hackers who lack deep knowledge and experience in numerical analysis or computational fluid dynamics. This book will cover the most classical and commonly used technologies with codes to help interested minds learn fluid dynamics and write their own engine. Once readers get used to the idea of simulating fluid dynamics, they will be able to extend the codebase to solve more sophisticated and unique problems.

Most of the core algorithms will be explained from a developer's perspective. Rather than abstract theories, practical and concrete code examples will be provided. The essential mathematics won't be omitted, and if necessary, in-depth details will be explained. After finishing this book, readers will be able to understand how each part of the engine works and write a working fluid simulation engine. This book, however, is not a collection of code snippets or an application programming interface (API) document. The purpose of this developer-friendly presentation is to deliver the idea of fluid engine algorithms as painlessly as possible and not to provide a black-box library.

This book comprises four major chapters. The first chapter covers the basics. It explains the main steps for writing a simulation code, such as vector and matrix operations and the concept of physics animation. Then the following two chapters introduce two major paradigms of simulating fluids – particles and grids. Those two methods have distinct features and clear pros and cons, and we will discuss these topics with various kinds of models and solvers within those two chapters. Finally, the idea of combining the two frameworks will be introduced with different hybrid methods in the final chapter.

I hope this book will inspire readers and help them build their own fluid engine or utilize the accompanied codebase to their applications. Even after this book is published, the source code will keep evolving with more feature additions and improvements. I also hope that the code repository at http://github.com/doyubkim/fluid-engine-dev becomes a place where the readers interact and share their ideas.

List of Figures

1

Basics

This chapter covers the most fundamental topics that will frequently be referred throughout the book. Before anything else, a minimal fluid simulator will be introduced to bring a basic understanding of building a simulation engine. We will then start building up the foundation for mathematical and geometric operations that are commonly used in this book. This chapter will also introduce the core concept of computer-generated animations as well as its implementation, which will then evolve to the physics-based animation. Finally, the general process of simulating fluid flow will be introduced at the end of the chapter.

1.1 Hello, Fluid Simulator

In this section, we will implement the simplest fluid simulator in this book. This minimal example may not be fancy at all, but it will cover the key ideas of the fluid simulation engine end to end. It is self-contained and doesn't depend on any other libraries other than the standard C++ library. Although we haven't discussed anything about the simulation yet, this hello-world example will provide insight into how to approach to writing a fluid engine code. The only prerequisite for this is some knowledge on C++ and ability to run it on a command line tool.

The goal of the example is simple: to simulate two traveling waves in a one-dimensional (1D) world as shown in Figure 1.1. When a wave hits the end of the container, it will bounce back to the opposite direction.

1.1.1 Defining State

Before we start coding, let's step back and imagine how we would describe the waves with code. At a given time, a wave is located at a certain position with its speed as illustrated in Figure 1.2. Also, as shown in the figure, the final shape can be constructed from the wave positions. Therefore, the state of a wave can be simply defined as a pair of the position and speed. Since we have two waves, we need two pairs of states. Extremely straightforward and nothing complicated.

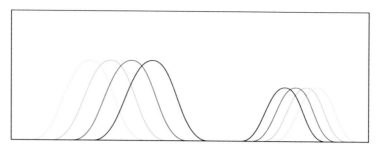

FIGURE 1.1
Simple 1D wave animation. Two different waves are moving back and forth.

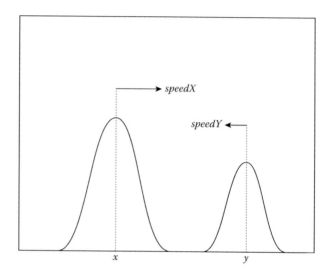

FIGURE 1.2
State of the two waves are described by their positions and speeds.

Now, it's time to code. Consider the following:

```
#include <cstdio>

int main() {
    double x = 0.0;
    double y = 1.0;
    double speedX = 1.0;
    double speedY = -0.5;

    return 0;
}
```

When naming the variables, we will use alphabet X to refer one of the waves and Y for the other one. As shown in the code, initial values assigned to those variables tells us that wave X starts from the left-most side (`double x = 0.0`) and travels to the right with 1.0 speed (`double speedX = 1.0`). Similarly, wave Y starts from the right-most side (`double y = 1.0`) and travels to the left (`double speedY = -0.5`) with half of the magnitude of wave X's speed.

Note that we just defined the "states" of the simulation using four variables which are the most crucial steps when designing a simulation engine. In this particular example, the simulation state is simply the positions and velocities of the waves. But in more complex systems, it is often implemented with a collection of various data structures. Thus, identifying the quantity to keep track of during the simulation is very important as well as finding the right data structure for storing the data. Once the data model is defined, the next step is to bring the life to it.

1.1.2   Computing Motion

To make the waves move, we should define "time". See the following code:

```
1   #include <cstdio>
2
3   int main() {
4       double x = 0.0;
5       double y = 1.0;
6       double speedX = 1.0;
7       double speedY = -0.5;
8
9       const int fps = 100;
10      const double timeInterval = 1.0 / fps;
11
12      for (int i = 0; i < 1000; ++i) {
13          // Update waves
14      }
15      return 0;
16  }
```

The code just got doubled in length, but still quite straightforward. First of all, the new variable `fps` stands for "frames-per-second (FPS)", and it defines how many frames we want to draw for each second. If we invert this FPS value, which is seconds-per-frame, we get time interval between the two frames. Right now, we set `fps` to 100 in the code. That means the interval between two frames is 0.01 seconds, which is stored as a separate variable `timeInterval`.

After initializing the new variables, we define a loop which iterates 1000 times at Line 12. Within this loop, we are now going to actually move wave X and Y. But before we fill in the loop, let's write the following function right above the main function.

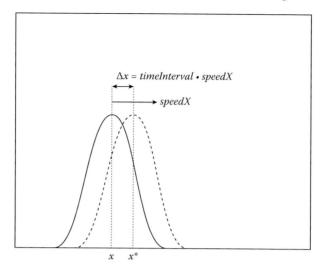

FIGURE 1.3
Image showing the translation of the wave from x to x^* after small time interval. The displacement Δx is equal to time interval $\times$ speed.

```
1    void updateWave(const double timeInterval, double* x, double* speed) {
2        (*x) += timeInterval * (*speed);
3    }
```

This function is just a single-liner but does an interesting thing. It takes the time interval and current center position of a wave. It also takes the speed of the wave as a parameter and multiply that to update the position of the wave. Thus, this code slightly translates the wave's position x for the given time duration, as shown in Figure 1.3, and the amount of that update depends on how fast it is (`speed`) and how long it moved (`timeInterval`). Also, the direction of the motion depends on the sign of `speed`.

This incremental update is how most of the physics simulation evolves the states of the system over time. As shown in the code, it updates the state by accumulation, or in other words, integration. The amount of integration per function call is the change rate of a physical quantity multiplied by time interval. This is actually one of the simplest ways of solving differential equation with computers, and we can describe many physical systems with differential equations. Thus, the idea behind this single line of code will persist throughout the book.

1.1.3   Boundary Handling

We now understand how to move the waves, but what if they hit the walls? The following code extends the code above to handle such a wall-hitting case by reflecting the wave to the opposite direction.

```
1   void updateWave(const double timeInterval, double* x, double* speed) {
2       (*x) += timeInterval * (*speed);
3
4       // Boundary reflection
5       if ((*x) > 1.0) {
6           (*speed) *= -1.0;
7           (*x) = 1.0 + timeInterval * (*speed);
8       } else if ((*x) < 0.0) {
9           (*speed) *= -1.0;
10          (*x) = timeInterval * (*speed);
11      }
12  }
```

After calculating the candidate position at the beginning of the function, the code first flips the sign of the speed if the new position is beyond the wall. It then recalculates the new position starting from the wall position. This is one of the simplest ways of handling wall reflection, but you can also design more sophisticated logic to detect and resolve collisions. The code is there to show the general idea on how to approach the problem. Anyway, now we can call this function `updateWave` from the main loop like this:

```
1   #include <cstdio>
2
3   void updateWave(const double timeInterval, double* x, double* speed) {
4       (*x) += timeInterval * (*speed);
5
6       // Boundary reflection
7       if ((*x) > 1.0) {
8           (*speed) *= -1.0;
9           (*x) = 1.0 + timeInterval * (*speed);
10      } else if ((*x) < 0.0) {
11          (*speed) *= -1.0;
12          (*x) = timeInterval * (*speed);
13      }
14  }
15
16  int main() {
17      double x = 0.0;
18      double y = 1.0;
19      double speedX = 1.0;
20      double speedY = -0.5;
21
22      const int fps = 100;
23      const double timeInterval = 1.0 / fps;
24
25      for (int i = 0; i < 1000; ++i) {
26          // Update waves
27          updateWave(timeInterval, &x, &speedX);
```

```
28          updateWave(timeInterval, &y, &speedY);
29      }
30      return 0;
31  }
```

We now have written all the necessary pieces to run the simulation. Now, let's visualize it.

1.1.4   Visualization

Just running a simulation is not enough, but we want to "see" the result with animation. That's the whole point of computer graphics. So let's finish up our code by adding some visualization code to our cool fluid simulator. We are not going to write any fancy OpenGL or DirectX renderers. You can try using third-party data visualization tools, such as Matplotlib [54] to show the data, but let's keep our code as simple as possible. In this example, we will simply display our result on the terminal screen.

```
1   #include <array>
2   #include <cstdio>
3
4   const size_t kBufferSize = 80;
5
6   using namespace std;
7
8   void updateWave(const double timeInterval, double* x, double* speed) {
9       ...
10  }
11
12  int main() {
13      const double waveLengthX = 0.8;
14      const double waveLengthY = 1.2;
15
16      const double maxHeightX = 0.5;
17      const double maxHeightY = 0.4;
18
19      double x = 0.0;
20      double y = 1.0;
21      double speedX = 1.0;
22      double speedY = -0.5;
23
24      const int fps = 100;
25      const double timeInterval = 1.0 / fps;
26
27      array<double, kBufferSize> heightField;
28
29      for (int i = 0; i < 1000; ++i) {
30          // Update waves
```

```
31          updateWave(timeInterval, &x, &speedX);
32          updateWave(timeInterval, &y, &speedY);
33     }
34     return 0;
35  }
```

Starting from the previous code, this is the new setup. Notice that we added five more variables: `waveLengthX`, `waveLengthY`, `maxHeightX`, `maxHeightY`, and `heightField`. Except for `heightField`, these variables define the shape properties of the waves. Variable `heightField`, however, is for something special. Each $0, 1, \ldots, N-1$ element of the array will store the height of the waves at $0.5/N, 1.5/N, \ldots, N-0.5/N$ location as shown in Figure 1.4. Using this setup, both x and y positions with wavelength and max height properties will be mapped into an array `heightField`. We will assume that the wave has a cosine shape, and Figure 1.5 shows the expected result of this mapping. To implement this mapping, let's add one more function to our code, above the `main` function.

```
1  #include <cmath>
2
3  void accumulateWaveToHeightField(
4      const double x,
5      const double waveLength,
6      const double maxHeight,
```

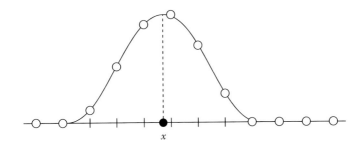

FIGURE 1.4
Constructing height field from wave position x.

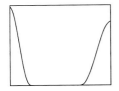 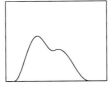 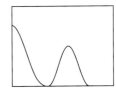

FIGURE 1.5
Wave animation sequence with overlapping.

```
7      array<double, kBufferSize>* heightField) {
8          const double quarterWaveLength = 0.25 * waveLength;
9          const int start = static_cast<int>((x - quarterWaveLength) *
               kBufferSize);
10         const int end = static_cast<int>((x + quarterWaveLength) *
               kBufferSize);
11
12         for (int i = start; i < end; ++i) {
13             int iNew = i;
14             if (i < 0) {
15                 iNew = -i - 1;
16             } else if (i >= static_cast<int>(kBufferSize)) {
17                 iNew = 2 * kBufferSize - i - 1;
18             }
19
20             double distance = fabs((i + 0.5) / kBufferSize - x);
21             double height = maxHeight * 0.5
22                 * (cos(min(distance * M_PI / quarterWaveLength, M_PI)) + 1.0);
23             (*heightField)[iNew] += height;
24         }
25     }
```

This new function takes position, length, and max height of a wave. A couple of local variables are defined at the beginning of the function and then makes a for-loop to accumulate the clamped cosine function to the input height field where the wave is touching. The integrated code can be written as below.

```
1    #include <array>
2    #include <cmath>
3    #include <cstdio>
4
5    const size_t kBufferSize = 80;
6
7    using namespace std;
8
9    void accumulateWaveToHeightField(
10       const double x,
11       const double waveLength,
12       const double maxHeight,
13       array<double, kBufferSize>* heightField) { ... }
14
15   void updateWave(const double timeInterval, double* x, double* speed) {
16       ...
17   }
18
19   int main() {
20       const double waveLengthX = 0.8;
```

```
21        const double waveLengthY = 1.2;
22
23        const double maxHeightX = 0.5;
24        const double maxHeightY = 0.4;
25
26        double x = 0.0;
27        double y = 1.0;
28        double speedX = 1.0;
29        double speedY = -0.5;
30
31        const int fps = 100;
32        const double timeInterval = 1.0 / fps;
33
34        array<double, kBufferSize> heightField;
35
36        for (int i = 0; i < 1000; ++i) {
37            // March through time
38            updateWave(timeInterval, &x, &speedX);
39            updateWave(timeInterval, &y, &speedY);
40
41            // Clear height field
42            for (double& height : heightField) {
43                height = 0.0;
44            }
45
46            // Accumulate waves for each center point
47            accumulateWaveToHeightField(x, waveLengthX, maxHeightX, &
                   heightField);
48            accumulateWaveToHeightField(y, waveLengthY, maxHeightY, &
                   heightField);
49        }
50
51        return 0;
52    }
```

What we have built so far is a code that maps the wave points to actual height field that can be visualized. This process is very similar to rasterizing points for visualizing the data on a bitmap screen, but in one dimension. Since we are not really drawing on a bitmap, the final code uses a simple ASCII code hack [1] to show the 1D height field in a terminal screen. The final code including this hack is shown below.

```
1    #include <algorithm>
2    #include <array>
3    #include <chrono>
4    #include <cmath>
5    #include <cstdio>
6    #include <string>
```

```
 7   #include <thread>
 8
 9   using namespace std;
10   using namespace chrono;
11
12   const size_t kBufferSize = 80;
13   const char* kGrayScaleTable = " .:-=+*#%@";
14   const size_t kGrayScaleTableSize = sizeof(kGrayScaleTable)/sizeof(char);
15
16   void updateWave(const double timeInterval, double* x, double* speed) {
17       (*x) += timeInterval * (*speed);
18
19       // Boundary reflection
20       if ((*x) > 1.0) {
21           (*speed) *= -1.0;
22           (*x) = 1.0 + timeInterval * (*speed);
23       } else if ((*x) < 0.0) {
24           (*speed) *= -1.0;
25           (*x) = timeInterval * (*speed);
26       }
27   }
28
29   void accumulateWaveToHeightField(
30       const double x,
31       const double waveLength,
32       const double maxHeight,
33       array<double, kBufferSize>* heightField) {
34       const double quarterWaveLength = 0.25 * waveLength;
35       const int start
36           = static_cast<int>((x - quarterWaveLength) * kBufferSize);
37       const int end
38           = static_cast<int>((x + quarterWaveLength) * kBufferSize);
39
40       for (int i = start; i < end; ++i) {
41           int iNew = i;
42           if (i < 0) {
43               iNew = -i - 1;
44           } else if (i >= static_cast<int>(kBufferSize)) {
45               iNew = 2 * kBufferSize - i - 1;
46           }
47
48           double distance = fabs((i + 0.5) / kBufferSize - x);
49           double height = maxHeight * 0.5
50               * (cos(min(distance * M_PI / quarterWaveLength, M_PI)) + 1.0);
51           (*heightField)[iNew] += height;
52       }
53   }
54
55   void draw(
```

```
56        const array<double, kBufferSize>& heightField) {
57        string buffer(kBufferSize, ' ');
58
59        // Convert height field to grayscale
60        for (size_t i = 0; i < kBufferSize; ++i) {
61            double height = heightField[i];
62            size_t tableIndex = min(
63                static_cast<size_t>(floor(kGrayScaleTableSize * height)),
64                kGrayScaleTableSize - 1);
65            buffer[i] = kGrayScaleTable[tableIndex];
66        }
67
68        // Clear old prints
69        for (size_t i = 0; i < kBufferSize; ++i) {
70            printf("\b");
71        }
72
73        // Draw new buffer
74        printf("%s", buffer.c_str());
75        fflush(stdout);
76    }
77
78    int main() {
79        const double waveLengthX = 0.8;
80        const double waveLengthY = 1.2;
81
82        const double maxHeightX = 0.5;
83        const double maxHeightY = 0.4;
84
85        double x = 0.0;
86        double y = 1.0;
87        double speedX = 1.0;
88        double speedY = -0.5;
89
90        const int fps = 100;
91        const double timeInterval = 1.0 / fps;
92
93        array<double, kBufferSize> heightField;
94
95        for (int i = 0; i < 1000; ++i) {
96            // March through time
97            updateWave(timeInterval, &x, &speedX);
98            updateWave(timeInterval, &y, &speedY);
99
100           // Clear height field
101           for (double& height : heightField) {
102               height = 0.0;
103           }
104
```

```
105          // Accumulate waves for each center point
106          accumulateWaveToHeightField(
107              x, waveLengthX, maxHeightX, &heightField);
108          accumulateWaveToHeightField(
109              y, waveLengthY, maxHeightY, &heightField);
110
111          // Draw height field
112          draw(heightField);
113
114          // Wait
115          this_thread::sleep_for(milliseconds(1000 / fps));
116      }
117
118      printf("\n");
119      fflush(stdout);
120
121      return 0;
122  }
```

Notice that we also added one more line of code after the `draw` call at Line 115. This is simply a sleep function call which let the app wait for a given time duration before proceeding to the next line. In this case, it let each iteration of the loop take `1000/fps` milliseconds.

1.1.5   Final Result

We finally finished writing our first fluid simulation code! You can run the app by running

```
bin/hello_fluid_sim
```

from the root of the source code repository. The source code (`main.cpp`) can be found from `src/examples/hello_fluid_sim/main.cpp`.

In summary, the goal of this hello-world example was to provide the core ideas you would need for developing a fluid engine. The code demonstrated how to define simulation states, update the states over time, handle the interaction with nonfluid objects, and, finally, visualize the result. We will see different kinds of simulation techniques for various phenomena throughout this book, but the basic idea will be the same.

1.2   How to Read This Book

To help reading and understanding this book, basic conventions for the codes and mathematical expressions will be covered in this section.

1.2.1 Getting the Codes

The codes from this book can be found from the GitHub page (`https://github.com/doyubkim/fluid-engine-dev`). You can also clone the latest version of the code from the repository, which is recommended since it may contain bug fixes and more features. You can clone the repository using a git command:

```
git clone https://github.com/doyubkim/fluid-engine-dev
```

The codebase depends on some third-party libraries and some of them are not available from the package managers like Homebrew or apt-get. Those libraries are included as a git submodule. Hence, you must initialize the submodule after cloning the main repository such that:

```
git submodule init
git submodule update
```

To build the code, SCons [73] is used for Mac OS X and Linux platforms. For Windows, Microsoft Visual Studio is used. See `README.md` and `INSTALL.md` in the repository for the latest build instruction.

1.2.2 Reading Codes

As we have already seen from our hello-world fluid simulation examples from the beginning, a text that indicates a code or a file path will be written in `fixed-width typefaces`. Multilines of codes will be written as:

```
1    void foo() {
2        printf("bar\n");
3    }
```

1.2.2.1 Languages

The code is mainly written in C++11 with some exception for the build tools and utility scripts that are written in Python. For example, lambda functions, template aliases, variadic templates, range-based loops, auto, and std::array are some of the features the code is using from C++11. This book, however, tries to make the code as readable as possible by avoiding fancy but cryptic codes. To get more information on C++11, find out more details from Bjarne Stroustrup's webpage [114] and Scott Meyers' recent book [84].

1.2.2.2 Source Code Structure

If not specified, most of the code can be found by the name of a class. For example, the header and source files for class `Collider3` can be found from `include/jet/collider3.h` and `src/jet/collider3.cpp`. The files and directories are named with lowercase letters and underscores such as `path_to/my/awesome_code.cpp`. For nonclass codes, such as the global functions and constants, they are grouped by their features. For example, math utility functions can be found from `include/jet/math_utils.h`.

In case of template class or functions, the declaration can be found under `include/jet` and the definition can be found under `include/jet/detail`. Since the definitions are inline implementations, the filenames have suffix `-inl.h`. For instance, template class `Vector3` has its declaration in `include/jet/vector3.h` and the implementation in `include/jet/vector3-inl.h`.

1.2.2.3   Naming Conventions

The code uses `CamelCase` for class names, `camelCase` for functions/variables, and `MACRO_NAME` for macros.

If a type needs to be distinguished by its dimension and value type, the code adds corresponding suffix to describe it. For example:

```
1   template <typename T, size_t N>
2   class Vector { ... };
```

In this case, we can define type aliases for specific value types and dimensions such as

```
1   template <typename T> using Vector3 = Vector<T, 3>;
2   typedef Vector3<float> Vector3F
3   typedef Vector3<double> Vector3D
```

Notice that suffix `3` is used to indicate that the dimension of this vector class is 3. Also, suffixes `F` and `D` are used to tell that they are using float and double for the value types, respectively.

Name of a private or protected member variable starts with underscore, such as

```
1   class MyClass {
2     ...
3
4     private:
5       double _data;
6   };
```

The code, especially the API, tries to be verbose if possible. For example, we prefer using `timeIntervalInSeconds` than `dt` or `viscosityCoefficient` than `mu`.

1.2.2.4 Constants

Frequently used constants are located in `jet/include/constants.h` header file. Names of the constants start with the letter `k`, followed by the value and type with camel-case naming convention. For example, unsigned size type zero constant is defined as:

```
1  const size_t kZeroSize = 0;
```

Similarly, double-precision floating point π is defined as:

```
1  const double kPiD = 3.14159265358979323846264338327950288;
```

There are also physics constants such as:

```
1  // Gravity
2  const double kGravity = -9.8;
3
4  // Speed of sound in water at 20 degrees celsius.
5  const double kSpeedOfSoundInWater = 1482.0;
```

1.2.2.5 Arrays

Arrays are the most frequently used primitives in the codebase. It provides several data types to access 1D, 2D, and 3D arrays. They are not extremely generic classes like NumPy [118] but supports most of the use cases.

To store 1D data, we define the following class:

```
1   template <typename T, size_t N>
2   class Array final {};
3
4   template <typename T>
5   class Array<T, 1> final {
6    public:
7       Array();
8
9       ...
10
11      T& operator[](size_t i);
12      const T& operator[](size_t i) const;
13
14      size_t size() const;
15
16      ...
17
18    private:
19      std::vector<T> _data;
```

```
20   };
21
22   template <typename T> using Array1 = Array<T, 1>;
```

The new data type, `Array<T, 1>`, is a wrapper around `std::vector` with some additions. See `jet/include/array1.h` for more details. We can extend this to 2D and 3D arrays as follows:

```
1    template <typename T>
2    class Array<T, 2> final {
3     public:
4        Array();
5
6        ...
7
8        T& operator()(size_t i, size_t j);
9        const T& operator()(size_t i, size_t j) const;
10
11       Size3 size() const;
12       size_t width() const;
13       size_t height() const;
14
15       ...
16
17    private:
18       Size2 _size;
19       std::vector<T> _data;
20   };
21
22   template <typename T> using Array2 = Array<T, 2>;
```

and

```
1    template <typename T>
2    class Array<T, 3> final {
3     public:
4        Array();
5
6        ...
7
8        T& operator()(size_t i, size_t j, size_t k);
9        const T& operator()(size_t i, size_t j, size_t k) const;
10
11       Size3 size() const;
12       size_t width() const;
13       size_t height() const;
14       size_t depth() const;
15
16       ...
```

```
17
18    private:
19        Size3 _size;
20        std::vector<T> _data;
21    };
22
23    template <typename T> using Array3 = Array<T, 3>;
```

Here, `Size2` and `Size3` are tuples holding two and three `size_t`s that represent the size of the multidimensional arrays. Range of i is $[0, width)$, j is $[0, height)$, and k is $[0, depth)$.* Note that both classes have operator `()` defined which returns array element at (i, j) in 2D and (i, j, k) in 3D. The data are stored as a 1D `std::vector`, but it is mapped to 2D or 3D by:

```
1     template <typename T>
2     T& Array<T, 2>::operator()(size_t i, size_t j) {
3         return _data[i + _size.x * j];
4     }
5
6     template <typename T>
7     const T& Array<T, 2>::operator()(size_t i, size_t j) const {
8         return _data[i + _size.x * j];
9     }
10
11    template <typename T>
12    T& Array<T, 3>::operator()(size_t i, size_t j, size_t k) {
13        return _data[i + _size.x * (j + _size.y * k)];
14    }
15
16    template <typename T>
17    const T& Array<T, 3>::operator()(size_t i, size_t j, size_t k) const {
18        return _data[i + _size.x * (j + _size.y * k)];
19    }
```

Note that we are taking i-major ordering. Thus, iterating a 3D array can be written as:

```
1     Array3<double> data = ...
2
3     for (size_t k = 0; k < data.depth(); ++k) {
4         for (size_t j = 0; j < data.height(); ++j) {
5             for (size_t i = 0; i < data.width(); ++i) {
6                 data(i, j, k) = ...
7             }
8         }
9     }
```

---

*Symbol [means inclusive and) means exclusive. Thus, $[0, width)$ means 0 to $width - 1$.

The innermost loop iterates i because it will maximize the cache hit. If writing three for-loops are too time-consuming for you, there are some helper functions to make the code shorter:

```
template <typename T>
class Array<T, 3> final {
 public:
    Array();

    ...

    void forEachIndex(
        const std::function<void(size_t, size_t, size_t)>& func) const;

    void parallelForEachIndex(
        const std::function<void(size_t, size_t, size_t)>& func) const;

    ...
};
```

Function `forEachIndex` takes function object and iterates every i, j, and k in the i-major order. Function `parallelForEachIndex` does the same iteration, but in parallel using multiple threads.[*] These two utility functions can be used as follows:

```
Array3<double> data = ...

data.forEachIndex([&] (size_t i, size_t j, size_t k) {
        data(i, j, k) = ...
    });

data.parallelForEachIndex([&] (size_t i, size_t j, size_t k) {
        data(i, j, k) = ...
    });
```

Here, we are using lambda functions to inline the function object. See C++11 lambda feature if this code is not quite obvious [114].

Another array-related types that are frequently used in the codebase are the array accessors. They are simple array wrappers that are very similar to a random access iterators. They do not provide any capability of allocating or deallocating heap memory, but simply carry array pointers and provide the same (i, j, k) indexing. For example, the 3D array accessor class

---

[*]The codebase utilizes `std::thread` for parallel processing. See `include/jet/parallel.h` and `include/jet/detail/parallel-inl.h` for the actual implementation.

is defined as follows:

```
1   template <typename T>
2   class ArrayAccessor<T, 3> final {
3    public:
4      ArrayAccessor();
5      explicit ArrayAccessor(const Size3& size, T* const data);
6
7      ...
8
9      T& operator()(size_t i, size_t j, size_t k);
10     const T& operator()(size_t i, size_t j, size_t k) const;
11
12     Size3 size() const;
13     size_t width() const;
14     size_t height() const;
15     size_t depth() const;
16
17     ...
18
19    private:
20     Size3 _size;
21     T* _data;
22   };
23
24   template <typename T> using ArrayAccessor3 = ArrayAccessor<T, 3>;
25
26   template <typename T>
27   class ConstArrayAccessor<T, 3> {
28    public:
29      ConstArrayAccessor();
30      explicit ConstArrayAccessor(const Size3& size, const T* const data);
31
32      ...
33
34      const T& operator()(size_t i, size_t j, size_t k) const;
35
36      Size3 size() const;
37      size_t width() const;
38      size_t height() const;
39      size_t depth() const;
40
41      ...
42
43    private:
44     Size3 _size;
45     const T* _data;
46   };
47
48   template <typename T> using ConstArrayAccessor3 = ConstArrayAccessor<T,3>;
```

These two classes are used to exchange data without allocating or deallocating the memory. Especially the second class, `ConstArrayAccessor<T, 3>`, is only for read operations, just like `const iterators` in C++ STL. In the codebase, all the multidimensional array types return the array accessors. For example, `Array<T, 3>` provides such member functions as follows:

```
1   template <typename T>
2   class Array<T, 3> final {
3    public:
4       ...
5
6       ArrayAccessor3<T> accessor();
7       ConstArrayAccessor3<T> constAccessor() const;
8
9       ...
10  };
11
12  template <typename T>
13  ArrayAccessor3<T> Array<T, 3>::accessor() {
14      return ArrayAccessor3<T>(size(), data());
15  }
16
17  template <typename T>
18  ConstArrayAccessor3<T> Array<T, 3>::constAccessor() const {
19      return ConstArrayAccessor3<T>(size(), data());
20  }
```

This coding pattern will frequently appear in the grid-base fluid simulation codes.

1.2.3 Reading Math Expressions

Mathematical expressions will be written using Serif font such as $e = mc^2$. Longer equations or even multiline expressions will be written as:

$$\frac{\partial \mathbf{u}}{\partial t} + \mathbf{u} \cdot \nabla \mathbf{u} = \nu \nabla^2 \mathbf{u} + \mathbf{g}$$

$$\nabla \cdot \mathbf{u} = 0$$

1.2.3.1 Scalar, Vector, and Matrix

We will cover what are vector and matrix in the upcoming sections. But in short, a vector is a list of numbers that represents a point or direction. Scalar, on the other hand, is a single number. A scalar value is written in plain style such as c, whereas a vector is written with bold lowercase typeface such as $\mathbf{f}$. A matrix uses uppercase boldfaced letter such as $\mathbf{M}$.

1.3   Math

This section will introduce the most commonly used mathematical operations, data structures, and concepts that are used throughout the book. If you are already familiar with linear algebra and vector calculus, you can skip this section.

1.3.1   Coordinate System

The coordinate system is a system for specifying points using coordinates measured in some specified way [119]. The simplest coordinate system consists of coordinate axes oriented perpendicularly to each other, known as Cartesian coordinates. There are other types of coordinate systems as well, such as polar coordinates, but we will only use Cartesian coordinates in this book.

Figure 1.6 shows both two-dimensional (2D) and three-dimensional (3D) spaces with arrows that represent the coordinate axes, and each axis is labeled with x, y, and z. The figure shows that x is tagged on the axis that points right, whereas y and z are put on the upward and forward axes, respectively. You can have different ordering for labeling x, y, and z. But in this book, we will follow the convention shown in Figure 1.6. This is called right-handed coordinate system because you can use your right hand to point your thumb, index, and middle finger in the direction of x, y, and z, respectively.

1.3.2   Vector

We have our axes defined for our space. Now, let's talk about points. From Figure 1.7, point A in the figure can be projected orthogonally onto both x- and y-axes, and the projected values can be written using a pair of numbers. In this particular example, it would be $(2, 3)$.

Similarly, we can also describe the difference between two points using pairs. From Figure 1.7, look at the arrow which points B from A. Point B is at $(7, 4)$, so it is two units away in the x-direction and four units away in the

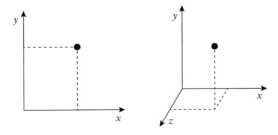

FIGURE 1.6
2D and 3D Cartesian coordinates.

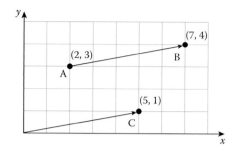

FIGURE 1.7
Three points A, B, and C in a 2D space.

y-direction from point A. We can also write this difference or delta in a pair form $(5, 1)$, and this can be expressed as a point as we can see from the figure (point C).

To generalize these ideas, we introduce a vector. As we can see from the previous example, a vector is simply a set of numbers that point the coordinates of that numbers from the origin. In a 3D case, for example, vector $(2, 3, 7)$ is an arrow that starts from points $(0, 0, 0)$ and ends at point $(2, 3, 7)$. A vector can be used to describe the coordinates of a point, and it also can be used to represent displacement. For instance, if you want to move a point by translating x coordinate by -1, y by 5, and z by 4, you can write a vector $(-1, 5, 4)$ to describe the translation. We can also have any dimension of vectors from one to N-dimension.

Now, let's see how we can define a class to represent a vector. Consider the class written below.

```
1   template <typename T, size_t N>
2   class Vector final {
3    public:
4       static_assert(
5           N > 0,
6           "Size of static-sized vector should be greater than zero.");
7       static_assert(
8           std::is_floating_point<T>::value,
9           "Vector only can be instantiated with floating point types");
10
11   private:
12       std::array<T, N> _elements;
13   };
```

The class takes two template parameters, the data type of element T and dimension of the vector N. Note that we will only allow floating points, `float` or `double`, for value type T because we want this vector class to be used only

for the mathematical calculation, rather than storing any arbitrary types.[*]
We are also limiting the range of N to be greater than zero.

After adding some constructors, setters, getters, and utility operators, the code would look as follows:

```
template <typename T, std::size_t N>
class Vector final {
 public:
    // static_asserts
    ...


    Vector();

    template <typename... Params>
    explicit Vector(Params... params);

    explicit Vector(const std::initializer_list<T>& lst);

    Vector(const Vector& other);

    void set(const std::initializer_list<T>& lst);

    void set(const Vector& other);

    Vector& operator=(const std::initializer_list<T>& lst);

    Vector& operator=(const Vector& other);

    const T& operator[](std::size_t i) const;

    T& operator[](std::size_t);

 private:
    std::array<T, N> _elements;

    // private helper functions
    ...
};
```

The complete implementation can be found from include/vector.h and include/detail/vector-inl.h. The basic usage example can be found from the unit tester which is located at src/tests/unit_tests/vector_tests.cpp.

In computer graphics, the most commonly used vectors are 2D, 3D, and four-dimensional (4D) vectors. For such dimensions, we can specialize the template class and have more useful structure and helper functions for our

---

[*]More generic data type to store an arbitrary set of values would be std::tuple.

frequent uses. That will also prevent overly generalizing vector class which may make the internal logic too complicated. Taking 3D vector as an example, we can write the specialized class as:

```
1   template <typename T>
2   class Vector<T, 3> final {
3    public:
4       ...
5
6       T x;
7       T y;
8       T z;
9   };
10
11  template <typename T> using Vector3 = Vector<T, 3>;
12
13  typedef Vector3<float> Vector3F;
14  typedef Vector3<double> Vector3D;
```

The most notable change is that instead of defining an array, the new class explicitly declares x, y, and z. This is a small change but provides easy access points to the coordinates which can be very handy for many situations. One can implement this by having an array of size 3, just like Vector<T, N>, and have dedicated getter and setter functions for x, y, and z components. That is totally fine, and it is just a matter of decision. Anyway, there are also aliases defined after the class definition that is also useful when trying to instantiate frequently used types. The final implementation of Vector<T, 3> can be found from include/vector3.h and include/detail/vector3-inl.h. Similar to Vector<T, N>, the examples are located in src/tests/unit_tests/vector3_tests.cpp.

So far we have seen the basic idea of vector and some codes to represent the vector data. From now on, we will cover frequently used operations with the vectors and their implementations.

1.3.2.1 Basic Operations

Let's start with the most basic stuff – the arithmetic operations. Just like scalar values, we can also add, subtract, multiply, and divide a vector with another vector. By extending the previous code, we can write:

```
1   template <typename T>
2   class Vector<T, 3> final {
3    public:
4       ...
5
6       // Binary operations: new instance = this (+) v
7       Vector add(T v) const;
8       Vector add(const Vector& v) const;
```

```
9      Vector sub(T v) const;
10     Vector sub(const Vector& v) const;
11     Vector mul(T v) const;
12     Vector mul(const Vector& v) const;
13     Vector div(T v) const;
14     Vector div(const Vector& v) const;
15  };
```

This code indicates that we can apply the arithmetic operations with scalar types as well. Taking add function for example, it can be written as:

```
1   template <typename T>
2   Vector<T,3> Vector<T,3>::add(T v) const {
3       return Vector(x + v, y + v, z + v);
4   }
5
6   template <typename T>
7   Vector<T,3> Vector<T,3>::add(const Vector& v) const {
8       return Vector(x + v.x, y + v.y, z + v.z);
9   }
```

It is also convenient to overload the operators so that we can use the class like:

```
1   Vector3D a(1.0, 2.0, 3.0), b(4.0, 5.0, 6.0):
2   Vector3D c = a + b;
```

We can easily implement such features by adding:

```
1   template <typename T>
2   Vector<T,3> operator+(const Vector<T,3>& a, T b) {
3       return a.add(b);
4   }
5
6   template <typename T>
7   Vector<T,3> operator+(T a, const Vector<T,3>& b) {
8       return b.add(a);
9   }
10
11  template <typename T>
12  Vector<T,3> operator+(const Vector<T,3>& a, const Vector<T,3>& b) {
13      return a.add(b);
14  }
```

The geometric meaning of addition, subtraction, and multiplication is shown in Figure 1.8.

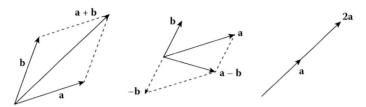

FIGURE 1.8
Left: Adding vector **a** and **b**. Middle: Subtracting vector **b** from **a**. Right:
Multiplying scalar 2 to vector **a**.

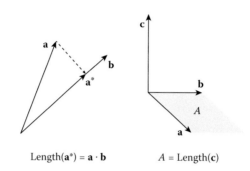

Length(**a***) = **a** · **b** A = Length(**c**)

FIGURE 1.9
Left: Vector **a*** is the projection of **a** to **b**. Length of **a*** is the result of the
dot product of **a** and **b**. Right: Vector **c** is the cross-product of **a** and **b**. The
length of **c** is equal to the area A.

1.3.2.2   Dot and Cross Product

Both dot and cross operations are binary operations, and they both have geometric meanings. Dot product projects one vector to another and returns the
length of the projected vector. By definition of the cosine function, taking dot
product with two unit-sized vectors gives cosine angle between the two. Cross
product produces perpendicular vector out of the parallelogram that the input
two vectors defines, and its magnitude is determined by the parallelogram's
area. Figure 1.9 illustrates how the two operations work.

Mathematical definition for dot product is

$$\mathbf{a} \cdot \mathbf{b} = a_x b_x + a_y b_y + a_z b_z \tag{1.1}$$

and cross product is defined as

$$\mathbf{a} \times \mathbf{b} = (a_y b_z - a_z b_y)\mathbf{i} + (a_z b_x - a_x b_z)\mathbf{j} + (a_x b_y - a_y b_x)\mathbf{k} \tag{1.2}$$

where **i**, **j**, and **k** represent x, y, and z axes, respectively. The equivalent code starts with declaring the interface:

```
1  template <typename T>
2  class Vector<T, 3> final {
3    public:
4      ...
5      T dot(const Vector& v) const;
6      Vector cross(const Vector& v) const;
7  };
```

And the actual implementation behind looks like this:

```
1  template <typename T>
2  T Vector<T,3>::dot(const Vector& v) const {
3      return x * v.x + y * v.y + z * v.z;
4  }
5
6  template <typename T>
7  Vector<T,3> Vector<T,3>::cross(const Vector& v) const {
8      return Vector(y*v.z - v.y*z, z*v.x - v.z*x, x*v.y - v.x*y);
9  }
```

It is worth to mention that dot product returns a scalar value out of two vectors while cross product gives a vector as a result. But in 2D, the cross product will also produce a scalar value. If you reinterpret 2D space as a xy-plane in 3D, performing the cross product on the plane will give a vector that either points in the $+z$ or $-z$ direction. In a 2D world, this is just a matter of sign. Thus, the cross product code simply becomes

```
1  template <typename T>
2  Vector<T,2> Vector<T,2>::cross(const Vector& v) const {
3      return x*v.y - v.x*y;
4  }
```

1.3.2.3 More Operations

Using the basic operators we have seen so far, we can also implement helper functions that are often used when manipulating vectors.

1.3.2.3.1 Length of a Vector

We can measure the length of a vector, $l = |\mathbf{v}|$, using Pythagorean theorem as shown in Figure 1.10. For a 3D vector, we can implement the function as shown in the following:

```
1  template <typename T>
2  T Vector<T,3>::length() const {
3      return std::sqrt(x * x + y * y + z * z);
4  }
```

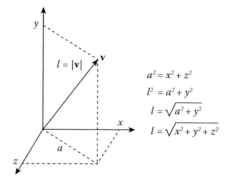

FIGURE 1.10
Measuring the length l of a vector $\mathbf{v}$.

This code implements simple formula $\sqrt{x^2 + y^2 + z^2}$. Now sometimes it is a bit more efficient to have *length*^{2} instead of *length* especially when you compare the lengths between two vectors. This is because you don't have to call std::sqrt which involves more operations than simpler operations like addition, and if $a < b$, then $a^2 < b^2$ is also true. Thus, we can write additional helper function as follows:

```
template <typename T>
T Vector<T,3>::lengthSquared() const {
    return x * x + y * y + z * z;
}
```

1.3.2.3.2   Normalization

A vector with its length equal to 1 is called a unit vector, and making a vector into a unit vector is called normalization. If a vector has a length of l, we can scale its size by $1/l$ and we get the normalized vector. So the code can be written as:

```
template <typename T>
void Vector<T,3>::normalize() {
    T l = length();
    x /= l;
    y /= l;
    z /= l;
}

Vector<T,3> Vector<T,3>::normalized() const {
    T l = length();
    return Vector(x / l, y / l, z / l);
}
```

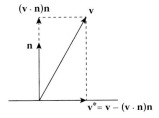

FIGURE 1.11
Vector **v** is projected on the surface with normal **n** resulting vector **v***.

The first function `normalize()` turns the given vector into a unit vector, while the second function `normalized()` creates a new vector that is the unit vector of the given one.

1.3.2.3.3 Projection

The next operation needs a bit of geometric sense. As shown in Figure 1.11, we want to project a vector on the surface that is defined by a surface normal vector. As we already know from Section 1.3.2.2, we can use the dot product to project a vector to another vector. But in this case, we want to project the vector onto the surface. To do so, we first need to decompose our vector into a vector that is parallel to the surface normal, and another vector that is the projected vector which we want to know. So if we subtract the normal component from the original vector, we can get the projected vector. We can write down this as an equation which is

$$\mathbf{v}^* = \mathbf{v} - (\mathbf{v} \cdot \mathbf{n})\mathbf{n} \tag{1.3}$$

where **n** is the surface normal vector. This equation can be directly implemented into:

```
1  template <typename T>
2  Vector<T, 3> Vector<T, 3>::projected(const Vector<T, 3>& normal) const {
3      return sub(dot(normal) * normal);
4  }
```

1.3.2.3.4 Reflection

We can take the same approach to calculate the reflection. As shown in Figure 1.12, we again decompose the input vector into surface normal and tangential components. We then subtract the scaled normal component of the input vector to get reflected vector. Writing down the equation, we get

$$\mathbf{v}^* = \mathbf{v} - 2\mathbf{v} \cdot \mathbf{n}\mathbf{n} \tag{1.4}$$

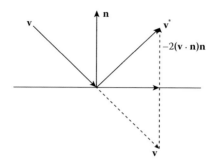

FIGURE 1.12
Vector **v** is reflected from the surface with normal **n** resulting in vector **v***.

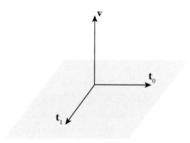

FIGURE 1.13
Vector **v** has two tangential vectors $\mathbf{t}_0$ and $\mathbf{t}_1$.

and the code can be written as:

```
template <typename T>
Vector<T, 3> Vector<T, 3>::reflected(const Vector<T, 3>& normal) const {
    return sub(normal.mul(2 * dot(normal)));
}
```

1.3.2.3.5   Tangential Vector

If a given vector defines the normal direction of a surface, we can think of computing tangential vectors from the normal as well. This is useful if you want to generate points on the surface that are defined by the surface normal. However, as shown in Figure 1.13, there can be an infinite number of tangential vectors on the surface so that we will pick two perpendicular vectors. By definition, these two tangential vectors are orthogonal to the normal vector as well. So these three vectors construct a coordinate system on the surface.

To compute the two tangential vectors, see the code below.

```
template <typename T>
std::tuple<Vector<T, 3>, Vector<T, 3>> Vector<T, 3>::tangential() const {
    Vector<T, 3> a = ((std::fabs(y) > 0 || std::fabs(z) > 0) ?
        Vector<T, 3>(1, 0, 0) :
        Vector<T, 3>(0, 1, 0)).cross(*this).normalized();
    Vector<T, 3> b = cross(a);
    return std::make_tuple(a, b);
}
```

Note that this vector is the surface normal vector. We first pick the x-directional vector $(1, 0, 0)$ if the normal is not parallel to the x-axis, but pick $y(0, 1, 0)$ if it is. This selected vector can be anything if it is not parallel to the normal vector. We just need it temporarily to compute a vector that is perpendicular to the surface normal. We compute this new vector a by taking the cross product with the selected vector and surface normal. Then, we apply the cross product again with the normal vector to get vector b, and return both a and b as a tuple.

1.3.2.3.6 *Operator Overloading and Others*

We can also add other helper functions such as operator overloadings. I won't go too deep into the details, but the code below lists what can be implemented. You can find out the details from `include/vector3.h` and `include/detail/vector3-inl.h` for a 3D vector. You can also find 2D and 4D implementations from `include/detail/vector2-inl.h` and `include/detail/vector4-inl.h`.

```
template <typename T>
class Vector<T, 3> final {
 public:
    ...

    // Constructors
    Vector();
    explicit Vector(T x, T y, T z);
    explicit Vector(const Vector2<T>& pt, T z);
    Vector(const std::initializer_list<T>& lst);
    Vector(const Vector& v);

    ...

    // Operators
    T& operator[](std::size_t i);
    const T& operator[](std::size_t i) const;

    Vector& operator=(const std::initializer_list<T>& lst);
```

```
20      Vector& operator=(const Vector& v);
21      Vector& operator+=(T v);
22      Vector& operator+=(const Vector& v);
23      Vector& operator-=(T v);
24      Vector& operator-=(const Vector& v);
25      Vector& operator*=(T v);
26      Vector& operator*=(const Vector& v);
27      Vector& operator/=(T v);
28      Vector& operator/=(const Vector& v);
29
30      bool operator==(const Vector& v) const;
31      bool operator!=(const Vector& v) const;
32  };
33
34
35  template <typename T> using Vector3 = Vector<T, 3>;
36
37  template <typename T>
38  Vector3<T> operator+(const Vector3<T>& a);
39
40  template <typename T>
41  Vector3<T> operator-(const Vector3<T>& a);
42
43  template <typename T>
44  Vector3<T> operator+(T a, const Vector3<T>& b);
45
46  template <typename T>
47  Vector3<T> operator+(const Vector3<T>& a, const Vector3<T>& b);
48
49  template <typename T>
50  Vector3<T> operator-(const Vector3<T>& a, T b);
51
52  template <typename T>
53  Vector3<T> operator-(T a, const Vector3<T>& b);
54
55  template <typename T>
56  Vector3<T> operator-(const Vector3<T>& a, const Vector3<T>& b);
57
58  template <typename T>
59  Vector3<T> operator*(const Vector3<T>& a, T b);
60
61  template <typename T>
62  Vector3<T> operator*(T a, const Vector3<T>& b);
63
64  template <typename T>
65  Vector3<T> operator*(const Vector3<T>& a, const Vector3<T>& b);
66
67  template <typename T>
68  Vector3<T> operator/(const Vector3<T>& a, T b);
```

```
69
70  template <typename T>
71  Vector3<T> operator/(T a, const Vector3<T>& b);
72
73  template <typename T>
74  Vector3<T> operator/(const Vector3<T>& a, const Vector3<T>& b);
75
76  template <typename T>
77  Vector3<T> min(const Vector3<T>& a, const Vector3<T>& b);
78
79  template <typename T>
80  Vector3<T> max(const Vector3<T>& a, const Vector3<T>& b);
81
82  template <typename T>
83  Vector3<T> clamp(const Vector3<T>& v, const Vector3<T>& low, const
        Vector3<T>& high);
84
85  template <typename T>
86  Vector3<T> ceil(const Vector3<T>& a);
87
88  template <typename T>
89  Vector3<T> floor(const Vector3<T>& a);
90
91  typedef Vector3<float> Vector3F;
92  typedef Vector3<double> Vector3D;
```

1.3.3 Matrix

Matrix is a 2D array that stores numbers at each row and column. For example, a matrix with M rows and N columns, namely $M \times N$ matrix, can be written as:

$$
\mathbf{A} = \begin{bmatrix}
a_{11} & a_{12} & a_{13} & \cdots & a_{1N} \\
a_{21} & a_{22} & a_{23} & \cdots & a_{2N} \\
\vdots & \vdots & \vdots & \ddots & \vdots \\
a_{M1} & a_{M2} & a_{M3} & \cdots & a_{MN}
\end{bmatrix}
\tag{1.5}
$$

Here, a_{ij} represents the matrix element at the ith row and jth column. An $M \times N$ matrix can be interpreted as a set of M-row vectors or N-column vectors.

1.3.3.1 Basic Matrix Operations

Next, let's find out the most frequently used matrix operators.

1.3.3.1.1 *Matrix–Vector Multiplication*

The first operator to cover is matrix–vector multiplication. Assume that we have an $M \times N$ matrix $\mathbf{A}$ and N-dimensional vector $\mathbf{x}$. Multiplying the vector to the matrix is denoted as

$$\mathbf{y} = \mathbf{Ax} \tag{1.6}$$

We can write the operation element-wise such as

$$\begin{bmatrix} y_1 \\ y_2 \\ \vdots \\ y_M \end{bmatrix} = \begin{bmatrix} a_{11} & a_{12} & a_{13} & \cdots & a_{1N} \\ a_{21} & a_{22} & a_{23} & \cdots & a_{2N} \\ \vdots & \vdots & \vdots & \ddots & \vdots \\ a_{M1} & a_{M2} & a_{M3} & \cdots & a_{MN} \end{bmatrix} \begin{bmatrix} x_1 \\ x_2 \\ \vdots \\ x_N \end{bmatrix} \tag{1.7}$$

where the output vector $\mathbf{y}$ is an M-dimensional vector. The output vector $\mathbf{y}$ can be computed by taking the dot product of ith column of the matrix and the input vector such as

$$y_i = \begin{bmatrix} a_{i1} & a_{i2} & a_{i3} & \cdots & a_{iN} \end{bmatrix} \cdot \begin{bmatrix} x_1 \\ x_2 \\ \vdots \\ x_N \end{bmatrix} \tag{1.8}$$

which is

$$y_i = a_{i1}x_1 + a_{i2}x_2 + \cdots + a_{iN}x_N \tag{1.9}$$

The time complexity of the matrix–vector multiplication is $O(M \times N)$.

1.3.3.1.2   Matrix–Matrix Multiplication

Extending the matrix–vector multiplication, we can also multiply two matrices. For example, the multiplication of matrices $\mathbf{A}$ and $\mathbf{B}$ can be written as:

$$\mathbf{C} = \mathbf{AB} \tag{1.10}$$

or

$$\begin{bmatrix} c_{11} & c_{12} & \cdots & c_{1L} \\ c_{21} & c_{22} & \cdots & c_{2L} \\ \vdots & \vdots & \ddots & \vdots \\ c_{M1} & c_{M2} & \cdots & c_{ML} \end{bmatrix} = \begin{bmatrix} a_{11} & a_{12} & \cdots & a_{1N} \\ a_{21} & a_{22} & \cdots & a_{2N} \\ \vdots & \vdots & \ddots & \vdots \\ a_{M1} & a_{M2} & \cdots & a_{MN} \end{bmatrix} \begin{bmatrix} b_{11} & b_{12} & \cdots & b_{1L} \\ b_{21} & b_{22} & \cdots & b_{2L} \\ \vdots & \vdots & \ddots & \vdots \\ b_{N1} & b_{N2} & \cdots & b_{NL} \end{bmatrix} \tag{1.11}$$

Each element in matrix $\mathbf{C}$ can then be calculated by taking a dot product for each ith row of matrix $\mathbf{A}$ and jth column of matrix $\mathbf{B}$ such as

$$c_{ij} = \begin{bmatrix} a_{i1} & a_{i2} & \cdots & a_{iN} \end{bmatrix} \begin{bmatrix} b_{1j} \\ b_{2j} \\ \vdots \\ b_{Nj} \end{bmatrix} \tag{1.12}$$

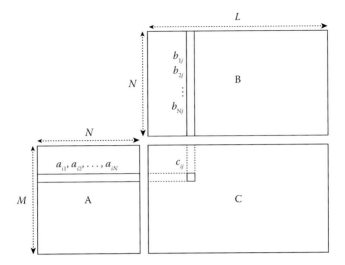

FIGURE 1.14
Visualization of matrix–matrix multiplication, $\mathbf{C} = \mathbf{AB}$. A row from $\mathbf{A}$ and a column from $\mathbf{B}$ constructs c_{ij}.

or

$$c_{ij} = a_{i1}b_{1j} + a_{i2}b_{2j} + \cdots + a_{iN}b_{Nj} \tag{1.13}$$

Figure 1.14 shows how the dot products are taken for each row and columns more visually. Note that the number of columns of matrix $\mathbf{A}$ should be equal to the number of rows of matrix $\mathbf{B}$. Also, the output matrix $\mathbf{C}$ will have $M \times L$ dimension if the dimension of $\mathbf{A}$ and $\mathbf{B}$ are $M \times N$ and $N \times L$. The time complexity of the matrix–matrix multiplication is $O(L \times M \times N)$.

1.3.3.1.3 Inverse

Finally, let's understand how to perform the inversion of a matrix. If we have a matrix $\mathbf{A}$, its inverse matrix can be written as $\mathbf{A}^{-1}$ which satisfies

$$\mathbf{A}^{-1}\mathbf{A} = \mathbf{A}\mathbf{A}^{-1} = \mathbf{I} \tag{1.14}$$

Here, $\mathbf{I}$ is an identity matrix where its diagonal elements are all one and others are zero, such as

$$\begin{bmatrix} 1 & 0 & 0 & \cdots & 0 \\ 0 & 1 & 0 & \cdots & 0 \\ 0 & 0 & 1 & \cdots & 0 \\ \vdots & \vdots & \vdots & \ddots & \vdots \\ 0 & 0 & 0 & \cdots & 1 \end{bmatrix} \tag{1.15}$$

Note that the input matrix $\mathbf{A}$ should be a square matrix, which means the number of rows and columns should be the same.

The most straightforward way to compute the inverse matrix is the Gauss–Jordan elimination method. It first starts with the original matrix A concatenated with an identity matrix with the same dimension. For example, if we have a 3×3 matrix

$$\begin{bmatrix} 2 & -1 & 0 \\ -1 & 2 & -1 \\ 0 & -1 & 2 \end{bmatrix} \tag{1.16}$$

then we can concatenate 3×3 matrix on the right, resulting

$$\left[\begin{array}{ccc|ccc} 2 & -1 & 0 & 1 & 0 & 0 \\ -1 & 2 & -1 & 0 & 1 & 0 \\ 0 & -1 & 2 & 0 & 0 & 1 \end{array}\right] \tag{1.17}$$

The Gauss–Jordan elimination method then iterates each row of this matrix and try to make the left 3×3 portion to be identity matrix by adding a linear combination of other rows. Take a look at the following step:

$$\left[\begin{array}{ccc|ccc} 2 & -1 & 0 & 1 & 0 & 0 \\ -1 & 2 & -1 & 0 & 1 & 0 \\ 0 & -1 & 2 & 0 & 0 & 1 \end{array}\right] \rightarrow \left[\begin{array}{ccc|ccc} 1 & -1/2 & 0 & 1/2 & 0 & 0 \\ 0 & 3/2 & -1 & 1/2 & 1 & 0 \\ 0 & -1 & 2 & 0 & 0 & 1 \end{array}\right] \tag{1.18}$$

You can notice that the first row is scaled by $1/2$. Then, the first row is added to the second row to cancel out the first column to zero. The similar process continues to the third row such that

$$\left[\begin{array}{ccc|ccc} 1 & -1/2 & 0 & 1/2 & 0 & 0 \\ 0 & 3/2 & -1 & 1/2 & 1 & 0 \\ 0 & -1 & 2 & 0 & 0 & 1 \end{array}\right] \rightarrow \left[\begin{array}{ccc|ccc} 1 & 0 & 1 & 1 & 1 & 1 \\ 0 & 1 & -2/3 & 1/3 & 2/3 & 0 \\ 0 & 0 & 1 & 1/4 & 1/2 & 3/4 \end{array}\right] \tag{1.19}$$

Now, using the third row, we now propagate upward to make the other rows' third column to zero such that

$$\left[\begin{array}{ccc|ccc} 1 & 0 & 1 & 1 & 1 & 1 \\ 0 & 1 & -2/3 & 1/3 & 2/3 & 0 \\ 0 & 0 & 4/3 & 1/3 & 2/3 & 1 \end{array}\right] \rightarrow \left[\begin{array}{ccc|ccc} 1 & 0 & 0 & 3/4 & 1/2 & 1/4 \\ 0 & 1 & 0 & 1/2 & 1 & 1/2 \\ 0 & 0 & 1 & 1/4 & 1/2 & 3/4 \end{array}\right] \tag{1.20}$$

After completing the step, the right 3×3 portion of the matrix becomes the inverse matrix. For $N \times N$ matrix, the time complexity of the Gauss–Jordan elimination is $O(N^3)$.

1.3.3.2 Sparse Matrix

The common use cases of the matrix in fluid simulation, such as solving diffusion or pressure problems, require very large dimensions which easily exceeds a million. This can be problematic even for a simple matrix–vector computation since the time complexity for the operation is $O(N^2)$ in a case of square

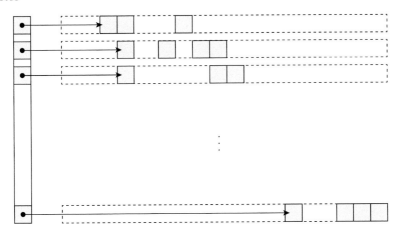

FIGURE 1.15
Illustration of a compressed sparse row matrix. Each row stores nonzero
elements (gray boxes) and a list of pointers.

matrices. Also, the space complexity of a matrix is $O(N^2)$ which is also very
expensive. But, the matrices from the fluid simulations are often mostly occupied with zeros. For example, a matrix to compute diffusion equation (see
Section 3.4.4) has at most seven nonzero columns per row. Such a matrix
is called "sparse" matrix whereas the conventional matrix is called "dense"
matrix. To improve both time and space complexity, we can think of storing
only the nonzero elements, and if it is possible, both the time complexity of
matrix–vector multiplication and space complexity will decrease to $O(N)$.

One of the data structures to efficiently represent a sparse matrix is to store
nonzero elements and their column indices per row. Each row is then stored as
a list as shown in Figure 1.15. This approach is called the compressed sparse
row (CSR) matrix. If the compression is done in column unit, then it is called
the compressed sparse column (CSC) matrix. To find out other compression
formats, see Saad's technical paper on the sparse matrices [99]. In this book,
the grid-based fluid simulators use sparse matrices to solve linear systems,
and for such use cases, we can further optimize the compression format. The
details can be found in Appendix C.1.

1.3.4   System of Linear Equations

When computing numerical problems, we often encounter linear equations.
For example, the diffusion or pressure equations from grid-based simulators
are often calculated by solving linear systems. We will cover the details in
Chapter 3, but those are the problems that require calculating the solution
with many constraints and knowing the bigger landscape view of the fluid
systems.

When we have a set of linear equations, we can represent the set, or the system, using a matrix. For example, consider the linear equations:

$$2x - y = 3$$
$$-x + 2y = 6$$

We can solve the equation above by multiplying the first row with 2, add it to the second row to eliminate y term, and then divide it by 3 to get $x = 4$ and $y = 5$. This can also be interpreted geometrically; find the intersection of two lines in a x–y plane. Alternatively, we can convert the equations into a matrix and a vector form, such that

$$\begin{bmatrix} 2 & -1 \\ -1 & 2 \end{bmatrix} \begin{bmatrix} x \\ y \end{bmatrix} = \begin{bmatrix} 3 \\ 6 \end{bmatrix} \tag{1.21}$$

Then, the solution can be calculated by multiplying the inverse matrix on both sides of the equation, such that

$$\begin{bmatrix} x \\ y \end{bmatrix} = \begin{bmatrix} 2 & -1 \\ -1 & 2 \end{bmatrix}^{-1} \begin{bmatrix} 3 \\ 6 \end{bmatrix} = \frac{1}{3}\begin{bmatrix} 2 & 1 \\ 1 & 2 \end{bmatrix}\begin{bmatrix} 3 \\ 6 \end{bmatrix} = \begin{bmatrix} 4 \\ 5 \end{bmatrix} \tag{1.22}$$

If we generalize the procedure to N-dimensional system, we can express the linear equations as

$$\mathbf{A}\mathbf{x} = \mathbf{b} \tag{1.23}$$

where $\mathbf{A}$ is the system matrix, $\mathbf{x}$ is the unknown solution, and $\mathbf{b}$ is the vector of the constant term of the linear equations.

1.3.4.1 Direct Methods

The example above using the inverse matrix to compute the solution is one way of solving the linear system. The key here is how to compute the inverse matrix, and we know from the previous section that we can use Gauss–Jordan elimination method. Such a method which computes the solution directly without approximation[*] is called a "direct" method. For small systems, the direct methods can be useful. But for the larger systems from many numerical problems, the direct methods are often impractical because of the time complexity. For instance, the Gauss–Jordan elimination method takes $O(N^3)$, where N is the dimension of the linear system.

1.3.4.2 Indirect Methods

Instead of computing the solution directly, an alternative way of getting the solution is to make an initial guess and iterate multiple times to approximate the answer. If it is determined to reach the predefined threshold that indicates the approximated solution is good enough, we can terminate the iteration and use the last-known answer. Such an approach is called an "indirect" method.

---

[*]Note that still there can be rounding-off errors because of the way computer handles floating numbers [25,117].

1.3.4.2.1 Jacobi Method

Imagine a case where the system matrix $\mathbf{A}$ is a diagonal matrix. It means only the diagonal elements, a_{ii}, are nonzero, and other off-diagonal elements are all zeros. In such case, getting the inverse matrix of $\mathbf{A}$ is very simple; the ith diagonal element of $\mathbf{A}^{-1}$ is just $1/a_{ii}$. If $\mathbf{A}$ is not a diagonal matrix, but still the diagonal components are dominant, we can expect that $\mathbf{A}^{-1}$ is similar to $\mathbf{D}^{-1}$ where $\mathbf{D}$ is the diagonal part of the matrix $\mathbf{A}$. Keeping that in mind, let's rewrite Equation 1.23, such that

$$(\mathbf{D} + \mathbf{R})\mathbf{x} = \mathbf{b} \tag{1.24}$$

where $\mathbf{R} = \mathbf{A} - \mathbf{D}$. This equation can be further evolved to

$$\mathbf{D}\mathbf{x} = \mathbf{b} - \mathbf{R}\mathbf{x} \tag{1.25}$$

and finally,

$$\mathbf{x} = \mathbf{D}^{-1}(\mathbf{b} - \mathbf{R}\mathbf{x}) \tag{1.26}$$

If $\mathbf{x}$ above is the right solution, the equation will hold. However, if $\mathbf{x}$ from the left-hand side and right-hand side are different, putting a new $\mathbf{x}$ to the right will result different $\mathbf{x}$ on the left. We can keep iterating this by passing the resulting $\mathbf{x}$ from the left-hand side to the right-hand side again until both $\mathbf{x}$ reach the same value, such that

$$\mathbf{x}^{k+1} = \mathbf{D}^{-1}(\mathbf{b} - \mathbf{R}\mathbf{x}^{k}) \tag{1.27}$$

or, if we write the same equation element-wise,

$$x_i^{k+1} = \frac{1}{a_{ii}} \left(b_i - \sum_{j \neq i} a_{ij} x_j^{k} \right) \tag{1.28}$$

where k is the number of iterations. This procedure is called Jacobi iteration, and the method is called Jacobi method. From the last equation above, if the system matrix is a pure diagonal matrix, $\mathbf{R}$ should be zero. Hence, we get the right solution with only one iteration. If the diagonal matrix $\mathbf{D}$ is less dominant, more nonzeros will flood in from $\mathbf{R}\mathbf{x}$, requiring more iterations to converge. In general, the Jacobi method has $O(N^2)$ time complexity [100].

1.3.4.2.2 Gauss–Seidel Method

To accelerate the convergence of the Jacobi method, let's try passing more information to the right-hand side of the equation than the diagonal. Similar to the Jacobi, we can rewrite Equation 1.23 as:

$$(\mathbf{L} + \mathbf{U})\mathbf{x} = \mathbf{b} \tag{1.29}$$

where **L** is the lower-triangular portion of the matrix including the diagonal and **U** is the strictly upper-triangular part. For instance,

$$\begin{bmatrix} 1 & 2 & 3 \\ 4 & 5 & 6 \\ 7 & 8 & 9 \end{bmatrix} = \begin{bmatrix} 1 & 0 & 0 \\ 4 & 5 & 0 \\ 7 & 8 & 9 \end{bmatrix} + \begin{bmatrix} 0 & 2 & 3 \\ 0 & 0 & 6 \\ 0 & 0 & 0 \end{bmatrix} \tag{1.30}$$

Here, the first matrix on the right-hand side is **L** and the last one is **U**. We can then write the iteration equation as:

$$\mathbf{Lx} = \mathbf{b} - \mathbf{Ux} \tag{1.31}$$

Now, unlike the diagonal matrix, knowing the inversion of the triangular matrix **L** is not a trivial task and would require the direct method. However, if you look into the equation carefully, you'll notice that the first element of **x**, x_1, can be easily computed by

$$x_1^{k+1} = \frac{1}{a_{11}} \left(b_1 - \sum_{j>1} a_{1j} x_j^k \right) \tag{1.32}$$

Since we now have x_1^{k+1}, we can assign this solution to the second row of the equation which is:

$$x_2^{k+1} = \frac{1}{a_{22}} \left(b_2 - a_{21} x_1^{k+1} - \sum_{j>1} a_{1j} x_j^k \right) \tag{1.33}$$

To generalize this procedure, we can write the iteration equation as follows:

$$x_i^{k+1} = \frac{1}{a_{ii}} \left(b_i - \sum_{j>i} a_{ij} x_j^{k+1} - \sum_{j>i} a_{ij} x_j^k \right) \tag{1.34}$$

So without inverting the matrix **L**, we can perform the iteration. This is called Gauss–Seidel method. Note that the term $\sum_{j>i} a_{ij} x_j^{k+1}$ from the equation above is the only difference between the Gauss–Seidel and Jacobi methods. This term is the contribution of the solution from the previous row which makes the iteration most up-to-date, and hence converges faster than Jacobi iteration. But still, the method has $O(N^2)$ time complexity which is the same as the Jacobi method.

1.3.4.2.3 *Gradient Descent Method*

Another approach to solve the linear system is by solving a minimization problem. From Equation 1.23,

$$F(\mathbf{x}) = |\mathbf{Ax} - \mathbf{b}|^2 \tag{1.35}$$

If the input **x** is the solution, this function will return zero. If not, we can iterate to find **x** that makes $F(\mathbf{x}) = 0$. For instance, imagine a 2D system where $F(\mathbf{x})$ can be plotted as shown in Figure 1.16. The point starting

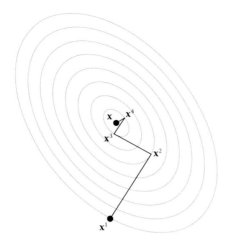

FIGURE 1.16
Illustration of the gradient descent process. The gray lines represent the isocontour of function F.

from $\mathbf{x}_1$ follows the steepest (or gradient) direction at each step, which is perpendicular to the isocontour.[*] After enough iterations, the solution will converge that minimizes the function F. This process is called gradient descent method. When solving linear systems in a fluid simulation, however, the gradient descent method is rarely used because of the slow convergence. For instance, if one of the semi-axes of the ellipsoid in Figure 1.16 is much longer than the other one, it would take a number of iterations to reach the final solution. This method, however, provides the foundation for one of the most frequently used methods, that is, the conjugate gradient.

1.3.4.2.4 Conjugate Gradient Method

In practice, the extended method called conjugate gradient (CG) is often used. Instead of taking the steepest direction at each iteration, the method follows the "conjugate" directions. When two vectors $\mathbf{a}$ and $\mathbf{b}$ satisfy

$$\mathbf{a} \cdot (\mathbf{A}\mathbf{b}) \tag{1.36}$$

we say the two vectors are conjugate. Note that the system matrix $\mathbf{A}$ is involved when determining the conjugacy. Thus, the characteristic of the system is reflected when finding the direction vectors. The maximum number of these conjugate vectors for an N-dimensional system is N. Thus, the CG method takes at most N iterations to fully converge to the solution. Figure 1.17 illustrates the CG procedure. Unlike the steepest gradient, the same solution can be found with only two iterations. For deeper insight and

---

[*]See Section 1.3.5.2 for more details on the definition of gradient.

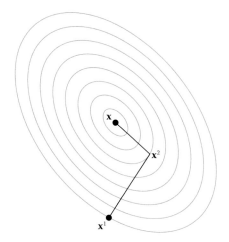

FIGURE 1.17
Illustration of the conjugate gradient process. The gray lines represent the isocontour of function F.

implementation details for the CG method, see the note from Shewchuk [107]. From our codebase, the implementation can be found from `jet/include/cg.h` and `jet/include/detail/cg-inl.h`.

To accelerate the computation even further, there's a method called "preconditioned" conjugate gradient. Again, the details of the algorithm are well explained in Shewchuk [107], but the idea is to apply a preconditioning filter to the system such as

$$\mathbf{M}^{-1}\mathbf{A}\mathbf{x} = \mathbf{M}^{-1}\mathbf{b} \qquad (1.37)$$

where $\mathbf{M}$ is the preconditioning matrix that is easy to compute the inverse matrix but still similar to $\mathbf{A}$. Having such $\mathbf{M}$ will make the term $\mathbf{M}^{-1}\mathbf{A}$ close to the identity matrix, and will make the convergence faster than normal CG method. See Appendix A.1 or `jet/include/detail/cg-inl.h` for the implementation.

1.3.5   Field

So far we have been dealing with one or two vectors. In this section, we are going to extend our focus to the entire space where a scalar or a vector value is defined at every point in the space. Such a mapping, a point to value, is called a field. If we map a point to a scalar value, such as temperature or pressure, that is a scalar field. If we map a point to a vector, then it becomes a vector field. The heat map we normally see from a weather report is a scalar field. Wind or ocean current are vector fields. In this book, field will be mostly used for describing physical quantities of fluids. But it can be used for any other general quantities, even if they don't have physical meanings such as colors.

To make the idea more meaningful, let's write some code. Here's the minimal interface for the scalar and vector fields:

```
1  class Field3 {
2   public:
3      Field3();
4
5      virtual ~Field3();
6  };
7
8  class ScalarField3 : public Field3 {
9   public:
10      ScalarField3();
11
12      virtual ~ScalarField3();
13
14      virtual double sample(const Vector3D& x) const = 0;
15  };
16
17  class VectorField3 : public Field3 {
18   public:
19      VectorField3();
20
21      virtual ~VectorField3();
22
23      virtual Vector3D sample(const Vector3D& x) const = 0;
24  };
```

We can see that we have base class `Field3` to represent a 3D field. It doesn't store any data nor perform any action, but it is just the root of the hierarchy. It is inherited by `ScalarField3` and `VectorField3`, which define specific scalar and vector field interfaces. We currently have one virtual function `sample` in both abstract base classes; this function represents the field which maps a point in 3D to a scalar or vector value.

We can now extend these base classes to implement actual fields. For example, let's define a scalar function which looks as follows:

$$f(\mathbf{x}) = f(x, y, z) = \sin x \sin y \sin z \qquad (1.38)$$

where vector $\mathbf{x}$ is (x, y, z) and $f(\mathbf{x})$ is the scalar function that maps $\mathbf{x}$ to a scalar value. Figure 1.18 shows how this function looks like. We can now implement this field by overriding the pure virtual function we defined earlier:

```
1  class MyCustomScalarField3 final : public ScalarField3 {
2   public:
3      double sample(const Vector3D& x) const override {
4          return std::sin(x.x) * std::sin(x.y) * std::sin(x.z);
5      }
6  };
```

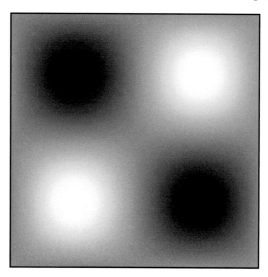

FIGURE 1.18
A cross-section of the example scalar field $f(x, y, z) = \sin x \sin y \sin z$ at $z = \pi/2$.

Similarly, we can also define simple vector field where

$$\mathbf{F}(\mathbf{x}) = \mathbf{F}(x, y, z) = (F_x, F_y, F_z) = (\sin x \sin y, \sin y \sin z, \sin z \sin x). \quad (1.39)$$

From the Equation 1.39, vector field $\mathbf{F}$ is written in boldface because it is mapping a vector to another vector. It is also written in an expanded vector form (F_x, F_y, F_z) where each of the elements corresponds to $\mathbf{F}(\mathbf{x})_x$, $\mathbf{F}(\mathbf{x})_y$, and $\mathbf{F}(\mathbf{x})_z$, respectively. Figure 1.19 illustrates how this field looks like, and the equivalent code can be written as:

```
1  class MyCustomVectorField3 final : public VectorField3 {
2  public:
3      Vector3D sample(const Vector3D& x) const override {
4          return Vector3D(std::sin(x.x) * std::sin(y),
5                          std::sin(x.y) * std::sin(z),
6                          std::sin(x.z) * std::sin(x));
7      }
8  };
```

It has been quite straightforward so far. We defined scalar and vector fields which map a given point to either a scalar or a vector value. From now on, we are going to see what kind of operations or measurements we can take from the fields. This operation will convert a field into another field that measures different characteristics of the given field. The most commonly used operations are gradient, Laplacian, divergence, and curl. The first two operations are

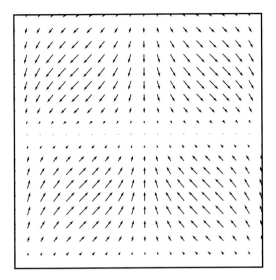

FIGURE 1.19
A cross-section of the example vector field $\mathbf{F}(x, y, z) = (\sin x \sin y, \sin y \sin z, \sin z \sin x)$ at $z = \pi/2$.

mostly applied to scalar fields, while the latter two only apply to vector fields. Let's find out what these operators mean and how to implement them.

1.3.5.1 Partial Derivative

Before we get started, let's talk about partial derivative which is the most important building block for defining and understanding all the operators we will cover in this section. Some readers may find this familiar while some others won't. So I'm going to explain the basic idea very briefly and informally, but if you are interested in learning more, see Vector Calculus textbooks [82,101] for detailed introductions.

The partial derivative is nothing but the way of measuring the tangent of a given field at a given location. But we call it a "partial" derivative because we are taking the derivative along the specific direction for a given multidimensional field. Assume that we have a scalar field $f(\mathbf{x})$. To evaluate the slope in x-axis at $\mathbf{x} = (x, y, z)$, we can start from the following equation:

$$\frac{f(x + \Delta, y, z) - f(x, y, z)}{\Delta} \tag{1.40}$$

where Δ is a reasonably small interval in the x-direction. The equation is simply using the field value from slightly left and right points and dividing the difference by the spacing between them. If Δ becomes very small, then the approximated tangent converges to the true tangent, and we say that is the partial derivative in the x-direction at point $\mathbf{x}$. This partial derivative is denoted by

$$\frac{\partial f}{\partial x}(\mathbf{x}) \tag{1.41}$$

Thus, the process is just like slicing the given scalar field parallel to the x-axis and measuring the tangent of the cross-section as shown in Figure 1.20. Similarly, we can write y- and z-directional derivatives as

$$\frac{\partial f}{\partial y}(\mathbf{x})$$

and

$$\frac{\partial f}{\partial z}(\mathbf{x})$$

Now imagine we have a scalar field, $f(x, y, z) = xy + yz$. When taking partial derivative for a certain axis, we simply consider other variables as constants in ordinary derivatives. Thus, $\frac{\partial f}{\partial x}(\mathbf{x})$ in this case would be

$$\frac{\partial f}{\partial x}(\mathbf{x}) = y \tag{1.42}$$

because $(xy)' = y$ and $(yz)' = 0$. For y and z, we can apply the same routine to get

$$\frac{\partial f}{\partial y}(\mathbf{x}) = x + z$$

and

$$\frac{\partial f}{\partial z}(\mathbf{x}) = y$$

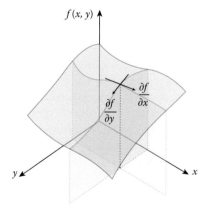

FIGURE 1.20
Partial derivatives for x and y axes are shown for 2D field $f(x, y)$. Each of the derivatives are the slopes of the cross-sections.

Also, the partial derivatives for the field from `MyCustomScalarField`, which is $f(x, y, z) = \sin x \sin y \sin z$, can be written as

$$\frac{\partial f}{\partial x}(\mathbf{x}) = \cos x \sin y \sin z$$

$$\frac{\partial f}{\partial y}(\mathbf{x}) = \sin x \cos y \sin z$$

and

$$\frac{\partial f}{\partial z}(\mathbf{x}) = \sin x \sin y \cos z$$

Now using these partial derivatives as our key foundation, let's find out how we can define other operators, starting from the gradient.

1.3.5.2 Gradient

The gradient operator measures the rate and direction of change in a scalar field as shown in Figure 1.21. From the figure, note that the arrows are pointing the "higher" region and are perpendicular to the isocontour. Those are the steepest slope directions at the sample locations.

The gradient operator is denoted by ∇, and we can define the operator as:

$$\nabla f(\mathbf{x}) = \left(\frac{\partial f}{\partial x}(\mathbf{x}), \frac{\partial f}{\partial y}(\mathbf{x}), \frac{\partial f}{\partial z}(\mathbf{x}) \right) \tag{1.43}$$

where $\partial/\partial x$, $\partial/\partial y$, and $\partial/\partial z$ are the partial derivatives as we saw earlier from Equation 1.41. So by definition, the gradient operator is simply a bundle of the partial derivatives in all directions.

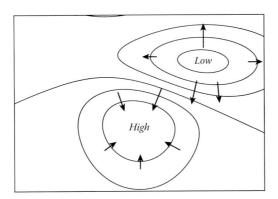

FIGURE 1.21
Isocontour is drawn to indicate the height, and the gradient vectors are shown by the arrows. The height field is from one of the Matplotlib examples [54].

If we apply the gradient equation (1.43) to our previous example scalar field, it becomes

$$\nabla f(\mathbf{x}) = (\cos x \sin y \sin z, \sin x \cos y \sin z, \sin x \sin y \cos z) \qquad (1.44)$$

To add this feature to our existing classes, let's first update `ScalarField3` as follows:

```
1  class ScalarField3 : public Field3 {
2   public:
3       ...
4       virtual Vector3D gradient(const Vector3D& x) const = 0;
5  };
```

We can also update our example class `MyCustomScalarField3` as:

```
1  class MyCustomScalarField3 : public ScalarField3 {
2   public:
3       ...
4       Vector3D gradient(const Vector3D& x) const {
5           return Vector3D(std::cos(x.x) * std::sin(x.y) * std::sin(x.z),
6                           std::sin(x.x) * std::cos(x.y) * std::sin(x.z),
7                           std::sin(x.x) * std::sin(x.y) * std::cos(x.z));
8       }
9  };
```

Figure 1.22 shows the result from the code. You can notice that the arrows are pointing toward the bright regions of Figure 1.18 which is expected from the definition of the gradient.

The gradient operator is often used together with an energy field. For example, if we place a ball on the uneven ground, it will roll from a higher to a lower level. The force acting on that ball is trying to minimize the potential energy from the gravity or, in other words, trying to find the lowest possible level nearby. Thus, the force is proportional to the gradient of the ground elevation. Another example is the pressure which we often see from the weather forecast. We know that the wind blows from higher to lower pressure region. This is also related to the gradient of the pressure field. We will revisit this topic in Section 1.7.2 where we will discuss fluid dynamics.

1.3.5.3 Divergence

Let's move our focus to the vector field. One of the important measurements from vector fields is divergence. For a given point in a vector field, the divergence operator measures incoming or outgoing flow with a scalar value. Imagine a very small cube and assume that we measure vectors from a given vector field at each face of the cube. If the sum of the magnitude of the vectors is greater than zero, then it means some flow is generated inside the cube; thus, it is a source. If the sum is less than zero, then something is sucking the

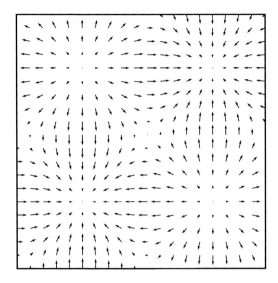

FIGURE 1.22
A cross-section of the example gradient field at $z = \pi/2$.

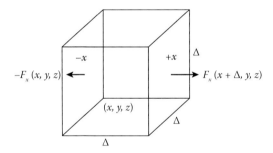

FIGURE 1.23
Image showing a cube with size $\Delta \times \Delta \times \Delta$. Two arrows represent the vector field at $+x$ and $-x$ faces.

flow which means it is a sink. And the magnitude of the sum gives the amount of the transaction. Figure 1.23 explains this idea more visually.

To measure the divergence, let's start from the cube in Figure 1.23. The size of the cube is Δ. Thus, the area of a face is Δ^2. Now the total amount of stream going in or out through $+x$ face will be

$$\Delta^2 F_x(x + \Delta, y, z) \tag{1.45}$$

where $\mathbf{F} = (F_x, F_y, F_z)$ is the input vector field. Thus, $F_x(x + \Delta, y, z)$ is the x-directional vector field at $+x$ face. Similarly, we can do the same for $-x$ face which will be

$$-\Delta^2 F_x(x, y, z) \tag{1.46}$$

Note that we put negative sign because $+$ is the inward direction in this case. Now let's sum these up for every cube faces. We will then have

$$
sum = \Delta^2 (F_x(x + \Delta, y, z) - F_x(x, y, z)
$$
$$
+ F_y(x, y + \Delta, z) - F_y(x, y, z)
$$
$$
+ F_z(x, y, z + \Delta) - F_z(x, y, z))
$$

The equation above measures the divergence for the cube. Actually, it measures the sum of the divergence for the whole volume of the cube. So we divide it up with the cube's volume, which is Δ^3, and we get

$$
\frac{\text{Sum}}{\text{Volume}} = \frac{F_x(x + \Delta, y, z) - F_x(x, y, z)}{\Delta}
$$
$$
+ \frac{F_y(x, y + \Delta, z) - F_y(x, y, z)}{\Delta}
$$
$$
+ \frac{F_z(x, y, z + \Delta) - F_z(x, y, z)}{\Delta}
$$

Noticed some pattern here? Yes, this is just like the sum of approximated partial derivatives (Equation 1.40) for x, y, and z. Thus, if Δ goes really small, we now have the divergence operator:

$$
\nabla \cdot \mathbf{F}(\mathbf{x}) = \frac{\partial F_x}{\partial x} + \frac{\partial F_y}{\partial y} + \frac{\partial F_z}{\partial z} \tag{1.47}
$$

Here, the divergence operator is denoted by $\nabla\cdot$. This equation is just like taking a dot product with the operator and the vector at a given point:

$$
\nabla \cdot \mathbf{F}(\mathbf{x}) = \left(\frac{\partial}{\partial x}, \frac{\partial}{\partial y}, \frac{\partial}{\partial z} \right) \cdot \mathbf{F}(\mathbf{x}) \tag{1.48}
$$

If we apply this divergence operator to our sample vector field $F(x, y, z) = (\sin x \sin y, \sin y \sin z, \sin z \sin x)$, it becomes $\cos x \sin y + \cos y \sin z + \cos z \sin x$.

To add this feature to `VectorField3`, let's add one more virtual function to the class:

```
1  class VectorField : public Field3 {
2   public:
3      ...
4      virtual double divergence(const Vector3D& x) const = 0;
5  };
```

Actual implementation of the function for our example class `MyCustomVectorField3` can then be written as:

```
1  class MyCustomVectorField3 : public VectorField3 {
2   public:
```

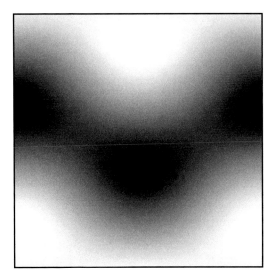

FIGURE 1.24
A cross-section of the example divergence field at $z = \pi/2$.

```
3        ...
4        double divergence(const Vector3D& x) const {
5            return std::cos(x.x) * std::sin(x.y)
6                + std::cos(x.y) * std::sin(x.z)
7                + std::cos(x.z) * std::sin(x.x);
8        }
9    };
```

Figure 1.24 shows the result from the code. The points where the original vector field $(\sin x \sin y, \sin y \sin z, \sin z \sin x)$ are pointing inward, the divergence tells us that those are sinks. Same for the points where the vectors are facing outward.

1.3.5.4 Curl

If divergence measures sink and source, curl evaluates the rotational flow of a vector field at a given point. As shown in Figure 1.25, imagine a small square in xy-plane. To measure the rotation around that square, we first evaluate the difference of x-directional vectors between $+y$ and $-y$ faces. Then, we do the same difference between $+x$ and $-x$ faces for y-directional vectors. Finally, these differences are summed up along the counterclockwise direction. We can write this as an approximated equation:

$$\left(\frac{F_y(x+\Delta, y, z) - F_y(x, y, z)}{\Delta} - \frac{F_x(x, y+\Delta, z) - F_z(x, y, z)}{\Delta} \right) \mathbf{k} \qquad (1.49)$$

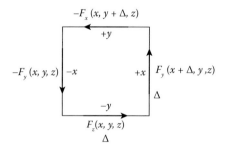

FIGURE 1.25
A square with size $\Delta \times \Delta$ is illustrated with the velocity field along the edges.

where again, Δ is the width of the square which we saw from the approximated partial derivative (Equation 1.40). If we extend this to nonapproximated version,[*] it becomes:

$$\text{rotation}_z = \left(\frac{\partial F_y}{\partial x} - \frac{\partial F_x}{\partial y} \right) \mathbf{k} \tag{1.50}$$

This equation measures rotation in the z-axis. If we further extend this evaluation to x- and y-axes, the curl operator can be defined as

$$\nabla \times \mathbf{F}(\mathbf{x}) = \left(\frac{\partial F_z}{\partial y} - \frac{\partial F_y}{\partial z} \right) \mathbf{i} + \left(\frac{\partial F_x}{\partial z} - \frac{\partial F_z}{\partial x} \right) \mathbf{j} + \left(\frac{\partial F_y}{\partial x} - \frac{\partial F_x}{\partial y} \right) \mathbf{k} \tag{1.51}$$

Similar to the divergence operator, the $\nabla \times$ operator can be interpreted as taking the cross product with the partial derivatives and the field.

$$\nabla \times \mathbf{F}(\mathbf{x}) = \left(\frac{\partial}{\partial x}, \frac{\partial}{\partial y}, \frac{\partial}{\partial z} \right) \times \mathbf{F}(\mathbf{x}) \tag{1.52}$$

The result of the curl operator is a vector. The direction and the magnitude of the vector correspond to the rotational axis and amount of the rotation, respectively. Thus, if you find a long $+x$-directional vector as an output, then it means the vector field around the given position has a lot of rotation around $+x$ axis. For instance, imagine a simple vector field

$$\mathbf{F}(x, y, z) = (-y, x, 0) \tag{1.53}$$

As shown in Figure 1.26, this field rotates counterclockwise around the z-axis. The curl for this field will be

$$\mathbf{F}(x, y, z) = (0, 0, 2) \tag{1.54}$$

which is parallel to the z-axis. If the curl operator is applied to our sample vector field function $\mathbf{F}(x, y, z) = (\sin x \sin y, \sin y \sin z, \sin z \sin x)$, it becomes

---

[*]This is not a very formal way to explain curl operator, but an attempt to bring the concept of the curl in a more friendly way. See Matthews [82] for a more detailed and formal explanation for curl and other operators.

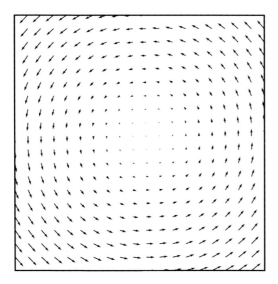

FIGURE 1.26
A simple rotating vector field around the z-axis.

$(-\sin y \cos z, -\sin z \cos x, -\sin x \cos y)$. To implement this, we also add a new virtual function to `VectorField3` and implement it from the subclasses. For example, our sample vector field class `MyCustomVectorField3` can be implemented as:

```
class MyCustomVectorField3 : public VectorField3 {
  public:
      ...
      Vector3D curl(const Vector3D& x) const {
          return Vector3D(-std::sin(x.y) * std::cos(x.z),
                          -std::sin(x.z) * std::cos(x.x),
                          -std::sin(x.x) * std::cos(x.y));
      }
};
```

The result of this code is shown in Figure 1.27.

1.3.5.5 Laplacian

Finally, let's meet Laplacian. The Laplacian operator measures how much the scalar field value at a given location is different from the average field value nearby. In other words, this operator evaluates the "bumps" on the scalar field. Take a look at the example scalar field from Figure 1.28. It shows a terrain-like 2D height field. The result of Laplacian operator then shows the tip of the mountains and the center line of the valleys are highlighted with white and

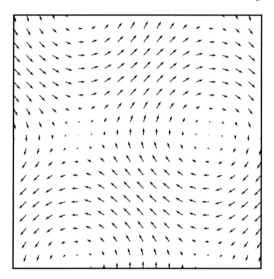

FIGURE 1.27
A cross-section of the example curl field at $z = \pi/4$.

black Laplacian values. The plane or slope that does not have any curvature has zero Laplacian value (the gray area in the image).

To get a deeper understanding, let's start with the gradient. Taking the previous example again, Figure 1.28b shows the gradient field, and we can notice that the vectors either converge or expand in the area where the non-flat features exist. Now, we already know that the operator that measures how much the vector field converges or expands is the divergence. Thus, we can first apply the gradient to the original scalar field to get an intermediate vector field, and then apply the divergence to get the final scalar field that describes the bumpiness of the input field. This is the definition of Laplacian operator, and we can write it as

$$\nabla^2 f(\mathbf{x}) = \nabla \cdot \nabla f(\mathbf{x}) = \frac{\partial^2 f(\mathbf{x})}{\partial x^2} + \frac{\partial^2 f(\mathbf{x})}{\partial y^2} + \frac{\partial^2 f(\mathbf{x})}{\partial z^2} \qquad (1.55)$$

Similar to the other operators, we can extend `ScalarField3` class to include the interface for measuring the Laplacian as:

```
class ScalarField3 : public Field3 {
public:
    ...
    virtual double laplacian(const Vector3D& x) const = 0;
};
```

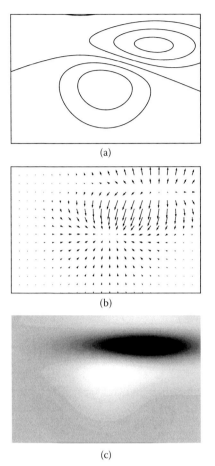

(a)

(b)

(c)

FIGURE 1.28
Image showing (a) the original scalar field, (b) the gradient field, and (c) the Laplacian field.

And our example class can be implemented as:

```
class MyCustomScalarField3 : public Field3 {
  public:
      ...
      double laplacian(const Vector3D& x) const {
          return -std::sin(x.x) * std::sin(x.y) * std::sin(x.z)
                 -std::sin(x.x) * std::sin(x.y) * std::sin(x.z)
                 -std::sin(x.x) * std::sin(x.y) * std::sin(x.z);
      }
};
```

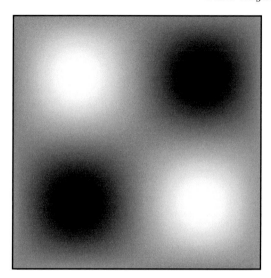

FIGURE 1.29
A cross-section of the example Laplacian field at $z = \pi/2$.

Since the Laplacian operator measures peaks and edges, one of the popular applications of the operator is the edge detection for a given scalar field since the output indicates where the edges are and how steep they are. Moreover, if we take that output and add or subtract from the original scalar field, we can either blur or sharpen the input. If we bring back the earlier terrain example, the tip of the mountain has negative Laplacian value. If we add the Laplacian field to the original terrain field, it will lower the sharpest point of the tip, thus making the feature point dull and blurry. Exactly the opposite thing happens when you subtract with the Laplacian field that will sharpen the original. Figure 1.29 shows the example results.

1.3.6   Interpolation

Interpolation is an approximation process that evaluates unknown value from known data values. Since the goal of this book is to model physics with computers, the continuous and infinite real world is represented by finite data points. Thus, to perform physics computations with such discrete samples, it is often required to evaluate values where the data are not available.

Imagine a car passing A to B as shown in Figure 1.30, and we only have its location recorded for those two checkpoints. To guess where the car was between those two, one of the options would be just drawing a line and assuming the car was on it (Figure 1.30b). For better guessing, we can think of using a curve based on the car's position and orientation as shown in Figure 1.30c.

Another application of the interpolation is the bitmap image scaling. Assume that we have a small image and would like to double the size.

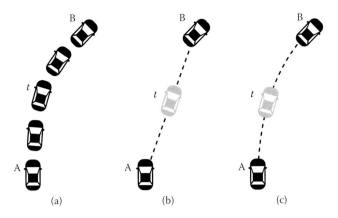

FIGURE 1.30
(a) The actual trace of the car, (b) the line approximation, and (c) the curve
approximation. The gray cars show the approximated location at time t for
two different approximation methods.

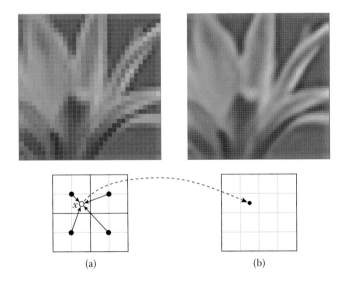

FIGURE 1.31
From the original image (a), a new pixel from image (b) interpolates the old
pixel values from A nearby its location x when performing the resizing.

Similar to the car example, we can approximate the pixel values for the higher-
resolution image by interpolating the pixels from the lower-resolution image.
As shown in Figure 1.31, the new pixel's value is determined by looking up
the nearby low-resolution pixels and averaging them with different weights.

There are different techniques for deciding the weights, but intuitively, we can imagine that closer neighboring pixels will contribute more to the weighted average.

The examples above show very common scenarios we encounter when processing discrete data, and we can write generic interpolation codes that can be applied to other calculations as well. Of course, there are a variety of algorithms with different characteristics. But from the following section, we will cover the most generic and commonly used methods that can be used for many other data-processing applications.

1.3.6.1   Nearest Point

Approximating a value at a random location by taking the nearest data point is the simplest method to perform interpolation. Consider the following code:

```
1   template<typename S, typename T>
2   inline S nearest(const S& f0, const S& f1, T t) {
3       return (t < 0.5) ? f0 : f1;
4   }
```

The code takes three parameters. The first parameter `f0` is the value at 0 and the second parameter `f1` is at 1. The last argument `f` is a value between 0 and 1. If this `f` is less than 0.5, which means it's closer to the first parameter, it returns `f0`. Otherwise, it is closer to `f1` and returns it. Figure 1.32 illustrates how the function looks like with sample data points. Notice that the resulting graph is a set of disjoint flat line segments. The segment starts and ends at the right middle point of the two data samples since the method takes the nearest data point for the interpolation. Because of this discontinuity, the method is not suitable for interpolating smooth functions but is good for fast evaluations.

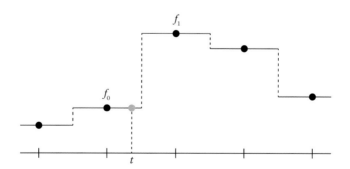

FIGURE 1.32

For given data points (black dots), the flat solid lines show the interpolation results using the nearest point approach.

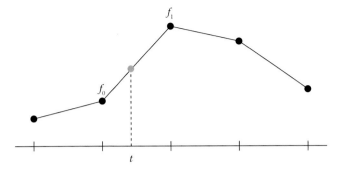

FIGURE 1.33
For given data points (black dots), the straight lines show the interpolation results using the linear approach.

1.3.6.2 Linear Interpolation

Linear interpolation, or often called "lerp" in short, is perhaps the most popular method because it is simple and efficient, but still gives reasonable results for many applications. As shown in Figure 1.33, it approximates values between two data points by connecting them with a line.

The code can be written in a straightforward manner. It is actually even simpler than the nearest point approximation above because the new code doesn't have such a conditional statement.

```
1   template<typename S, typename T>
2   inline S lerp(const S& f0, const S& f1, T t) {
3       return (1 - t) * f0 + t * f1;
4   }
```

Now, let's consider multidimensional cases. We would like to perform linear approximation inside a rectangle or box. This can be done by cascading the linear interpolation per dimension. As shown in Figure 1.34, it first starts with interpolating along the x-axis and then perform the interpolation for the remaining axes. The 2D linear interpolation is often called bilinear interpolation, and the following code shows the implementation.

```
1   template<typename S, typename T>
2   inline S bilerp(
3       const S& f00,
4       const S& f10,
5       const S& f01,
6       const S& f11,
7       T tx, T ty) {
8       return lerp(
9           lerp(f00, f10, tx),
```

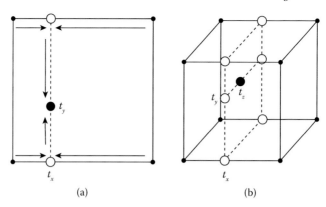

(a)   (b)

FIGURE 1.34
Image showing bilinear at point (t_x, t_y) (a) and trilinear interpolation at point (t_x, t_y, t_z) (b).

```
10              lerp(f01, f11, tx),
11              ty);
12   }
```

The same idea can be extended to 3D (which is called trilinear interpolation) as shown below.

```
1   template<typename S, typename T>
2   inline S trilerp(
3       const S& f000,
4       const S& f100,
5       const S& f010,
6       const S& f110,
7       const S& f001,
8       const S& f101,
9       const S& f011,
10      const S& f111,
11      T tx,
12      T ty,
13      T tz) {
14      return lerp(
15          bilerp(f000, f100, f010, f110, tx, ty),
16          bilerp(f001, f101, f011, f111, tx, ty),
17          tz);
18   }
```

You can easily verify that the results are the same regardless in which order you perform the interpolation. The codes above took x-axis first, followed by y and z. But it doesn't matter you reverse the order. If you expand the cascaded function call, you will notice that each corner value is multiplied by

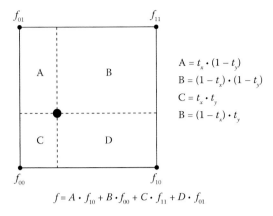

$$A = t_x \cdot (1 - t_y)$$
$$B = (1 - t_x) \cdot (1 - t_y)$$
$$C = t_x \cdot t_y$$
$$B = (1 - t_x) \cdot t_y$$

$$f = A \cdot f_{10} + B \cdot f_{00} + C \cdot f_{11} + D \cdot f_{01}$$

FIGURE 1.35
Bilinear interpolation explained by weighted average.

the area (2D) or volume (3D) of the opposite side of the interpolation point. Figure 1.35 illustrates what this means more visually in 2D.

1.3.6.3 Catmull–Rom Spline Interpolation

To perform linear interpolation, we only need two data points. But what if we have more data so that we can feed more information to the interpolation code? Will it produce better approximation?

Catmull–Rom spline interpolation is one of the classic interpolation methods [27] that generates a spline curve to interpolate intermediate values. Assuming that we have four data points with uniform spacing, we can first start with a 3rd order polynomial function that passes the points:

$$f(t) = a_3 t^3 + a_2 t^2 + a_1 t + a_0 \qquad (1.56)$$

The input of this function is a parametric variable t, which is between 0 and 1. The output, $f(t)$, is then defined by the polynomial function. We currently don't know what a_0, a_1, a_2, and a_3 are, but let's say the four given points, f_0, f_1, f_2, and f_3, correspond to $v(t)$ at $t = -1, 0, 1,$ and 2, respectively. Thus, we now know that a_0 is f_1.

We can also take the derivative of $v(t)$:

$$v'(t) = d(t) = 3a_3 t^2 + 2a_2 t + a_1 \qquad (1.57)$$

We approximate this $d(t)$ at $t = 0$ and 1 by

$$d(0) = d_1 = (f_2 - f_0)/2$$
$$d(1) = d_2 = (f_3 - f_1)/2$$

This means $d1$ and $d2$ are averaged slopes at 0 and 1. This also gives us the solution for a_1 which is $d1 = (f_2 - f_0)/2$. Now the remaining unknowns are a_2 and a_3. These values can be calculated by setting $t = 1$ and solving the linear equations:

$$f_2 = a_3 + a_2 + a_1 + a_0$$
$$d_2 = 3a_3 + 2a_2 + a_1$$

Solving these equations will lead us to the following code:

```cpp
template <typename S, typename T>
inline S catmullRomSpline(
    const S& f0,
    const S& f1,
    const S& f2,
    const S& f3,
    T f) {
    S d1 = (f2 - f0) / 2;
    S d2 = (f3 - f1) / 2;
    S D1 = f2 - f1;

    S a3 = d1 + d2 - 2 * D1;
    S a2 = 3 * D1 - 2 * d1 - d2;
    S a1 = d1;
    S a0 = f1;

    return a3 * cubic(f) + a2 * square(f) + a1 * f + a0;
}
```

As we can observe from Figure 1.36, the code gives smoother and continuous approximation compared to the linear interpolation. There are, of course, various kinds of interpolation methods other than the linear or Catmull–Rom spline methods. Depending on the application and constraint from the

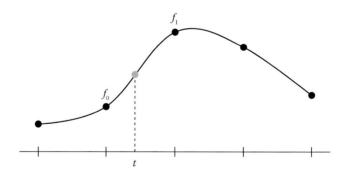

FIGURE 1.36
For given data points (black dots), the splines show the interpolation results using the Catmull–Rom approach.

data set, a more suitable interpolation method can be selected. Read Boor's book [18] or visit Bourke's website [19] to find out more details on the interpolation.

1.4 Geometry

When simulating fluids, we often want to set the initial shape of the fluid or define the solid objects that interact with the fluid body. In this section, we will implement common geometric data types and operations that are frequently used when developing fluid engines.

1.4.1 Surface

In this book, the topmost geometry type is surface. Some of the basic operations supported by a surface are querying for the closest point on the surface from an arbitrary point, measuring the surface normal from the point, and performing ray–surface intersection tests. Ray is the data type that represents a line with one endpoint as shown in Figure 1.37.

To support the basic queries, class `Surface3` can be defined as shown below.

```
1   struct SurfaceRayIntersection3 {
2       bool isIntersecting;
3       double t;
4       Vector3D point;
5       Vector3D normal;
6   };
7
8   class Surface3 {
9     public:
10        Surface3();
11
```

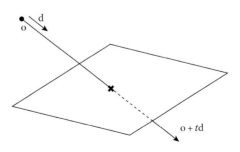

FIGURE 1.37
Surface, ray, and their intersection.

```
12      virtual ~Surface3();
13
14      virtual Vector3D closestPoint(const Vector3D& otherPoint) const = 0;
15
16      virtual Vector3D closestNormal(const Vector3D& otherPoint) const = 0;
17
18      virtual BoundingBox3D boundingBox() const = 0;
19
20      virtual void getClosestIntersection(
21          const Ray3D& ray,
22          SurfaceRayIntersection3* intersection) const = 0;
23
24      virtual bool intersects(const Ray3D& ray) const;
25
26      virtual double closestDistance(const Vector3D& otherPoint) const;
27  };
28
29  bool Surface3::intersects(const Ray3D& ray) const {
30      SurfaceRayIntersection3 i;
31      getClosestIntersection(ray, &i);
32      return i.isIntersecting;
33  }
34
35  double Surface3::closestDistance(const Vector3D& otherPoint) const {
36      return otherPoint.distanceTo(closestPoint(otherPoint));
37  }
```

Note that `BoundingBox3` is a 3D axis-aligned bounding box representation that is essentially a class of two corner points of the box. Class `Ray3D` is the type that has the origin and direction of a ray. Finally, `SurfaceRayIntersection3` is a simple struct that holds ray–surface intersection information such as the distance from the ray origin to the intersection point (t), the intersection point itself, and the surface normal at the intersection.

The base class above can be extended by overriding the virtual functions that are shown above. For example, a sphere geometry can be implemented as:

```
1   class Sphere3 final : public Surface3 {
2   public:
3       Sphere3(const Vector3D& center, double radius);
4
5       Vector3D closestPoint(const Vector3D& otherPoint) const override;
6
7       Vector3D closestNormal(const Vector3D& otherPoint) const override;
8
9       void getClosestIntersection(
10          const Ray3D& ray,
11          SurfaceRayIntersection3* intersection) const override;
12
```

```
13      BoundingBox3D boundingBox() const override;

15  private:
16      Vector3D _center;
17      double _radius = 1.0;
18  };

20  Vector3D Sphere3::closestPoint(const Vector3D& otherPoint) const {
21      return _radius * closestNormal(otherPoint) + _center;
22  }

24  Vector3D Sphere3::closestNormal(const Vector3D& otherPoint) const {
25      if (_center.isSimilar(otherPoint)) {
26          return Vector3D(1, 0, 0);
27      } else {
28          return (_center - otherPoint).normalized();
29      }
30  }

32  BoundingBox3D Sphere3::boundingBox() const {
33      Vector3D r(_radius, _radius, _radius);
34      return BoundingBox3D(_center - r, _center + r);
35  }
```

Another frequently used surface type is triangle mesh as shown in Figure 1.38. Using the mesh, you can provide a wide range of geometries such as artist-created objects or reconstructed scenes from computer vision algorithms. From the code base, triangle and its mesh are implemented as `Triangle3` and `TriangleMesh3`, respectively. The implementation details for

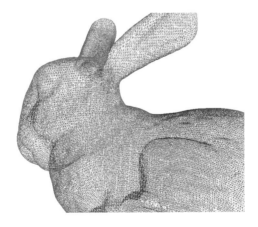

FIGURE 1.38
Example triangle mesh from the Stanford Bunny model [6].

these two classes won't be listed in this book, but the basic interfaces look like the following:

```cpp
class Triangle3 final : public Surface3 {
 public:
    std::array<Vector3D, 3> points;
    std::array<Vector3D, 3> normals;
    std::array<Vector2D, 3> uvs;

    Triangle3();

    Triangle3(
        const std::array<Vector3D, 3>& newPoints,
        const std::array<Vector3D, 3>& newNormals,
        const std::array<Vector2D, 3>& newUvs);

    Vector3D closestPoint(const Vector3D& otherPoint) const override;

    Vector3D closestNormal(const Vector3D& otherPoint) const override;

    void getClosestIntersection(
        const Ray3D& ray,
        SurfaceRayIntersection3* intersection) const override;

    bool intersects(const Ray3D& ray) const override;

    BoundingBox3D boundingBox() const override;

    ...
};

class TriangleMesh3 final : public Surface3 {
 public:
    typedef Array1<Vector2D> Vector2DArray;
    typedef Array1<Vector3D> Vector3DArray;
    typedef Array1<Point3UI> IndexArray;

    TriangleMesh3();

    TriangleMesh3(const TriangleMesh3& other);

    Vector3D closestPoint(const Vector3D& otherPoint) const override;

    Vector3D closestNormal(const Vector3D& otherPoint) const override;

    void getClosestIntersection(
        const Ray3D& ray,
        SurfaceRayIntersection3* intersection) const override;

```

```
47      BoundingBox3D boundingBox() const override;
48
49      bool intersects(const Ray3D& ray) const override;
50
51      double closestDistance(const Vector3D& otherPoint) const override;
52
53      ...
54
55  private:
56      Vector3DArray _points;
57      Vector3DArray _normals;
58      Vector2DArray _uvs;
59      IndexArray _pointIndices;
60      IndexArray _normalIndices;
61      IndexArray _uvIndices;
62
63      ...
64  };
```

Other surface types, such as `Box3` and `Plane3`, are also available from the code base. See the code base to find out more.

1.4.2 Implicit Surface

The surfaces like planes or triangle meshes, a point on the surface is defined explicitly, which means we can write an equation such as

$$\mathbf{x} = f(t_1, t_2, \cdots) \tag{1.58}$$

where t_i are input parameters and $\mathbf{x}$ is the point on the surface. In the case of a sphere-type surface, for example, two parameters can be used to locate a point. As shown in Figure 1.39, imagine a pair of latitude and longitude that can define a geo-coordinate on the earth. Such surfaces are good at certain operations like measuring the bounding box of the geometry or visualizing its shape. However, operations like testing whether an arbitrary point is inside the surface or measuring the closest surface normal are not trivial or are often inefficient with such a representation.

An alternative way of defining the surface to efficiently handle such computations is to use an implicit function. Instead of mapping the parameters directly to the point on the surface, the implicit approach uses a function which tells whether the input point is on the surface or not. For instance, a sphere can be expressed using the distance function which is

$$f(\mathbf{x}) = |\mathbf{x} - \mathbf{c}| - r \tag{1.59}$$

where $\mathbf{x}$ is an arbitrary point in space, $\mathbf{c}$ is the center of the sphere, and r is the radius of the sphere. This function measures the closest distance to the surface and hence a set of points that satisfies $f(\mathbf{x}) = 0$ are on the sphere surface. Notice that if $f(\mathbf{x}) < 0$, it means the point is *inside* the surface,

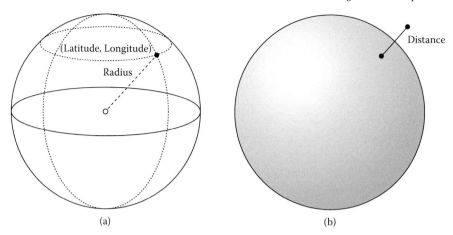

(a)   (b)

FIGURE 1.39
A sphere with two different surface types. (a) Explicit representation of a
sphere using radius, latitude, and longitude. (b) Implicit representation using
distance field.

and $f(\mathbf{x}) > 0$ means outside. Therefore, evaluating inside/outside of the surface becomes extremely simple. Such a function is called "signed-distance"
function or field (SDF).

It is not required to define implicit surfaces with SDF, but using SDF has
many advantages for many other operations. For example, simply subtracting
a constant from an SDF will extrude the surface as shown in Figure 1.40. One
of the applications of such an operation can be found from the text rendering.
To draw nicely styled text with outlines or glow effect, a font in a vector
format is converted into a signed-distance field [61].

Another example is the evaluation of the surface normal. Since an SDF
always returns the distance to the closest point on the surface, the gradient
of an SDF at the surface is the surface normal such that:

$$\mathbf{n} = \frac{\nabla f(\mathbf{x})}{|\nabla f(\mathbf{x})|} \tag{1.60}$$

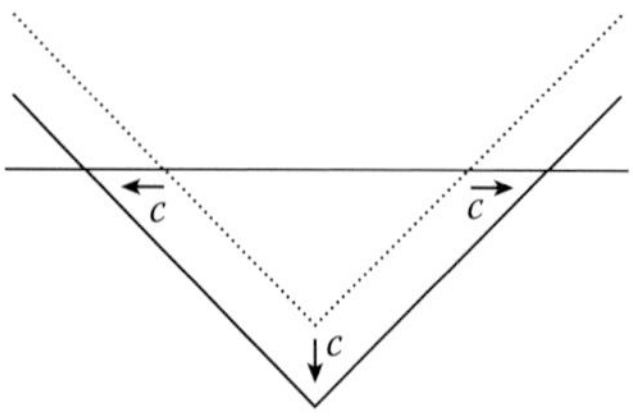

FIGURE 1.40
Extruding 1D signed-distance field by c is equivalent to subtracting a constant
value c.

This also means that the magnitude of the gradient is always one:

$$|\nabla f(\mathbf{x})| = 1 \qquad (1.61)$$

Finally, the boolean operations between two SDFs are simply a matter of taking min or max from the two functions. For instance, $h = \min(f, g)$ means the union of two SDFs, f and g. To subtract g from f, $h = \max(f, -g)$ can be used.

To implement implicit surface, we can use the following base class:

```
1  class ImplicitSurface3 : public Surface3 {
2   public:
3      ImplicitSurface3();
4
5      virtual ~ImplicitSurface3();
6
7      virtual double signedDistance(const Vector3D& otherPoint) const = 0;
8  };
```

As you can see, the class adds one more virtual function, `signedDistance`, to the abstract base class `Surface3`. For example, the implicit version of a sphere can be written as:

```
1  class ImplicitSphere3 final : public ImplicitSurface3 {
2   public:
3      ImplicitSphere3(const Vector3D& center, double radius);
4
5      double signedDistance(const Vector3D& otherPoint) const override;
6
7      ...
8  };
9
10 double ImplicitSphere3::signedDistance(const Vector3D& otherPoint) const
       {
11     return _center.distanceTo(otherPoint) - _radius;
12 }
```

1.4.3 Implicit Surface to Explicit Surface

Since both explicit and implicit surfaces have their own strength, it is often required to convert one into another. For instance, visualizing the implicit surface directly is only possible by performing ray tracing [74]. But the classical or rendering pipeline using rasterization, including OpenGL® or DirectX®, often requires explicit representation, especially using triangle mesh. Thus, we need a method to convert an implicit surface to an explicit mesh.

The most popular approach for such a conversion is the marching cubes method [76]. The method starts with a grid where each grid point has the sampled implicit surface function. Then, the algorithm iterates the grid cells and creates triangles if there are sign differences among the eight grid cell corners.

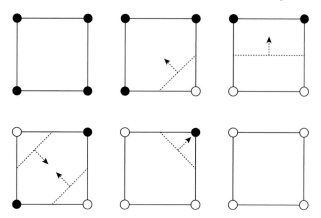

FIGURE 1.41
Six possible cases from 2D implicit field. The black and white dots at the corners represent positive and negative values, respectively. The dotted lines are the reconstructed explicit surfaces, and the arrows are the surface normal.

To simplify the problem, let's consider a 2D surface. Figure 1.41 illustrates all the possible cases a grid cell can have. Among those cases, notice that if there are any grid points that has a different sign than the others, it means the surface is passing through that grid cell. In such cases, we can draw lines (triangles in 3D) between the edges that contain different signs, and the collection of those lines (again, triangles in 3D) from every grid cell will be the explicit representation of the implicit function. When determining the location of the newly created vertices on the edge, a linear approximation

$$x = \frac{|\phi_{left}|}{|\phi_{left}| + |\phi_{right}|} \tag{1.62}$$

can be used. Figure 1.42 shows a sample result from 2D marching cubes (or marching squares) from an implicit surface field.

1.4.4 Explicit Surface to Implicit Surface

Converting a generic explicit surface to implicit surface is simple. Consider the code below.

```
1   class SurfaceToImplicit3 final : public ImplicitSurface3 {
2   public:
3       explicit SurfaceToImplicit3(const Surface3Ptr& surface);
4
5       double signedDistance(const Vector3D& otherPoint) const override;
6
7       ...
8
```

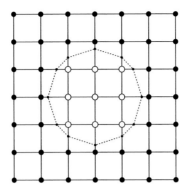

FIGURE 1.42
A sample result from marching squares. The black and white dots at the corners represent positive and negative values, respectively. The smaller dots and dotted lines represent the reconstructed explicit surface.

```
9    private:
10       Surface3Ptr _surface;
11   };
12
13   double SurfaceToImplicit3::signedDistance(
14       const Vector3D& otherPoint) const {
15       Vector3D x = _surface->closestPoint(otherPoint);
16       Vector3D n = _surface->closestNormal(otherPoint);
17       if (n.dot(otherPoint - x) < 0.0) {
18           return -x.distanceTo(otherPoint);
19       } else {
20           return x.distanceTo(otherPoint);
21       }
22   }
```

The adapter class, `SurfaceToImplicit3`, takes an explicit surface and returns signed-distance from the surface. From a given point, it first measures the closest point and normal to the explicit surface. If the vector from the closest point to the given point is facing the opposite direction from the surface normal, it is *inside* the surface, hence returning negative distance. If not, the point is *outside* of the surface, returning positive distance. This approach, however, assumes `closestPoint` and `closestNormal` are computationally less expensive.

Measuring the closest distance to the triangle mesh is also the same. To determine the sign, we can also query for the surface normal of the closest point and see if the point is on the other side of the surface using a dot product. Then, we can also set up a grid and assign the measured distance and sign to each grid point. The most problematic part is to determine the sign, though. Especially when the surface is not completely enclosed (has a hole) or the surface normal of the mesh is not well defined, the formation of a signed-distance field is not guaranteed (only distance field can be robustly generated). To handle such a wide range of arbitrary inputs, a robust surface reconstruction technique [106] can be considered. For the sake of simplicity, we can assume that the input mesh does not have any holes,[*] and apply the angle-weighted normal method from Bærentzen and Aanæs [8].

1.5   Animation

In computer graphics, an animation is created by generating a series of images for a given time sequence [81]. For example, Figure 1.43 shows a couple of images from an animation of a bouncing ball. For the given time sequence 0, 1, and 2 seconds, corresponding positions and shapes of the ball are drawn to the images. In this particular example, the time interval between two adjacent images is 1 second. In general, we use much lower time intervals, such as $1/24$, $1/30$, or $1/60$, so that it looks smoother when you playback the image sequence with the same speed. When referring the time stamps for the image sequence, we use "frame". For Figure 1.43, frame 0 corresponds to the first image, and frame 1 to the next one. Since this example has 1 a time interval 1 second, the playback will show 1 frame per second, or in short, 1 FPS. If the time interval between two frames is $1/60$, then we say the animation has 60 FPS of frame rate.

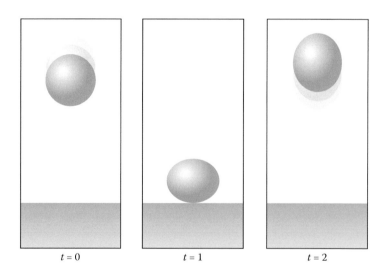

$t = 0$ $\qquad\qquad\qquad\qquad$ $t = 1$ $\qquad\qquad\qquad\qquad$ $t = 2$

FIGURE 1.43
Sequence of images from a bouncing ball animation.

---

[*]Meshes that are perfectly closed without any holes are often called "watertight" meshes.

Now it is time to code again. Let's start from a very simple struct for holding frame data:

```cpp
struct Frame final {
    unsigned int index = 0;
    double timeIntervalInSeconds = 1.0 / 60.0;

    double timeInSeconds() const {
        return count * timeIntervalInSeconds;
    }

    void advance() {
        ++index;
    }

    void advance(unsigned int delta) {
        index += delta;
    }
};
```

This code is pretty straightforward. This struct contains an integer `index` which represents its chronological order in timeline (Figure 1.44). Also, member variable `timeIntervalInSeconds` stores the time interval between frames. We are going to assume that the system is using fixed time interval for entire animation, so if we want to know current time in seconds unit, we can simply multiply variable `count` and `timeIntervalInSeconds` as shown in the member function `timeInSeconds`. Also, the last two functions are simple helper functions which treat this frame class as a forward iterator of a frame sequence.

As shown in Figure 1.44, the heart of the animation process is displaying the sequence of frames. If we write a pseudo code for such a process, it will look like this:

```cpp
Frame frame;

while (!quit) {
    processInput();
    updateScene(frame);
    renderScene(frame);

    frame.advance();
}
```

For each frame, the while-loop first processes the incoming user input, updates scene objects, and then renders the result. Function `updateScene` simply iterates all scene objects and updates their states with current frame

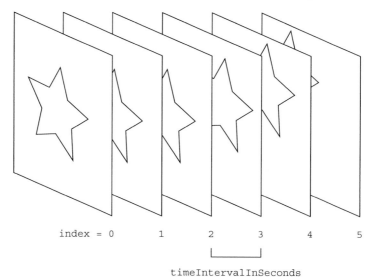

index = 0   1   2   3   4   5

timeIntervalInSeconds

FIGURE 1.44
Sequence of frames, frame index, and time interval are shown.

information. In this book, the focus will be on the `updateScene` function which can be written as:

```
1   void updateScene(const Frame& frame) {
2       for (auto& animation: animations) {
3           animation->update(frame);
4       }
5   }
```

We are assuming that all the animations in the scene are stored in the list, and we simply iterate it to update individual animation by calling `update` function which presumably updates the internal data for each animation object. To define the animation object type, we can write:

```
1   class Animation {
2   public:
3       ...
4
5       void update(const Frame& frame) {
6           // Some pre-processing here..
7
8           onUpdate(frame);
9
10          // Some post-processing here..
11      }
```

```
12
13   protected:
14       virtual void onUpdate(const Frame& frame) = 0;
15   };
```

This is the abstract base class for all the objects that define animation in this book. As you can see, we have one public function update and one protected but purely virtual function called onUpdate. When "update" is called externally, it will do some internal preprocessing work (such as logging) and call onUpdate which is subclass-specific. Goal of this onUpdate function is to "update" the internal state for a given frame.

For example, you can inherit class Animation as shown below to define your own animation class:

```
1    class SineAnimation final : public Animation {
2    public:
3        double x = 0.0;
4
5    protected:
6        void onUpdate(const Frame& frame) override {
7            x = std::sin(frame.timeInSeconds());
8        }
9    };
```

As we can see, this class has one double-type variable to store the current animation state. You can imagine this represents the center position of a ball. The implementation of onUpdate map's current time to the position using sine function which will create oscillatory motion. You can test out SineAnimation class instance as shown below.

```
1    SineAnimation sineAnim;
2    for (Frame frame; frame.index < 240; frame.advance()) {
3        sineAnim.update(frame);
4
5        // Write data to disk
6    }
```

This code can be found i src/manual_tests/animation_tests.cpp and Figure 1.45a shows the result of this simple code. You can see that the code produces an animation of a sine wave, and it can be used for generating spring-like motion. Based on this minimal example, let's add some tweak to the code as shown below.

```
1    class SineWithDecayAnimation final : public Animation {
2    public:
3        double x = 0.0;
4
5    protected:
```

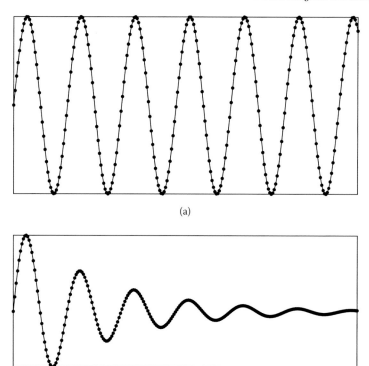

(a)

(b)

FIGURE 1.45
Traces of the state from the custom animation classes (a) `SineAnimation` test
and (b) `SineWithDecayAnimation` are shown. The horizontal axis represents
time while the vertical axis shows the value of `x`.

```
6      void onUpdate(const Frame& frame) override {
7          double decay = 1.0 / frame.timeInSeconds();
8          x = std::sin(frame.timeInSeconds()) * decay;
9      }
10  };
```

As you can see from Figure 1.45b, we have now made the sine function
to decay over time. The new animation looks like a spring with a damping
motion.

From the following sections, we will see how we can extend this basic
interface to create physics animation which is going to be the foundation of
the fluid simulation engine.

1.6 Physics-Based Animation

In computer graphics, a physics-based animation is an imitation of the natural phenomena such as fire, smoke, rain, or winds. It can model various types of materials like solids, water, gas, and even fabric or hairs. A large portion of the idea behind the fluid animation is thus inherited from the physics-based animation, and this section will introduce how to implement a physics-based animation engine in general.

1.6.1 Getting Started

If you recall our first animation example, `SineAnimation`, we directly mapped the input time to the position state using sine function. It does not depend on other data or states from any frames. Therefore, you can randomly pick a frame to know the corresponding position without calling `update` function in chronological order. Other types of animation, such as key-frame animation, has the same characteristic as well. Physics-based animation, on the contrary, depends on the states from the previous frames. Before we get into more details, let's take a look at the code below which defines the key interface for physics animations:

```
1  class PhysicsAnimation : public Animation {
2    ...
3
4  protected:
5    virtual void onAdvanceTimeStep(double timeIntervalInSeconds) = 0;
6
7  private:
8    Frame _currentFrame;
9
10   void onUpdate(const Frame& frame) final;
11
12   void advanceTimeStep(double timeIntervalInSeconds);
13 };
14
15 void PhysicsAnimation::onUpdate(const Frame& frame) {
16   if (frame.index > _currentFrame.index) {
17     unsigned int numberOfFrames = frame.index - _currentFrame.index;
18
19     for (unsigned int i = 0; i < numberOfFrames; ++i) {
20       advanceTimeStep(frame.timeIntervalInSeconds);
21     }
22
23     _currentFrame = frame;
24   }
25 }
```

As you can see, we are overriding `onUpdate` function from `Animation`, and it again calls private member function `advanceTimeStep` which advances one frame if input `frame` is newer than the current frame. But in rewinding situations where new input frame is older than the previous frame, it doesn't perform any simulations.[*]

It will become more natural once we go through some codes, but unlike the previous `SineAnimation` example, physics-based animations are history dependent—the next state is defined by the previous state. Think about the dynamics of a pool billiard. A cue ball will hit the other ball, and that event propagates to other balls. It is a series of cause and effect which evolves through time. This is one of the fundamentals of dynamics which is mostly about the cause and effect between force and motion. This is why `PhysicsAnimation` class takes a progressive approach for updating its state.

Also note that we are taking multiple steps with fixed time intervals when the input frame is away from the last simulated frame by more than a frame (i.e. fast-forward scenario), instead of taking a single giant time-step. It will be clearer once we see how actual simulation code works, but in general, taking three small time-steps is not equivalent to taking a three times larger time-step. Therefore, multiple steps are used so that the simulation output is consistent.

1.6.2   Physics Animation with Example

The base class `PhysicsAnimation` does give us some insights on physics animation, but it is still too abstract. To help better understand physics-based animation, we are going to implement a simple, yet fully functional, physics solver. This implementation will cover:

1. How to represent physical states?

2. How to compute forces?

3. How to compute motion?

4. How to apply constraints and interact with obstacles?

These are the core topics you would mostly need for any kind of physics engine development and the code we will develop throughout the book will also follow the same idea.

1.6.2.1   Choosing a Model

To get started, we first need to select the simulation model to be animated. It would be great if we can start with one of the fluid models right away, but let's start with something simpler. In this particular example, we are going to use the mass-spring model to demonstrate how those key ideas are

---

[*]You can implement cache-loading logic here, so that the class instance can rewind the animation. But still, we are not performing any simulation.

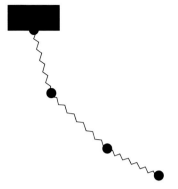

FIGURE 1.46
A sample mass-spring system configuration is shown. The black dots are mass points and the zig-zag segments are springs. Note that the topmost point is attached to the fixed block.

implemented. In the model, we have mass points which are connected by springs like a chain, and this system is under the influence of gravity and air. Due to those springs, each mass point can keep the relative distance to its neighbors. Also, gravity pulls the points toward the ground and air drag slows down the motion of the points. The points can collide with obstacles such as walls or floors. Figure 1.46 illustrates this configuration in detail. Although this is not exactly a fluid simulator, it is one of the simplest and most widely used models to simulate deformable objects.

1.6.2.2   Simulation State

We now have a model to simulate. The next step is to define the simulation state. As we can see from Figure 1.46, the system consists of many mass points under motion. Thus, there should be an array to store the positions of the points as well as the velocities. Also, the points can have accelerating or decelerating motion depending on the force acting on the points, and we can add another array to hold the force data. Finally, the connectivity between two points, like an edge of a graph, also should be stored. Based on these requirements, the first look of our new class `SimpleMassSpringAnimation` is shown below.

```
1   class SimpleMassSpringAnimation : public PhysicsAnimation {
2    public:
3      struct Edge {
4          size_t first;
5          size_t second;
6      };
7
8      std::vector<Vector3D> positions;
```

```
 9        std::vector<Vector3D> velocities;
10        std::vector<Vector3D> forces;
11        std::vector<Edge> edges;
12
13        SimpleMassSpringAnimation(size_t numberOfPoints = 10) {
14            size_t numberOfEdges = numberOfPoints - 1;
15
16            positions.resize(numberOfPoints);
17            velocities.resize(numberOfPoints);
18            forces.resize(numberOfPoints);
19            edges.resize(numberOfEdges);
20
21            for (size_t i = 0; i < numberOfPoints; ++i) {
22                positions[i].x = static_cast<double>(i);
23            }
24
25            for (size_t i = 0; i < numberOfEdges; ++i) {
26                edges[i] = Edge{i, i + 1};
27            }
28        }
29
30    protected:
31        void onAdvanceTimeStep(double timeIntervalInSeconds) override {
32            ...
33        }
34    };
```

In this class, we are representing the position, velocity, and force as 3D vectors. Each ith element of an array represents the ith mass point, and the spring connectivity is represented by an array of index pairs. Theses state data are initialized in the constructor. In this example, the code is chaining the points horizontally, but you can let it have arbitrary position and connectivity. For the unit, we will use MKS—meter for length, kilogram for mass, and second for time. Other than the member data, we can also notice that the class is overriding the virtual function from `PhysicsAnimation` class, `onAdvanceTimeStep`. This will be the place where we implement core logic for the mass-spring model, updating the state we just defined every frame.

1.6.2.3   Force and Motion

Since we now have states, let's talk about motion. According to Newton's second law of motion, the acceleration is determined by the mass of the point and the force acting on the point:

$$\mathbf{F} = m\mathbf{a} \qquad (1.63)$$

where $\mathbf{F}$, m, and $\mathbf{a}$ are the force, mass, and acceleration, respectively. In most of the cases, the force and acceleration are the inputs, and the acceleration is a calculated quantity. So the process of tracking the motion and updating the state starts from knowing the forces in the system. There are different kinds of forces that we are going to accumulate within this example, but let's assume that we know how much force is being applied to the points for now. Take a look at the code below.

```cpp
double mass = 1.0;
...
void onAdvanceTimeStep(double timeIntervalInSeconds) override {
    size_t numberOfPoints = positions.size();

    // Compute force
    for (size_t i = 0; i < numberOfPoints; ++i) {
        forces[i] = ...
    }

    // Update states
    for (size_t i = 0; i < numberOfPoints; ++i) {
        // Compute new states
        Vector3D newAcceleration = forces[i] / mass;
        Vector3D newVelocity = ...
        Vector3D newPosition = ...

        // Update states
        velocities[i] = newVelocity;
        positions[i] = newPosition;
    }

    // Apply constraints
    ...
}
```

This code shows the implementation of the function `onAdvanceTimeStep` for the class `SimpleMassSpringAnimation`. Again, the purpose of this function is to incrementally update the state for the given time interval `timeIntervalInSeconds`. Inside the code, there's a loop which iterates over points, and inside the loop, there are three major blocks. The first one computes the force, which we will soon discuss. The second part of the code computes the new velocity and position and then assigns the new states to the member data. The final part of the code applies constraints to the points so that some points have constrained position or velocity. For example, we can imagine a point is nailed on a wall, and the other points are moving freely.

Now let's talk about the first block which computes the force. As mentioned earlier, we are considering three different forces—gravity, spring, and air drag. The variable `force` is going to be an accumulation of these three different forces. Starting from gravity, which we consider as the earth's gravitational force, defined as

$$\mathbf{F}_g = m\mathbf{g} \tag{1.64}$$

where m is the mass and $\mathbf{g}$ is the gravity acceleration vector which points downward. The magnitude of $\mathbf{g}$ depends on where you are at, but we will use -9.8 m/sec^2. Thus, our system with the gravity force looks like this:

```
1  Vector3D gravity = Vector3D(0.0, -9.8, 0.0);
2  ...
3  void onAdvanceTimeStep(double timeIntervalInSeconds) override {
4      size_t numberOfPoints = positions.size();
5
6      for (size_t i = 0; i < numberOfPoints; ++i) {
7          forces[i] = mass * gravity;
8      }
9
10     ...
11 }
```

Pretty straight forward so far. Now let's consider the spring force. When two points are attached with a spring, the force is applied to the points if the spring gets compressed or elongated than the original rest length. As shown in Figure 1.47, the direction of the spring force applied to a point depends on whether the spring is being compressed or not, and the magnitude of the force is proportional to the compressed or elongated length. This is the Hooke's law, and the equation that encompasses all these properties can be written as:

$$\mathbf{F}_{s0} = -k(d-l)\mathbf{r}_{10} \tag{1.65}$$

Force $\mathbf{F}_{s1}$ is the force being applied to point 1, d is the distance between two points, l is the rest length of the spring, and vector $\mathbf{r}$ is the directional vector facing point 0 from 1. Constant k is the stiffness of the spring. Thus, larger k will produce stronger spring force. The same force is also applied to point 1, but in the opposite direction:

$$\mathbf{F}_{s1} = k(d-l)\mathbf{r}_{01} \tag{1.66}$$

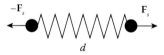

FIGURE 1.47
For a spring with rest length l, if the distance between two connected points changes to d, a spring force is generated and applied to the points.

Based on the equations above, the code that computes the spring force can be written as:

```
1   double stiffness = 500.0;
2   double restLength = 1.0;
3   ...
4   void onAdvanceTimeStep(double timeIntervalInSeconds) override {
5       size_t numberOfPoints = positions.size();
6       size_t numberOfEdges = edges.size();
7
8       // Compute forces
9       for (size_t i = 0; i < numberOfPoints; ++i) {
10          // Compute gravity force
11          forces[i] = mass * gravity;
12      }
13
14      for (size_t i = 0; i < numberOfEdges; ++i) {
15          size_t pointIndex0 = edges[i].first;
16          size_t pointIndex1 = edges[i].second;
17
18          // Compute spring force
19          Vector3D pos0 = positions[pointIndex0];
20          Vector3D pos1 = positions[pointIndex1];
21          Vector3D r = pos0 - pos1;
22          double distance = r.length();
23          if (distance > 0.0) {
24              Vector3D force = -stiffness * (distance - restLength) * r.
                    normalized();
25              forces[pointIndex0] += force;
26              forces[pointIndex1] -= force;
27          }
28      }
29
30      ...
31  }
```

Note that the `// compute force` block is now divided into two loops. The first one is the gravity part from the previous code. The second part is the novel code that iterates over the edges (or the springs), computes the spring force, and then accumulates to the force array. The code is implementing the equation almost as is. One small difference is the "if statement" which prevents the divide-by-zero case.

There is one more thing to consider in the spring force, which is the damping. If you imagine a real spring, it does not oscillate forever, but the motion decays over time, just like `SineWithDecayAnimation` we saw in Section 1.5.[*]

---

[*]In fact, `SineWithDecayAnimation` is one the solutions of the mass-spring system with one spring.

This damping force tries to reduce the "relative" velocity between two points. But whenever the points are moving with different velocities, the damping force kicks in. If we write this as an equation, it becomes

$$\mathbf{F}_{d0} = -c(\mathbf{v}_0 - \mathbf{v}_1). \tag{1.67}$$

Force $\mathbf{F}_{d0}$ is the damping force for point 0, and $\mathbf{v}_0$ and $\mathbf{v}_1$ are the velocities of points 0 and 1, respectively. We can see that the velocity difference between points 0 and 1, which is point 0's relative velocity, is scaled with constant $-c$. For example, if point 1 is not moving (zero velocity) and point 0 is moving in some direction, the force that point 0 will get is proportional to its own velocity but in the opposite direction. So point 0 will slow down until it reaches zero velocity. The symmetric force is also applied to point 1, which is

$$\mathbf{F}_{d1} = -c(\mathbf{v}_1 - \mathbf{v}_0). \tag{1.68}$$

Now let's write this equation into the code.

```
1   double dampingCoefficient = 1.0;
2   ...
3   void onAdvanceTimeStep(double timeIntervalInSeconds) override {
4       size_t numberOfPoints = positions.size();
5       size_t numberOfEdges = edges.size();
6
7       // Compute gravity force
8       ...
9
10
11      for (size_t i = 0; i < numberOfEdges; ++i) {
12          size_t pointIndex0 = edges[i].first;
13          size_t pointIndex1 = edges[i].second;
14
15          // Compute spring force
16          ...
17
18          // Add damping force
19          Vector3D vel0 = velocities[pointIndex0];
20          Vector3D vel1 = velocities[pointIndex1];
21          Vector3D damping = -dampingCoefficient * (vel0 - vel1);
22          forces[pointIndex0] += damping;
23          forces[pointIndex1] -= damping;
24      }
25
26      ...
27  }
```

From lines 19 to 23, the code shows how the damping force can be accumulated. The version of the code we have so far is quite enough for simulating

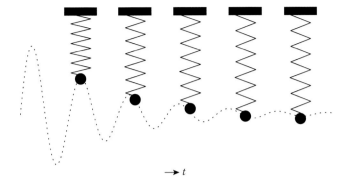

FIGURE 1.48
Sequence of frames from mass-spring animation with gravity and damping force are shown. The dotted line shows the trajectory of the mass point's position as time evolves.

the mass-spring system—we have enough components to create motion for chained mass points with springs. Figure 1.48 shows the image sequence of the points with gravity, spring, and damping forces.

As an additional feature, let's add the effect of the air to the code, the air drag. There are various kinds of models for the air drag, but we will take the simplest one. When an object moves inside the air, it experiences a friction force from the air which is proportional to the speed of the object. Thus, faster object gets higher drag force, and we can write this relation as

$$\mathbf{F}_a = -b\mathbf{v}, \tag{1.69}$$

where $\mathbf{v}$ is the velocity of the object and b is the air drag coefficient. The equation is very similar to the damping force we saw earlier. It creates a force in the opposite direction of the object's motion and becomes stronger if the speed is higher. This equation, however, doesn't take into account the shape of the object and simplifies the property of the air into a single constant, so it may not be very accurate. But for this introductory example, this equation works just fine. To incorporate this into our code, we can update the code as shown below.

```
1   double dragCoefficient = 0.1;
2   ...
3   void onAdvanceTimeStep(double timeIntervalInSeconds) override {
4       ...
5
6       // Compute forces
7       for (size_t i = 0; i < numberOfPoints; ++i) {
8           // Gravity force
9           forces[i] = mass * gravity;
```

```
10
11          // Air drag force
12          forces[i] += -dragCoefficient * velocities[i];
13      }
14
15      ...
16  }
```

Now, we can extend this a little bit further to make our system interact with the wind. The code above assumes that the air is stationary, and only the points are moving. If the air is moving, which is the wind, we can assume that the "relative" velocity can be used to compute the drag force. By adding a couple of lines of code, we can implement the wind effect, which is shown below.

```
1   VectorField3Ptr wind;
2
3   void onAdvanceTimeStep(double timeIntervalInSeconds) override {
4       ...
5
6       // Compute forces
7       for (size_t i = 0; i < numberOfPoints; ++i) {
8           // Gravity force
9           forces[i] = mass * gravity;
10
11          // Air drag force
12          Vector3D relativeVel = velocities[i];
13          if (wind != nullptr) {
14              relativeVel -= wind->sample(positions[i]);
15          }
16          forces[i] += -dragCoefficient * relativeVel;
17
18      }
19
20      ...
21  }
```

The wind is defined as a vector field, `VectorField3Ptr wind`, which is the shared pointer of `VectorField3`. Checkout Section 1.3.5 for information about fields. Anyway, if the field is set, the relative velocity is computed from the wind velocity, and then applied to the drag force. For example, we can apply a wind function to the animation object as shown below.

```
1   SimpleMassSpringAnimation anim;
2   anim.wind = std::make_shared<ConstantVectorField3>(Vector3D(10.0, 0.0,
        0.0));
```

This code will let wind blows from left to right at 10 meters per second. Class `ConstantVectorField3` is one of the built-in `VectorField3` types, and the code can be found i `include/jet/constant_vector_field3.h` and `src/jet/constant_vector_field3.cpp`. You can also assign your own custom vector field object to create interesting behaviors.

1.6.2.4 Time Integration

So far we have computed forces. We now need to update the states—positions and velocities—using the force we have calculated. At the beginning of the section, there were two major blocks in `onAdvanceTimeStep` function as shown here:

```
1   void onAdvanceTimeStep(double timeIntervalInSeconds) override {
2       // Compute force
3       ...
4
5       // Update states
6       for (size_t i = 0; i < numberOfPoints; ++i) {
7           // Compute new states
8           Vector3D newAcceleration = forces[i] / mass;
9           Vector3D newVelocity = ...
10          Vector3D newPosition = ...
11
12          // Update states
13          velocities[i] = newVelocity;
14          positions[i] = newPosition;
15      }
16  }
```

We are now going to fill in the second block. As shown in the skeleton code above, we first convert the force into the acceleration using Newton's second law of motion, $\mathbf{F} = m\mathbf{a}$. Since acceleration is the rate of change of velocity and velocity is the rate of change of position, velocity is the integral of acceleration and position is the integral of velocity. We can then write equations to calculate new velocity and position as

$$\mathbf{v}_{new} = \mathbf{v}_{old} + \Delta t \mathbf{a}_{new} \qquad (1.70)$$

and

$$\mathbf{x}_{new} = \mathbf{x}_{old} + \Delta t \mathbf{v}_{new} \qquad (1.71)$$

where Δt is the time interval of a frame. For example, if a car is moving at a speed of 50 miles per hour, it will be 100 miles away after two hours has passed. This is an approximation of integrals by extending the function with its derivative as shown in Figure 1.49, which assumes that the rate of change is constant within the given time interval. We are using the term "approximation" because our time interval is finite ($1/60$ seconds or less in general), which means we are missing some information in between. From the figure, you can notice the gap between the approximated value versus ground truth which is

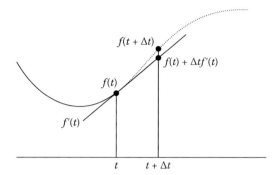

FIGURE 1.49
For a function $f(t)$, $f'(t)$ is its time derivative. From $f(t)$ and $f'(t)$, future value $f(t + \Delta t)$ is approximated by extending the derivative. The gap between the actual value $f(t + \Delta t)$ and $f(t) + \Delta t f'(t)$ is the approximation error.

the approximation error. This particular example uses a linear approximation, and such an approximation method is called the Euler method. There are many other methods as well, which improve the performance of the method. In general, such methods that compute the integration using computers is called numerical integration. And since we are integrating physical quantities over time, the process is called numerical time integration.

For certain types of problems where solutions can be derived analytically, such numerical integrations may not be necessary. For instance, if a mass point is attached to a single spring, the motion for the point can be described with a well-known solution, such as `SineWithDecayAnimation`. However, if the system gets complicated, it is often impossible to get the solution without numerical methods.

Anyway, let's get back to the code. We can implement the Euler method as shown below.

```
1   void onAdvanceTimeStep(double timeIntervalInSeconds) override {
2       // Compute force
3       ...
4
5       // Update states
6       for (size_t i = 0; i < numberOfPoints; ++i) {
7           // Compute new states
8           Vector3D newAcceleration = forces[i] / mass;
9           Vector3D newVelocity
10              = velocities[i] + timeIntervalInSeconds * newAcceleration;
11          Vector3D newPosition
12              = positions[i] + timeIntervalInSeconds * newVelocity;
13
14          // Update states
```

```
15        velocities[i] = newVelocity;
16        positions[i] = newPosition;
17    }
18 }
```

Note that this Euler method was already used in our hello-world example from Section 1.1 to update the positions and velocities of the waves.

1.6.2.5 Constraints and Collisions

The final stage is about applying constraints. Without any constraints, the code we currently have won't create any interesting animations because it will simply free-fall to negative infinity. In fact, the example result shown in Figure 1.48 was already using constraints by fixing the position of a point. This is a point constraint, but there can be many other types of constraints such as line or plane constraints. Please checkout Baraff and Witkin [9] for more details. In this example, we will implement the point constraint as well as a simple floor collision.

For the point constraints, we will fix specified points at given positions and assign predefined velocities. The updated code looks as follows:

```
1  struct Constraint {
2      size_t pointIndex;
3      Vector3D fixedPosition;
4      Vector3D fixedVelocity;
5  };
6  std::vector<Constraint> constraints;
7
8  ...
9
10 void onAdvanceTimeStep(double timeIntervalInSeconds) override {
11     // Compute force
12     ...
13
14     // Update states
15     ...
16
17     // Apply constraints
18     for (size_t i = 0; i < constraints.size(); ++i) {
19         size_t pointIndex = constraints[i].pointIndex;
20         positions[pointIndex] = constraints[i].fixedPosition;
21         velocities[pointIndex] = constraints[i].fixedVelocity;
22     }
23
24 }
```

The modified class has an array of constraints, and each constraint object specifies which point to fix and its state. Then after updating the position and velocity in every frame, it post-processes the new position and velocity by enforcing the specified state. The code below shows how we can fix the first point of the system at $(0, 0, 0)$ with zero velocity.

Now let's consider collisions. We will assume that there is a floor at the specified y-position so that the points cannot fall below that level. To implement the feature, we need to first check if the newly updated position of a point is lower than the floor. If so, we push the point on the floor. We can also make the point to bounce if it hits the floor, and to achieve it, we need to flip the y-direction of velocity in floor's normal direction. Take a look at the code below which implements this logic.

```
1   double floorPositionY = -7.0;
2   double restitutionCoefficient = 0.3;
3
4   ...
5
6   void onAdvanceTimeStep(double timeIntervalInSeconds) override {
7       // Compute force
8       ...
9
10      // Update states
11      for (size_t i = 0; i < numberOfPoints; ++i) {
12          // Compute new states
13          ...
14
15          // Collision
16          if (newPosition.y < floorPositionY) {
17              newPosition.y = floorPositionY;
18
19              if (newVelocity.y < 0.0) {
20                  newVelocity.y *= -restitutionCoefficient;
21                  newPosition.y += timeIntervalInSeconds * newVelocity.y;
22              }
23          }
24
25          // Update states
26          ...
27      }
28
29      // Apply constraints
30      ...
31  }
```

You can see that if the new position is below the floor plane, the y-position is clamped to zero and the y-velocity is flipped by multiplying the restitution coefficient. The parameter restitutionCoefficient is a value that controls how much energy will the point lose after the collision. If it is set to 1, then the point won't lose any energy and will make a perfect bounce. If set to 0, then the point will not bounce and will stick on the floor as it collides.

And that's it! We've just finished building a mass-spring animation solver. Figure 1.50 shows the complete code and test examples can be found in `src/tests/manual_tests/physics_animation_tests.cpp`. This is one of the simplest physics-based animation solvers, but yet practically usable simulation engine. You can further extend this code to simulate deformable objects including cloth and hair. But as mentioned earlier, the key takeaway from this example is the process of making physics-based animation engine. Starting from a model, we defined the data structure for storing the physical state, implemented force computation, wrote how to turn the force into motion, and finally made the system interactive to obstacles and user constraints. Even the details may vary, but the same idea will flow into the fluid engine development. The following section will provide a basic understanding of the fluid dynamics and simulation, and from the next chapter, we will see how the actual fluid simulation engine can be built with various techniques.

1.7 Fluid Animation

A fluid motion is generated by the combination of different forces and constraints. Just like the mass-spring system is governed by the spring, damping, and drag forces, there are forces derived from observing and analyzing the nature of fluid dynamics. Also, there are physical constraints that limit the freedom of the flow. For instance, the fluid should not lose any mass unless we model vaporization or something similarly exceptional. These forces and constraints vary depending on the phenomena. Even though the Navier–Stokes equations are the equations that describe fluid dynamics, the dominating factors can be different if you are looking at a cup of glass instead of a space shuttle entering the atmosphere.

In this book, we will mostly assume small- to mid-scale fluid dynamics as our target which are around the level of a bathtub or a water fountain. This implies the time scale as well as the size scale. Our time scale is around seconds to minutes, not days or months. It can be extended to a larger scale, such as breaking waves from the ocean, but not to the level of a weather forecast. We are not considering any micro-scale phenomena as well, such as a drop of ink from an inkjet printer nozzle. So in summary, our target is to create human-scale fluid animations, imitating something that we can observe with our eyes in daily life.

Based on the assumptions above, we get three dominating forces and one constraint. That includes (1) gravity, (2) pressure, and (3) viscosity as the main driving forces, and density preservation for the constraint. There could be a couple of additions depending on the phenomena we simulate, but those are the most essential pieces. Throughout this book, you will see different

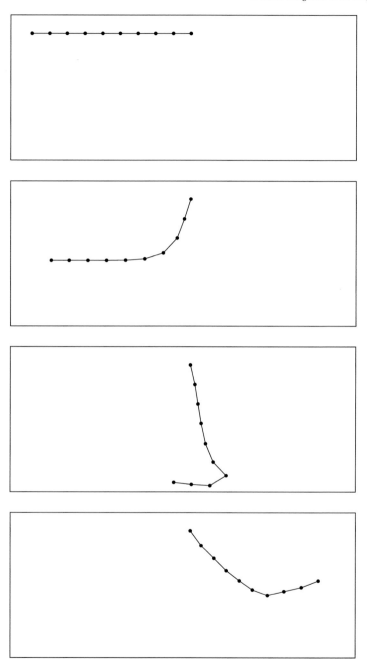

FIGURE 1.50
Sequence of frames from a mass-spring system simulation. The chain of mass points are horizontally positioned at the beginning, and then dropped on the floor except the end point, which is fixed at the original location.

kinds of fluid simulators with different approaches, but they all share the same idea—compute the three forces under the density constraint. I will leave the details on how to write the codes to other chapters. In the rest of the sections in this chapter, we will focus on the general idea of each of the forces and constraints to understand fluid dynamics and ultimately get an idea of building a fluid animation engine.

1.7.1 Gravity

In the human-scale fluid dynamics, the gravity force is the most obvious and dominant factor that affects the motion. It gives a downward acceleration to the entire fluid body uniformly, and we can write this as following:

$$\mathbf{F}_g = m\mathbf{g} \tag{1.72}$$

Vector $\mathbf{F}_g$ represents the gravity force acting on the fluid, m the mass of a portion of the fluid, and $\mathbf{g}$ the gravity constant. This is exactly the same as we observed from the mass-spring example (Section 1.6.2), and just like the earlier example, other types of forces will get accumulated in addition to the gravity, and then the final net force $\mathbf{F}$ creates the acceleration as we already know from Newton's second law of motion:

$$\mathbf{a} = \mathbf{F}/m = (\mathbf{F}_g + \dots)/m \tag{1.73}$$

Vector $\mathbf{a}$ is the final acceleration of the fluid motion. So we can see that the same physics principles are applied everywhere, even for the fluids.

One thing to note here is that the force is acting on some fraction of fluid that has mass m. But since the fluid is a material that deforms very easily, every tiny fraction of fluid can have a different motion. Thus, we want the fraction to be as small as possible so that it almost becomes a point. Therefore, it is quite common to use the acceleration and density instead of the force and mass when describing a fluid motion. This will turn the latest equation into:

$$\mathbf{a} = \mathbf{g} + \dots \tag{1.74}$$

which is in fact even simpler. Depending on the context, the book will occasionally use acceleration to imply force if it's more convenient.

1.7.2 Pressure

Next, let's talk about the pressure and pressure gradient force. As we often see in the weather forecast, the wind blows from higher to lower pressure region, and the same rule applies to other types of fluids in different scales as well. Another example of the pressure gradient force in action is the steady water (e.g. the water in a swimming pool). As you go deeper into the water, the pressure (not the pressure gradient force) increases. This pressure difference along the depth generates an up-force in the opposite direction of the gravity,

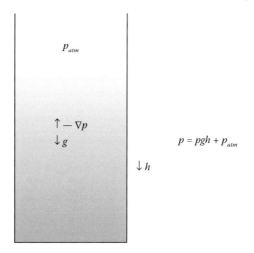

FIGURE 1.51
A water tank with atmosphere pressure p_{atm}, water density ρ, gravity g, and depth h.

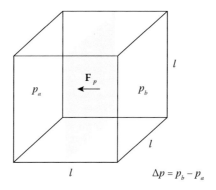

FIGURE 1.52
A small cube with size $l \times l \times l$ with pressure difference Δp.

and because of this, the water can keep its state without shrinking. Figure 1.51 illustrates these examples more visually.

The definition of pressure is a force per unit area, $p = F/area$, and the gradient of the pressure creates the gradient force. (Checkout Section 1.3.5.2 for the gradient.) Consider a small cubic portion of fluid with size l as shown in Figure 1.52. Let's assume that the pressure varies along the x-axis only. If the pressure difference between left and right is Δp, the force F that is applied to the square interface is $\Delta p l^2$ (again, pressure is force/area). Since $F = ma$ and mass m is volume times density, we can say:

$$F_p = -\Delta p l^2 = m a_p = l^3 \cdot \rho \cdot a_p \tag{1.75}$$

where ρ and a_p are the density and acceleration. If we clean up the above equation, we get:

$$a_p = -\frac{\Delta p}{\rho l} \qquad (1.76)$$

Now, if we shrink the size of this cube as much as possible, the equation above becomes:

$$a_p = -\frac{\partial p}{\partial x}\frac{1}{\rho} \qquad (1.77)$$

What this equation is trying to say is that the acceleration of a fraction of the fluid is proportional to the pressure difference along the x-axis and is inverse of the fluid density. In other words, fluid will accelerate faster with higher pressure contrast and lighter density. If we generalize the equation above to three dimension, the partial derivative becomes the gradient as shown below:

$$\mathbf{a}_p = -\frac{\nabla p}{\rho} \qquad (1.78)$$

If we accumulate this acceleration generated by the pressure gradient to Equation 1.74, it becomes:

$$\mathbf{a} = \mathbf{g} - \frac{\nabla p}{\rho} + \ldots \qquad (1.79)$$

1.7.3 Viscosity

Our third force is viscosity. We have already seen this in our earlier mass-spring example. From the simulation, the damping force tries to minimize the velocity difference between two points. The viscosity force is the same kind of force. This is the force that makes honey thick and lets it flow differently with less viscous fluids like water.

Imagine that we are trying to stir a thick, steady-state fluid using a thin straw so that a peak velocity is generated at a point in the fluid. Now that every other point nearby is still steady, we can see the velocity difference between the point we stir and its neighbors. The viscosity force then kicks in and tries to reduce the velocity difference between the points. As a result, the velocity at the stir point spreads out to its neighbors. Thus, applying the viscosity force is like blurring the velocity field.

Luckily, we already know how to "blur" a field. If you recall the Laplacian operator from Section 1.3.5.5, adding the Laplacian to the original field is equal to blurring out the field. So we can take that operator to define the viscosity force, such that:

$$\mathbf{v}_{new} = \mathbf{v} + \Delta t \mu \nabla^2 \mathbf{v} \qquad (1.80)$$

Vector $\mathbf{v}$ is the velocity of the fluid, and μ is a positive, scaling constant that controls how much Laplacian-filtered velocity we want to add. Similarly, time interval Δt is also multiplied to the Laplacian field as well. Vector $\mathbf{v}_{new}$

is the new velocity field due to the viscosity after this short time interval, Δt. If we move $\mathbf{v}$ and Δt to the left-hand side of the equation, it becomes:

$$\frac{\mathbf{v}_{new} - \mathbf{v}}{\Delta t} = \mu \nabla^2 \mathbf{v} \qquad (1.81)$$

The left-hand side becomes the acceleration if Δt is very small, because the time derivative of velocity is acceleration, and the left-hand side is exactly the derivative as Δt get close to zero. So the equation finally becomes:

$$\mathbf{a}_v = \mu \nabla^2 \mathbf{v} \qquad (1.82)$$

At last, we gathered the three dominating forces for fluid dynamics (in the human-scale of course), and our final acceleration becomes:

$$\mathbf{a} = \mathbf{g} - \frac{\nabla p}{\rho} + \mu \nabla^2 \mathbf{v} \qquad (1.83)$$

1.7.4   Density Constraint

I mentioned earlier that we have one constraint to keep when animating fluids, and that is density preservation. In other words, the fluids we are dealing with are incompressible. Imagine a two-sided piston filled with air as shown in Figure 1.53. Once you push or pull one end of the piston, it will immediately push or pull the other side because the air inside the piston tries to preserve its density. Note that the preservation of the density means that the volume is also maintained, because the mass of the air will be conserved within the piston. To represent such characteristics with equations, we can write:

$$\rho = \rho_c \qquad (1.84)$$

and

$$\nabla \cdot \mathbf{v} = 0. \qquad (1.85)$$

The first equation is straight forward—the density is constant. What about the next equation?

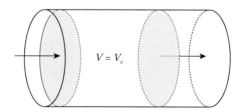

FIGURE 1.53
The volume inside the cylinder between pistons is V. If the fluid is incompressible and one side of the piston gets pressed or pulled, the other side of the piston moves immediately and preserves the density.

If you recall Figure 1.23 from Section 1.3.5.3, zero divergence means there is no inward or outward flow from the small portion of the fluid. Similar illustration can be found in Figure 1.53. Thus, this simple equation, $\nabla \cdot \mathbf{u} = 0$, means the density is preserved for every fraction of the fluid.

Now, I have to admit that this is an ideal assumption, and in real world, the fluids do get compressed or they expand a bit. If the fluids get involved into thermodynamics, like inside a gasoline engine, compression or expansion becomes quite noticeable even in our daily life, human-scale phenomena. Still, it is safe to make such an assumption for most of the real situations that our fluid engine will target, such as water splash, breaking waves, or fountains. If we want to handle something that compresses or expands significantly so that we can observe with our eyes, let's treat that as a special case.

In summary, the equations that describe fluid motion can be written as:

$$\mathbf{a} = \mathbf{g} - \frac{\nabla p}{\rho} + \mu \nabla^2 \mathbf{v}$$

$$\nabla \cdot \mathbf{v} = 0,$$

and this is one of the most famous equations in Physics, the Navier–Stokes equations for incompressible flow. The equations might be overwhelming for some of the readers, and it is quite natural. But if you try to break down the equations into individual terms, you will notice that the message is relatively simpler—gravity, pressure, viscosity, and density preservation makes fluid flow. If we follow the same process as Section sec:basics-pba-ex, the next step would be applying these three forces to the fluid state and performing time integration. There are multiple options for the data structure for defining a fluid state, and the actual implementation of the force computation and time integration will be different depending on the approach we take. This book introduces two different data structures, particles, and grids. These two approaches have distinct views of interpreting the fluid, and each of them has its pros and cons. From the following chapters, we will see how the fluid engine can be built using both particles and grids.

2

Particle-Based Simulation

2.1 Seeing the World Like Seurat

Georges Seurat is one of the most famous painters, known for his unique style of painting. As shown in Figure 2.1, he used a technique called Pointillism, which uses many small dots to construct an image. Each dot has its own color with round shape, but when viewed from a distance, a beautiful Sunday afternoon on the Island of La Grande Jatte appears. His technique of drawing images with points has inspired many artists, but the way he saw the world also deeply connects to how we want to describe our virtual physics world.

In the human eye-scale, fluids are continuous material. Fluid is not like the sand which can be broken down into "reasonably" countable elements. We can go deeply into the molecular level of fluids, but if you think of how many molecules are there inside a small cup of water and how much memory you have on your computer, you will soon realize that it is impractical even trying to simulate fluids from the microscopic scale. Thus, we need to approximate the real physical world with finite data points, just like the painter draws his masterpiece with many, but a measurable number of dots.

There are many different approaches to discretize the volume of fluids with a set of points. Some methods use particles and some use grids. There are even hybrid ways that combine different discretization techniques. A particle-based approach sees the world like Seurat. It discretizes the world with scattered particles, and they are freely distributed without any structure. On the contrary, a grid-based method is more like a digital bitmap image. It is structured, and each data point is connected to each other. The particle-based methods are often classified as a Lagrangian framework—a framework that solves the fluid motion by following the fluid parcel, such as particles. On the contrary, the grid-based methods we cover in the next chapter is called Eulerian framework—a framework that sees the fluid flow from fixed grid points. Both approaches have their own pros and cons, and we will discuss on their characteristics throughout the book.

In this chapter, we will cover the particle-based method. Let's find out how we can define the data structures, design the solver, and implement the dynamics.

FIGURE 2.1
A Sunday afternoon on the Island of La Grande Jatte by Georges Seurat, 1884 [31].

2.2 Data Structures

In this section, we will cover the core data structures for simulating fluids with particles. We will first cover how to store a collection of particles. Then, we see how we can find nearby particles at any random location and build a network of particles so that we can compute the interaction between the particles.

2.2.1 Particle System Data

As discussed in Section 1.6, building a physics-animation engine starts with defining the state of the animation and its data structure. The key element of a particle-based engine is obviously a particle, and just like the mass point in Section 1.6.2, the particle state includes position, velocity, and force. So we can write Particle3 struct as:

```
1  struct Particle3 {
2      Vector3D position;
3      Vector3D velocity;
4      Vector3D force;
5  };
```

The name of the struct ends with 3 to indicate this is a 3D particle. Since we want many particles, we can have an array of particles to define particle set, as follows:

```
1    typedef std::vector<Particle3> ParticleSet3;
```

Such an approach is called array of structure (AOS) since it is an array of `Particle3` struct. Alternatively, we can rewrite the same data as:

```
1    struct ParticleSet3 {
2        std::vector<double> positionsX, positionsY, positionsZ;
3        std::vector<double> velocitiesX, velocitiesY, velocitiesZ;
4        std::vector<double> forcesX, forcesY, forcesZ;
5    };
```

This representation is called structure of array (SOA) because literally it is a struct of arrays. In general, the choice between AOS and SOA depends on the performance, such as the memory access pattern and vectorization of the computation [16]. The decision is also based on the code design as well since it directly affects how to access the data from the code.

In this book, we will take the semi-SOA approach, which is similar to:

```
1    struct ParticleSet3 {
2        std::vector<Vector3D> positions;
3        std::vector<Vector3D> velocities;
4        std::vector<Vector3D> forces;
5    };
```

Since the x, y, and z components are normally accessed simultaneously, the code grouped them together to avoid cache misses. However, since different simulator can require a different set of attributes, each attribute is defined as a separate vector. Speaking of having different attributes, we want it to be flexible enough so that we can assign attributes to the particles dynamically. For instance, some particle-solvers may only require positions, velocity, and force for the computation. But as mentioned, some other solvers may require more attributes. To develop the extensible structure, let's define a new class called `ParticleSystemData3` which has the interface as shown below.

```
1    class ParticleSystemData3 {
2    public:
3        typedef std::vector<Vector3D> VectorArray;
4
5        ParticleSystemData3();
6        virtual ~ParticleSystemData3();
7
8        void resize(size_t newNumberOfParticles);
```

```
9        size_t numberOfParticles() const;
10
11       const Vector3D* const positions() const;
12       const Vector3D* const velocities() const;
13       const Vector3D* const forces() const;
14
15       void addParticle(
16           const Vector3D& newPosition,
17           const Vector3D& newVelocity = Vector3D(),
18           const Vector3D& newForce = Vector3D());
19       void addParticles(
20           const VectorArray& newPositions,
21           const VectorArray& newVelocities = VectorArray(),
22           const VectorArray& newForces = VectorArray());
23
24   private:
25       VectorArray _positions;
26       VectorArray _velocities;
27       VectorArray _forces;
28   };
```

The implementation details for all these member functions won't be covered in this section. Take a look at `src/jet/particle_system_data3.cpp` to see how the actual implementations are written.

To make this code more generic so that we can add any custom particle attribute data (other than position, velocity, and force), we can update the code as follows:

```
1    class ParticleSystemData3 {
2    public:
3        ...
4
5        size_t addScalarData(double initialVal = 0.0);
6
7        size_t addVectorData(const Vector3D& initialVal = Vector3D());
8
9        ConstArrayAccessor1<double> scalarDataAt(size_t idx) const;
10
11       ArrayAccessor1<double> scalarDataAt(size_t idx);
12
13       ConstArrayAccessor1<Vector3D> vectorDataAt(size_t idx) const;
14
15       ArrayAccessor1<Vector3D> vectorDataAt(size_t idx);
16
17   private:
18       ...
19
20       std::vector<ScalarData> _scalarDataList;
```

```
21     std::vector<VectorData> _vectorDataList;
22 };
```

For example, if an SDK user wants to add "life" attribute so that particles can vanish after a certain time duration, `addScalarData` can be used. This function will return the index of the data which can be used later on to access the data using `scalarDataAt` function. The same idea applies to the functions `addVectorData` and `vectorDataAt` that are used for adding custom vector attribute data, such as 3D texture coordinates.

2.2.2 Particle System Example

To demonstrate how to make a particle system solver using the data layout we discussed earlier, we will build a simple particle system solver which will also become the base solver for the other simulators. This simulator models a particle system that does not consider particle-to-particle interactions; only external forces like gravity or wind/drag forces will be taken into account. Still, this can be useful when simulating secondary spray effects.

To get started, let's start with the scaffolding code shown below.

```
1  class ParticleSystemSolver3 : public PhysicsAnimation {
2  public:
3      ParticleSystemSolver3();
4
5      virtual ~ParticleSystemSolver3();
6
7      ...
8
9  protected:
10     void onAdvanceTimeStep(double timeIntervalInSeconds) override;
11
12     virtual void accumulateForces(double timeStepInSeconds);
13
14     void resolveCollision();
15
16     ...
17
18 private:
19     ParticleSystemData3Ptr _particleSystemData;
20     ...
21
22     void beginAdvanceTimeStep();
23
24     void endAdvanceTimeStep();
25
26     void timeIntegration(double timeIntervalInSeconds);
27 };
```

```
28
29   ParticleSystemSolver3::ParticleSystemSolver3() {
30       _particleSystemData = std::make_shared<ParticleSystemData3>();
31       _wind = std::make_shared<ConstantVectorField3>(Vector3D());
32   }
33
34   ParticleSystemSolver3::~ParticleSystemSolver3() {
35   }
36
37   void ParticleSystemSolver3::onAdvanceTimeStep(double
            timeIntervalInSeconds) {
38       beginAdvanceTimeStep();
39
40       accumulateForces(timeIntervalInSeconds);
41       timeIntegration(timeIntervalInSeconds);
42       resolveCollision();
43
44       endAdvanceTimeStep();
45   }
46
47   ...
```

As you can see from the code above, all the physics logic will be implemented in `ParticleSystemSolver3`, whereas the `ParticleSystemData3` instance will be the data model. Since `ParticleSystemSolver3` is inheriting `PhysicsAnimation` class, we are also overriding `onAdvanceTimeStep` function. Refer to Section 1.6 if this is not familiar to you. The function `onAdvanceTimeStep` takes a single time-step and advances the simulation for the given time interval. Within the function, you can see there are pre- and postprocessing functions (`beginAdvanceTimeStep` and `endAdvanceTimeStep`). Between those two functions, there are the three core subroutines that compute forces, time integration, and collision. These steps have the same structure as the mass–spring example in Section 1.6.2. Notice that `accumulateForces` is a virtual function that can be overridden by the subclasses. That is because the forces are different depending on which physics model we would take. But other functions are nonvirtual protected functions which can be invoked from the subclasses.

Again, the implementation of the new functions are very similar to the mass–spring example (Section 1.6.2). Let's take a look at `accumulateForces` and `accumulateExternalForces` first.

```
1   class ParticleSystemSolver3 : public PhysicsAnimation {
2       ...
3   private:
4       double _dragCoefficient = 1e-4;
5       Vector3D _gravity = Vector3D(0.0, -9.8, 0.0);
```

```
6       VectorField3Ptr _wind;

7

8       ...

9   };

10

11  void ParticleSystemSolver3::accumulateForces(double timeStepInSeconds) {

12      accumulateExternalForces();

13  }

14

15  void ParticleSystemSolver3::accumulateExternalForces() {

16      size_t n = _particleSystemData->numberOfParticles();

17      auto forces = _particleSystemData->forces();

18      auto velocities = _particleSystemData->velocities();

19      auto positions = _particleSystemData->positions();

20      const double mass = _particleSystemData->mass();

21

22      parallelFor(

23          kZeroSize,

24          n,

25          [&] (size_t i) {

26              // Gravity

27              Vector3D force = mass * _gravity;

28

29              // Wind forces

30              Vector3D relativeVel

31                  = velocities[i] - _wind->sample(positions[i]);

32              force += -_dragCoefficient * relativeVel;

33

34              forces[i] += force;

35          });

36  }
```

accumulateForces is a virtual function that aggregates all the forces that the particles will get for the current time-step. As mentioned earlier, this example solver will only consider the external forces. Thus, the function invokes subroutine accumulateExternalForces. Later on, accumulateForces will have a list of function calls that accumulate various kinds of forces that fluid will experience. Function accumulateForces accepts function parameter timeIntervalInSeconds which is not used at this moment. We are reserving the parameter for any potential customers in the future.

Moving on to accumulateExternalForces, you can see we are adding the gravity and drag forces to the force array. The air drag force is the same as discussed in Section 1.6.2; Take the relative velocity of the surrounding air, scale it, and then apply the vector in the opposite direction of the particle's motion. You may wonder what parallelFor is doing, but it is a helper function that executes the given function object with multithreads for given range.

Now let's find out how the rest of the code is implemented. The time-integration and collision resolution can be written as follows:

```
1    class ParticleSystemSolver3 : public PhysicsAnimation {
2        ...
3     private:
4        ...
5
6        ParticleSystemData3::VectorData _newPositions;
7        ParticleSystemData3::VectorData _newVelocities;
8        Collider3Ptr _collider;
9        VectorField3Ptr _wind;
10
11       ...
12   };
13
14   void ParticleSystemSolver3::timeIntegration(double timeIntervalInSeconds)
         {
15       size_t n = _particleSystemData->numberOfParticles();
16       auto forces = _particleSystemData->forces();
17       auto velocities = _particleSystemData->velocities();
18       auto positions = _particleSystemData->positions();
19       const double mass = _particleSystemData->mass();
20
21       parallelFor(
22           kZeroSize,
23           n,
24           [&] (size_t i) {
25               // Integrate velocity first
26               Vector3D& newVelocity = _newVelocities[i];
27               newVelocity = velocities[i]
28                   + timeIntervalInSeconds * forces[i] / mass;
29
30               // Integrate position.
31               Vector3D& newPosition = _newPositions[i];
32               newPosition = positions[i] + timeIntervalInSeconds *
                      newVelocity;
33           });
34   }
35
36   void ParticleSystemSolver3::resolveCollision() {
37       resolveCollision(
38           _particleSystemData->positions(),
39           _particleSystemData->velocities(),
40           _newPositions.accessor(),
41           _newVelocities.accessor());
42   }
43
```

```
44  void ParticleSystemSolver3::resolveCollision(
45      const ConstArrayAccessor1<Vector3D>& positions,
46      const ConstArrayAccessor1<Vector3D>& velocities,
47      ArrayAccessor1<Vector3D> newPositions,
48      ArrayAccessor1<Vector3D> newVelocities) {
49      if (_collider != nullptr) {
50          size_t numberOfParticles
51              = _particleSystemData->numberOfParticles();
52          const double radius = _particleSystemData->radius();
53
54          parallelFor(
55              kZeroSize,
56              numberOfParticles,
57              [&] (size_t i) {
58                  _collider->resolveCollision(
59                      newPositions[i],
60                      newVelocities[i],
61                      radius,
62                      _restitutionCoefficient,
63                      &newPositions[i],
64                      &newVelocities[i]);
65              });
66      }
67  }
```

The function `timeIntegration` is also very similar to what we discussed in Section 1.6.2. It takes the final force array, computes acceleration, and then integrates the velocity and position. Notice that we don't apply the changes directly to the position and velocity arrays from `_particleSystemData` since the data will be postprocessed by `resolveCollision` and we need both current and new data during the process. So we are keeping the current and new states by assigning new values to the buffers, `_newPositions` and `_newVelocities`. Speaking of collisions, the actual collision resolution is abstracted within the `Collider3` instance, `_collider`, and the collider-side function `Collider3::resolveCollision` will be covered in Section 2.5. Let's treat it as a black box for now, but you can see we have a wrapper function `ParticleSystemSolver3::resolveCollision`, which resolves collisions for each particle in parallel. Notice that we have another layer inside `ParticleSystemSolver3::resolveCollision` which accepts arbitrary position and velocity arrays. This additional layer can be useful if a subclass would like to perform collision resolution in custom states (see Section 2.4).

Finally, let's wrap up our example by implementing the pre- and postprocessing part of the code.

```
1  void ParticleSystemSolver3::beginAdvanceTimeStep() {
2      // Allocate buffers
3      size_t n = _particleSystemData->numberOfParticles();
4      _newPositions.resize(n);
```

```
5        _newVelocities.resize(n);
6
7        // Clear forces
8        auto forces = _particleSystemData->forces();
9        setRange1(forces.size(), Vector3D(), &forces);
10
11       onBeginAdvanceTimeStep();
12   }
13
14   void ParticleSystemSolver3::endAdvanceTimeStep() {
15       // Update data
16       size_t n = _particleSystemData->numberOfParticles();
17       auto positions = _particleSystemData->positions();
18       auto velocities = _particleSystemData->velocities();
19       parallelFor(
20           kZeroSize,
21           n,
22           [&] (size_t i) {
23               positions[i] = _newPositions[i];
24               velocities[i] = _newVelocities[i];
25           });
26
27       onEndAdvanceTimeStep();
28   }
```

For the preprocessing, `beginAdvanceTimeStep`, we allocate memory for `_newPositions` and `_newVelocities`, which are required from the time-integration and collision handling. Also, the force array is cleared by setting zeros so that we can accumulate different forces. For postprocessing, we update the position and velocity states with the buffers to complete the time-step. For both functions, you can see the callback functions, `onBeginAdvanceTimeStep` and `onEndAdvanceTimeStep`, which can be overriden by the subclasses to perform extra pre- and postprocessing.

So far we have covered how to build a simulator using `ParticleSystemData3`. Figure 2.2 shows sample results from the solver, and the sample code to generate the animation can be found in `src/tests/manual_tests/particle_system_solver3_tests.cpp`. Again, this baseline simulator does not consider particle-to-particle interactions. In the following section, we will see what additional data structures are needed to make the particles interact with each other.

2.2.3 Neighbor Search

One of the most common operations in a particle-based simulation is to find nearby particles for a given location. In the mass–spring example from Section 1.6.2, we predefined the connectivity between two mass points with edges. Forming such a mesh was possible because the connectivity of the system does not change over time. We can also construct a particle set with

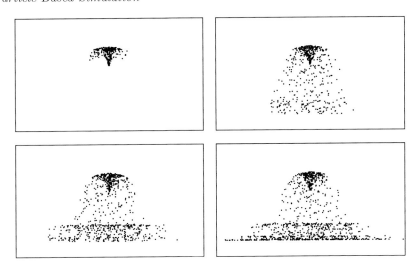

FIGURE 2.2
Sequence of a spray simulation using `ParticleSystemSolver3`. Particles are emitted from a point like a fountain. When collided with the floor, particles bounce up.

initial connectivity. Because of the nature of fluids, however, the volume that particles represent can break, merge, or deform radically from the original shape. Thus, the connectivity will change over time, requiring a continuous update for every time-step. The purpose of the neighbor search data structure and algorithm that we will cover in this section is to accelerate such location-based queries and cache the connectivity between a particle and its neighbor.

2.2.3.1 Searching Nearby Particles

An ad hoc way to search nearby particles from a given location is to iterate over entire particle list and see whether a particle is located within a given search radius. This algorithm has $O(N^2)$ time complexity, and obviously, we want a better method.

One of the commonly used algorithm to accelerate the neighbor search is hashing. The hashing algorithm maps particles into a grid of buckets based on their positions, and the size of the buckets is equal to the diameter of the search region. The mapping is determined by a spatial hashing function, which can be anything that converts 3D coordinates to bucket index. Now whenever a search query comes in, the query location can also be hashed to find the corresponding bucket. Then we can look up the nearby buckets and see whether the particles stored in those buckets are inside the search radius. All the other buckets need not be tested because it is clear that the particles in those buckets are outside the search range. Figure 2.3 illustrates the process more visually. To implement the hashing algorithm and the bucket data structure, let's first see how the

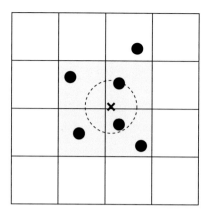

FIGURE 2.3
Neighbor search using hash grid data structure. When finding the nearby points from x-marked location within the radius represented by the dashed circle, the overlapping grid cells (colored with gray) are only looked up. Then, the points registered on each of the four grid cells are tested whether the points are inside the circle.

interface of a neighbor search class should look like:

```
1  class PointNeighborSearcher3 {
2   public:
3      typedef std::function<void(size_t, const Vector3D&)>
4          ForEachNearbyPointFunc;
5
6      PointNeighborSearcher3();
7      virtual ~PointNeighborSearcher3();
8
9      virtual void build(const ConstArrayAccessor1<Vector3D>& points) = 0;
10
11     virtual void forEachNearbyPoint(
12         const Vector3D& origin,
13         double radius,
14         const ForEachNearbyPointFunc& callback) const = 0;
15  };
```

This code is the base class for neighbor search classes, assuming that we can have multiple implementations of search algorithms. The class is using the word "point" instead of a particle, because we don't want to restrict the use case of this class to particles only, but would like to have more generic API that can be used for any other scenarios involving a spatial point search. Anyway, the base class has two virtual functions to be overridden, one for building the internal data structure, and the other for looking up the nearby points. Virtual function `build` takes an array of points and its size as input parameters.

Query function `forEachNearbyPoint` invokes the given callback function if there is a point near `origin` within `radius`. The two parameters in the callback function are the index and location of the nearby points.

To implement the hashing algorithm, we will inherit the base class and add hashing-specific members. As we can see in Figure 2.3, input parameters to construct the grid of buckets can be grid resolution and grid size. For each bucket, we are going to store the indices of the points that fall into the bucket. Now the class interface for the hashing can be written as:

```
1   class PointHashGridSearcher3 final : public PointNeighborSearcher3 {
2    public:
3       PointHashGridSearcher3(const Size3& resolution, double gridSpacing);
4       PointHashGridSearcher3(
5           size_t resolutionX,
6           size_t resolutionY,
7           size_t resolutionZ,
8           double gridSpacing);
9
10      void build(const ConstArrayAccessor1<Vector3D>& points) override;
11
12      void forEachNearbyPoint(
13          const Vector3D& origin,
14          double radius,
15          const ForEachNearbyPointFunc& callback) const override;
16
17      ...
18
19    private:
20      double _gridSpacing = 1.0;
21      Point3I _resolution = Point3I(1, 1, 1);
22      std::vector<Vector3D> _points;
23      std::vector<std::vector<size_t>> _buckets;
24
25      ...
26   };
```

Starting from the constructor above, the class instance can be initialized by providing the resolution and spacing of the grid. Then, there are two public functions that override virtual functions from the base class. For member data, the class stores grid shape information as well as the buckets. Also, it keeps the copy of the points that are passed to `forEachNearbyPoint` function. The implementation of the function `build` is quite simple as you can see below:

```
1   void PointHashGridSearcher3::build(
2       const ConstArrayAccessor1<Vector3D>& points) {
3       _buckets.clear();
4       _points.clear();
5
```

```
 6        if (points.size() == 0) {
 7            return;
 8        }
 9
10        // Allocate memory chuncks
11        _buckets.resize(_resolution.x * _resolution.y * _resolution.z);
12        _points.resize(points.size());
13
14        // Put points into buckets
15        for (size_t i = 0; i < points.size(); ++i) {
16            _points[i] = points[i];
17            size_t key = getHashKeyFromPosition(points[i]);
18            _buckets[key].push_back(i);
19        }
20    }
```

The key part of this code is in the last couple of lines. In the for-loop in the end, you can notice a point is passed to the member function, getHashKeyFromPosition, which returns the corresponding hash key. The hash function that maps the point to an integer key value can be anything that satisfies this input and output, but it is preferred to scatter the mapping spatially so that the number of points inside the buckets is as similar as possible. See Ihmsen et al. [55] for more discussion on the hash function. Once the hash key is determined, the index of the point is added to the corresponding bucket. The function getHashKeyFromPosition and necessary helper functions can be implemented as follows:

```
 1    Point3I PointHashGridSearcher3::getBucketIndex(const Vector3D& position)
          const {
 2        Point3I bucketIndex;
 3        bucketIndex.x = static_cast<ssize_t>(
 4            std::floor(position.x / _gridSpacing));
 5        bucketIndex.y = static_cast<ssize_t>(
 6            std::floor(position.y / _gridSpacing));
 7        bucketIndex.z = static_cast<ssize_t>(
 8            std::floor(position.z / _gridSpacing));
 9        return bucketIndex;
10    }
11
12    size_t PointHashGridSearcher3::getHashKeyFromPosition(
13        const Vector3D& position) const {
14        Point3I bucketIndex = getBucketIndex(position);
15        return getHashKeyFromBucketIndex(bucketIndex);
16    }
17
18    size_t PointHashGridSearcher3::getHashKeyFromBucketIndex(
19        const Point3I& bucketIndex) const {
20        Point3I wrappedIndex = bucketIndex;
```

```
21      wrappedIndex.x = bucketIndex.x % _resolution.x;
22      wrappedIndex.y = bucketIndex.y % _resolution.y;
23      wrappedIndex.z = bucketIndex.z % _resolution.z;
24      if (wrappedIndex.x < 0) { wrappedIndex.x += _resolution.x; }
25      if (wrappedIndex.y < 0) { wrappedIndex.y += _resolution.y; }
26      if (wrappedIndex.z < 0) { wrappedIndex.z += _resolution.z; }
27      return static_cast<size_t>(
28          (wrappedIndex.z * _resolution.y + wrappedIndex.y) * _resolution.x
29          + wrappedIndex.x);
30  }
```

From the code, the function `getBucketIndex` converts the input position to integer coordinate that corresponds to the bucket at grid cell (x, y, z). It is, however, an imaginary coordinate, which gets wrapped around if it lies outside the grid. Then the wrapped coordinate is hashed into a single integer, and the hash function in this code simply maps the 3D integer coordinate to 1D index as if the volumetric grid is mapped into a linear array. Again, Figure 2.3 shows how this hashing works.

Once the buckets are initialized, we can use this class to query neighbor search. For the given query location, it first figures out which buckets are overlapping with the search sphere (or circle in 2D). For 3D, there will be eight overlapping buckets, and for 2D, there will be four. Then, the code iterates for each overlapping bucket to test whether the points within the bucket lie inside the search radius. The code below implements these steps:

```
1   void PointHashGridSearcher3::forEachNearbyPoint(
2       const Vector3D& origin,
3       double radius,
4       const std::function<void(size_t, const Vector3D&)>& callback) const {
5       if (_buckets.empty()) {
6           return;
7       }
8
9       size_t nearbyKeys[8];
10      getNearbyKeys(origin, nearbyKeys);
11
12      const double queryRadiusSquared = radius * radius;
13
14      for (int i = 0; i < 8; i++) {
15          const auto& bucket = _buckets[nearbyKeys[i]];
16          size_t numberOfPointsInBucket = bucket.size();
17
18          for (size_t j = 0; j < numberOfPointsInBucket; ++j) {
19              size_t pointIndex = bucket[j];
20              double rSquared
21                  = (_points[pointIndex] - origin).lengthSquared();
22              if (rSquared <= queryRadiusSquared) {
23                  callback(pointIndex, _points[pointIndex]);
```

```
24                }
25              }
26          }
27    }

29    void PointHashGridSearcher3::getNearbyKeys(
30          const Vector3D& position,
31          size_t* nearbyKeys) const {
32          Point3I originIndex
33              = getBucketIndex(position), nearbyBucketIndices[8];

35          for (int i = 0; i < 8; i++) {
36              nearbyBucketIndices[i] = originIndex;
37          }

39          if ((originIndex.x + 0.5f) * _gridSpacing <= position.x) {
40              nearbyBucketIndices[4].x += 1; nearbyBucketIndices[5].x += 1;
41              nearbyBucketIndices[6].x += 1; nearbyBucketIndices[7].x += 1;
42          } else {
43              nearbyBucketIndices[4].x -= 1; nearbyBucketIndices[5].x -= 1;
44              nearbyBucketIndices[6].x -= 1; nearbyBucketIndices[7].x -= 1;
45          }

47          if ((originIndex.y + 0.5f) * _gridSpacing <= position.y) {
48              nearbyBucketIndices[2].y += 1; nearbyBucketIndices[3].y += 1;
49              nearbyBucketIndices[6].y += 1; nearbyBucketIndices[7].y += 1;
50          } else {
51              nearbyBucketIndices[2].y -= 1; nearbyBucketIndices[3].y -= 1;
52              nearbyBucketIndices[6].y -= 1; nearbyBucketIndices[7].y -= 1;
53          }

55          if ((originIndex.z + 0.5f) * _gridSpacing <= position.z) {
56              nearbyBucketIndices[1].z += 1; nearbyBucketIndices[3].z += 1;
57              nearbyBucketIndices[5].z += 1; nearbyBucketIndices[7].z += 1;
58          } else {
59              nearbyBucketIndices[1].z -= 1; nearbyBucketIndices[3].z -= 1;
60              nearbyBucketIndices[5].z -= 1; nearbyBucketIndices[7].z -= 1;
61          }

63          for (int i = 0; i < 8; i++) {
64              nearbyKeys[i] = getHashKeyFromBucketIndex(nearbyBucketIndices[i]);
65          }
66    }
```

Note that the function `getNearbyKeys` determines which buckets overlap with the search sphere by checking where the input location lies within the bucket with respect to the center of the cube.

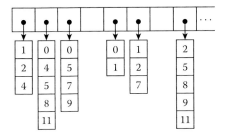

FIGURE 2.4
Illustration of the neighbor list data structure. It is represented by the point indices list. For example, point 0's neighbors are points 1, 2, and 4.

2.2.3.2 Caching Neighbors

The data structure we have built so far is efficient for searching nearby points for any random input location. But one of the common use cases from the particle-based animation is to iterate neighboring particles for a given particle. In such case, it would be even more efficient to cache the nearby particles and create a neighbors list as shown in Figure 2.4, instead of running a bucket search for every step in the loop. The code below demonstrates how we can build neighbors lists within `ParticleSystemData3` class:

```cpp
class ParticleSystemData3 {
 public:
    ...

    void buildNeighborSearcher(double maxSearchRadius);
    void buildNeighborLists(double maxSearchRadius);

 private:
    ...

    PointNeighborSearcher3Ptr _neighborSearcher;
    std::vector<std::vector<size_t>> _neighborLists;
};

void ParticleSystemData3::buildNeighborSearcher(double maxSearchRadius) {
    // Use PointHashGridSearcher3 by default
    _neighborSearcher = std::make_shared<PointHashGridSearcher3>(
        kDefaultHashGridResolution,
        kDefaultHashGridResolution,
        kDefaultHashGridResolution,
        2.0 * maxSearchRadius);

    _neighborSearcher->build(positions());
}
```

```
26  void ParticleSystemData3::buildNeighborLists(double maxSearchRadius) {
27      _neighborLists.resize(numberOfParticles());
28
29      auto points = positions();
30      for (size_t i = 0; i < numberOfParticles(); ++i) {
31          Vector3D origin = points[i];
32          _neighborLists[i].clear();
33
34          _neighborSearcher->forEachNearbyPoint(
35              origin,
36              maxSearchRadius,
37              [&](size_t j, const Vector3D&) {
38                  if (i != j) {
39                      _neighborLists[i].push_back(j);
40                  }
41              });
42      }
43  }
```

2.3 Smoothed Particles

One of the most popular approaches for representing fluid with particles is to use smoothed particles, namely Smoothed Particle Hydrodynamics (SPH). It is a method of partitioning the fluid volume with many particles, and single particle represents a small fraction of the volume. It's called "smoothed" because the method blurs out the boundaries of a particle so that we get a smooth distribution of physical quantities. It is just like an airbrush, as you can see in Figure 2.5. Note that the idea of smoothing enables "painting" the region with a finite number of blurry dots, which means you can fill the gap between particles with the smoothed profile. With a small number of dots or particles, you would need bigger airbrush nozzle. With more particles, the smaller dot would be sufficient to fill the blanks. This feature is important because it turns finite data points into a continuous field; remember we have limited computational resource, whereas fluids are continuous material. Also, once we can measure the value (or the color using our painting analogy) at any arbitrary point in the domain, we can define mathematical operators as well, such as gradient or Laplacian, that are required for computing fluid motion.

The SPH method was originally introduced in astrophysics community by Monaghan [86] and actively studied in computational fluid dynamics field as well [87]. Soon after, computer animation started to adopt the idea of SPH [34,89] and also became one of the core frameworks for commercial products like RealFlow [3]. In this book, we will also use SPH framework as our main particle-based simulation engine.

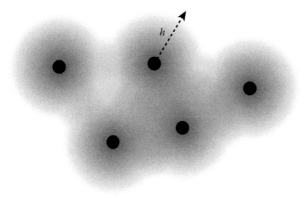

FIGURE 2.5
Illustration of smoothed particles. Each particle has its influence radius h, and any values assigned to the particle is blurred to that extent.

2.3.1 Basics

This section will cover the basic SPH operations and their codes including interpolation, gradient, and Laplacian, which are essential building blocks for implementing SPH-based fluid simulations.

2.3.1.1 Kernel

In SPH, we are going to describe the "smoothness" using a function called "kernel." When a particle position is given, this kernel function spreads out any values stored in the particle nearby, as shown in Figure 2.6. Starting from the center point of a particle, the function fades out to zero as the distance from the center reaches the kernel radius. For high-resolution simulation using many particles, the radius is usually set smaller. For coarse simulation with less number of particles, we use a larger radius. In such cases, the peak of the kernel function also changes so that the area below the function remains constant, which is 1 (see Figure 2.6).

For the function itself, we can use any functions if the integral of a function is 1 and it decays monotonically to 0 as we get further from the center point. For example,

$$W_{std}(r) = \frac{315}{64\pi h^3} \begin{cases} (1 - \frac{r^2}{h^2})^3 & 0 \le r \le h \\ 0 & \text{otherwise} \end{cases} \tag{2.1}$$

is one of the popular kernels for 3D that was first proposed by Müller et al. [89]. From the sample code in Adams and Wicke [7], the code for the kernel can be

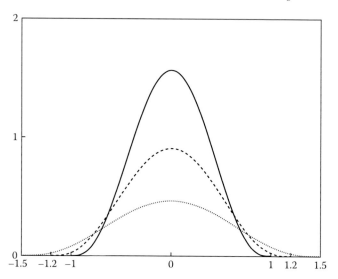

FIGURE 2.6
Kernel functions with different radii –1.0, 1.2, and 1.5. As radius increases,
the maximum value decreases.

written as:

```
 1  struct SphStdKernel3 {
 2      double h, h2, h3;
 3
 4      SphStdKernel3();
 5
 6      explicit SphStdKernel3(double kernelRadius);
 7
 8      SphStdKernel3(const SphStdKernel3& other);
 9
10      double operator()(double distance) const;
11
12      ...
13  };
14
15  inline SphStdKernel3::SphStdKernel3()
16      : h(0), h2(0), h3(0) {}
17
18  inline SphStdKernel3::SphStdKernel3(double kernelRadius)
19      : h(kernelRadius), h2(h*h), h3(h2*h) {}
20
21  inline double SphStdKernel3::operator()(double distance) const {
22      if (distance*distance >= h2) {
23          return 0.0;
```

```
24        } else {
25            double x = 1.0 - distance * distance / h2;
26            return 315.0 / (64.0 * kPiD * h3) * x * x * x;
27        }
28    }
```

As mentioned earlier, the integral of any valid kernel functions should be 1. That is:

$$\int W(r) = 1 \tag{2.2}$$

You can verify Equation 2.1 using the integral above, and you will need this if you want to invent your own kernel function. In the end, we also create a couple of more kernel functions in this book. To see how to calculate the integral together with other kernels, see Appendix B.1.

2.3.1.2   Data Model

Since we now have the kernel function, we can evaluate smoothed physical quantities for a single particle. The next step is to extend the data structure to the multiple particles.

If you recall the class, `ParticleSystemData3` from the previous section, you may agree that it is a good starting point because it stores particles and has neighbor-search capability. So let's extend the class and add a couple of new features as shown below.

```
1    class SphSystemData3 : public ParticleSystemData3 {
2      public:
3        SphSystemData3();
4
5        virtual ~SphSystemData3();
6
7        ConstArrayAccessor1<double> densities() const;
8
9        ArrayAccessor1<double> densities();
10
11     private:
12        ...
13    };
```

Notice that the constructor is adding density data to the system. As we will discover soon, the density is required from many SPH operators, so we are reserving it from the beginning. A couple of simple getters are also included in the skeleton code as well. Return types `ArrayAccessor1` and `ConstArrayAccessor1` are just simple 1D array pointer wrappers, just like a simple random access iterator.

From the following sections, we will keep adding more features to this class. Similar to the particle system example in Section 2.2.2, we are going to decouple the data model from the physics. Thus, most of the data evaluation-related functions will be implemented in SphSystemData3, and dynamics-related functions will be implemented in a different class which will inherit ParticleSystemSolver3 from the previous section.

2.3.1.3 Interpolation

The basic idea of SPH interpolation is to measure any physical quantities at any given location by looking up the nearby particles. It is a weighted average, where the weight is the mass times kernel function divided by neighboring particles' density. So what does that mean? Take a look at the following code.

```
1   class SphSystemData3 : public ParticleSystemData3 {
2   public:
3       ...
4
5       Vector3D interpolate(
6           const Vector3D& origin,
7           const ConstArrayAccessor1<Vector3D>& values) const;
8       ...
9   };
10
11  Vector3D SphSystemData3::interpolate(
12      const Vector3D& origin,
13      const ConstArrayAccessor1<Vector3D>& values) const {
14      Vector3D sum;
15      auto d = densities();
16      SphStdKernel3 kernel(_kernelRadius);
17
18      neighborSearcher()->forEachNearbyPoint(
19          origin,
20          _kernelRadius,
21          [&] (size_t i, const Vector3D& neighborPosition) {
22              double dist = origin.distanceTo(neighborPosition);
23              double weight = _mass / d[i] * kernel(dist);
24              sum += weight * values[i];
25          });
26
27      return sum;
28  }
```

To our data model, SphSystemData3, we are adding a new public function, interpolate. The function takes two parameters: the location where we want to perform interpolation (origin) and the array of values we want to interpolate (values). Each ith element of values corresponds to the ith particle. Also, the variables _kernelRadius and _mass represent the kernel radius and the mass of a particle. We are going to assume that the kernel radius and mass are the same for every particle. You can also define varying kernel radii and mass, but we won't cover that in this book.

From the function call, `forEachNearbyPoint`, the code iterates nearby points and computes sum of weights using the mass, density, and kernel weight. If this sounds unfamiliar, take a look at Section 2.2.3 for the neighbor search. Note that mass is divided by density `d[i]` which means volume. Hence, this interpolation is putting more weight to a value that is closer to the origin (`kernel(dist)`) and larger in terms of volume. The code can also be written in mathematical expression as well:

$$\phi(\mathbf{x}) = m \sum_j \frac{\phi_j}{\rho_j} W((x) - \mathbf{x}_j) \qquad (2.3)$$

where $\mathbf{x}$, m, ϕ, ρ, and $W(\mathbf{r})$ are location for the interpolation, mass, quantity that we want to interpolate, density, and kernel function, respectively. Subscript j represents jth neighboring particle.

2.3.1.4 Density

Density is a quantity that changes every time-step (or for every `onAdvanceTimeStep` call) since the positions of the particles can change. So for each time-step, we need to compute the densities with updated positions, and use the values for other SPH operations. For instance, the interpolation function above already depends on the density. So in fact, we must compute the density prior to any interpolation steps, and this applies to the other operators like the gradient and Laplacian as well. To get the density for each particle, imagine that we want to "interpolate" the density for each particle's location. But wait, didn't we just discuss that we need densities for the interpolation? Sounds like an infinite recursion, but let's just try it. If we replace `values` array with the density from `interpolate` function, the code can be written as:

```
1   ...
2
3   neighborSearcher()->forEachNearbyPoint(
4       origin,
5       _kernelRadius,
6       [&](size_t i, const Vector3D& neighborPosition) {
7           double dist = origin.distanceTo(neighborPosition);
8           double weight = _mass / d[i] * kernel(dist);
9           sum += weight * d[i];
10      });
11
12  ...
```

This can be further simplified as:

```
1   ...
2
3   neighborSearcher()->forEachNearbyPoint(
```

```
4      origin,
5      _kernelRadius,
6      [&](size_t i, const Vector3D& neighborPosition) {
7          double dist = origin.distanceTo(neighborPosition);
8          double weight = _mass * kernel(dist);
9          sum += weight;
10     });
11
12 ...
```

Notice that the density part is now gone! So that breaks the infinite loop and enables us to compute density before anything else. Thus, measuring the density is just a kernel-weighted summation of the mass for each particle. The code can be written in an equation form as well:

$$\rho(\mathbf{x}) = m \sum_j W(\mathbf{x} - \mathbf{x}_j) \qquad (2.4)$$

In SphSystemData3, we can implement a helper function updateDensities to update the density with some minor code clean-ups:

```
1  class SphSystemData3 : public ParticleSystemData3 {
2   public:
3       ...
4
5       void updateDensities();
6
7       double sumOfKernelNearby(const Vector3D& position) const;
8
9   private:
10      ...
11  };
12
13  void SphSystemData3::updateDensities() {
14      auto p = positions();
15      auto d = densities();
16
17      parallelFor(
18          kZeroSize,
19          numberOfParticles(),
20          [&](size_t i) {
21              double sum = sumOfKernelNearby(p[i]);
22              d[i] = _mass * sum;
23          });
24  }
25
26  double SphSystemData3::sumOfKernelNearby(const Vector3D& origin) const {
27      double sum = 0.0;
28      SphStdKernel3 kernel(_kernelRadius);
```

```
29    neighborSearcher()->forEachNearbyPoint(
30        origin,
31        _kernelRadius,
32        [&] (size_t, const Vector3D& neighborPosition) {
33            double dist = origin.distanceTo(neighborPosition);
34            sum += kernel(dist);
35        });
36    return sum;
37  }
```

Thus, to use an SPH-type operation like interpolation, `updateDensities` function must be called to initialize the density field.

2.3.1.5 Differential Operators

We now have basic tools to perform mathematical computation in the SPH world. To compute fluid dynamics, however, we need the differential operators we covered in Section 1.3.5. Let's find out how we can implement the gradient and Laplacian operators, the most frequently used operators in this chapter, based on the kernel interpolation.

2.3.1.5.1 Gradient

To calculate the gradient, ∇f, using SPH particles, let's first start with just one particle. If we have a particle, we know that we can make a Gaussian-like distribution using the SPH kernel as shown in Figure 2.7a. From the interpolation code we wrote earlier, we know that the field can be computed by:

```
1   result = value * mass / density * kernel(distance);
```

The gradient vector's magnitude would be proportional to the derivative of the kernel, and its direction will point toward the center of the kernel as

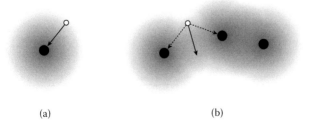

(a)   (b)

FIGURE 2.7
Illustration of (a) a gradient vector with a single particle and (b) with many particles. From image (b), the gradient vectors from two particles form the net gradient particle.

shown in Figure 2.7a. Thus, the code for computing the gradient with single particle would look like:

```
1   result = value * mass / density * kernel.firstDerivative(distance) *
        directionToParticle;
```

Note that everything else is kept the same from the interpolation, but we are multiplying first derivative of the kernel instead of the kernel itself together with the direction from the sample location to the particle's center. The new function firstDerivative can be added to the existing class SphStdKernel3:

```
1   struct SphStdKernel3 {
2       ...
3       double firstDerivative(double distance) const;
4
5       Vector3D gradient(double distance, const Vector3D& direction) const;
6   };
7
8   inline double SphStdKernel3::firstDerivative(double distance) const {
9       if (distance >= h) {
10          return 0.0;
11      } else {
12          double x = 1.0 - distance*distance / h2;
13          return -945.0 / (32.0 * kPiD * h5) * distance * x * x;
14      }
15  }
16
17  inline Vector3D SphStdKernel3::gradient(
18      double distance,
19      const Vector3D& directionToCenter) const {
20      return -firstDerivative(distance) * directionToCenter;
21  }
```

This code implements the first derivative of Equation 2.1 and the gradient of the smoothed field.

Extending the idea to multiple particles is easy. As shown in Figure 2.7b, simply iterating over the nearby neighbors and adding the gradient vectors will work. Thus, we can write a new function that is very similar to interpolate:

```
1   class SphSystemData3 : public ParticleSystemData3 {
2   public:
3       ...
4
5       Vector3D gradientAt(
6           size_t i,
7           const ConstArrayAccessor1<double>& values) const;
8
9   private:
```

```
10        ...
11   };
12
13   Vector3D SphSystemData3::gradientAt(
14       size_t i,
15       const ConstArrayAccessor1<double>& values) const {
16       Vector3D sum;
17       auto p = positions();
18       auto d = densities();
19       const auto& neighbors = neighborLists()[i];
20       Vector3D origin = p[i];
21       SphSpikyKernel3 kernel(_kernelRadius);
22
23       for (size_t j : neighbors) {
24           Vector3D neighborPosition = p[j];
25           double dist = origin.distanceTo(neighborPosition);
26           if (dist > 0.0) {
27               Vector3D dir = (neighborPosition - origin) / dist;
28               sum += values[j] * _mass / d[j] * kernel.gradient(dist, dir);
29           }
30       }
31
32       return sum;
33   }
```

The new function, `gradientAt`, returns the gradient for the input `values` for a given particle index `i`. The code above is equivalent to the equation below:

$$\nabla \phi(\mathbf{x}) = m \sum_j \frac{\phi_j}{\rho_j} \nabla W(|\mathbf{x} - \mathbf{x}_j|) \tag{2.5}$$

This implementation of the gradient, however, is not symmetric. It means the gradient calculated from two nearby particles with respect to each other can be different. For example, assume that we have only two particles in the system, and see what's the return value of the code or equation. It can result in different magnitude of gradient vectors if particles have different ϕ (or `value`) and density. This can be a problem if you compute the force out of this gradient. Nonsymmetric gradient means two different magnitude of forces will be applied depending on which particle you are looking at, and that will violate Newton's third law of motion – for every action, there is an equal and opposite action.

To solve this issue, different versions of gradient implementations have been proposed [86,89,7]. One of the most commonly used methods is:

$$\nabla \phi(\mathbf{x}) = \rho_i m \sum_j \left(\frac{\phi_i}{\rho_i^2} + \frac{\phi_j}{\rho_j^2} \right) \nabla W(|\mathbf{x} - \mathbf{x}_j|) \tag{2.6}$$

and we can also replace a part of the previous code as follows:

```
Vector3D SphSystemData3::gradientAt(
    size_t i,
    const ConstArrayAccessor1<double>& values) const {
    Vector3D sum;
    auto p = positions();
    auto d = densities();
    const auto& neighbors = neighborLists()[i];
    Vector3D origin = p[i];
    SphSpikyKernel3 kernel(_kernelRadius);

    for (size_t j : neighbors) {
        Vector3D neighborPosition = p[j];
        double dist = origin.distanceTo(neighborPosition);
        if (dist > 0.0) {
            Vector3D dir = (neighborPosition - origin) / dist;
            sum += d[i] * _mass * (values[i] / square(d[i]) + values[j] /
                square(d[j])) * kernel.gradient(dist, dir);
        }
    }

    return sum;
}
```

You can see the detailed derivation of this new gradient equation in Appendix B.1. But we can easily confirm that the new gradient is symmetric.

2.3.1.5.2 Laplacian

To compute the Laplacian $\nabla^2 f$ from the given particles, we take similar steps as we did from the gradient calculation. So starting from the evaluation of a single particle's profile:

```
result = value * mass / density * kernel(distance);
```

If we apply second derivative along the variable `distance`, it becomes:

```
result = value * mass / density * kernel.secondDerivative(distance);
```

where the function, `secondDerivative`, can be implemented as:

```
struct SphStdKernel3 {
    double h5;
    ...

    double secondDerivative(double distance) const;
};
```

```
7
8    inline SphStdKernel3::SphStdKernel3()
9        : h(0), h2(0), h3(0), h5(0) {}
10
11   inline SphStdKernel3::SphStdKernel3(double kernelRadius)
12       : h(kernelRadius), h2(h * h), h3(h2 * h), h5(h2 * h3) {}
13
14   inline double SphStdKernel3::secondDerivative(double distance) const {
15       if (distance*distance >= h2) {
16           return 0.0;
17       } else {
18           double x = distance*distance / h2;
19           return 945.0 / (32.0 * kPiD * h5) * (1 - x) * (3 * x - 1);
20       }
21   }
```

Similar to the gradient code, if we put all together within the neighbor iteration, the code can be written as:

```
1    double SphSystemData3::laplacianAt(
2        size_t i,
3        const ConstArrayAccessor1<double>& values) const {
4        double sum = 0.0;
5        auto p = positions();
6        auto d = densities();
7        const auto& neighbors = neighborLists()[i];
8        Vector3D origin = p[i];
9        SphSpikyKernel3 kernel(_kernelRadius);
10
11       for (size_t j : neighbors) {
12           Vector3D neighborPosition = p[j];
13           double dist = origin.distanceTo(neighborPosition);
14           sum += _mass * values[j] / d[j] * kernel.secondDerivative(dist);
15       }
16
17       return sum;
18   }
```

As discussed in other literatures [7,88], the code above does not return zero for constant fields. Even if `values[j]` has the same nonzero value for each particle, `sum` will be nonzero in the end of the loop. This can be a problem because we are going to use the Laplacian mostly for the viscosity computation, and to have proper viscosity force, constant input should have a zero field as an output. As suggested by Monaghan and others [7,88], however, one minor tweak will solve this problem which is simply subtracting the value from the origin particle as shown below.

```
1    double SphSystemData3::laplacianAt(
2        size_t i,
3        const ConstArrayAccessor1<double>& values) const {
```

```
4        double sum = 0.0;
5        auto p = positions();
6        auto d = densities();
7        const auto& neighbors = neighborLists()[i];
8        Vector3D origin = p[i];
9        SphSpikyKernel3 kernel(_kernelRadius);
10
11       for (size_t j : neighbors) {
12           Vector3D neighborPosition = p[j];
13           double dist = origin.distanceTo(neighborPosition);
14           sum += _mass * (values[j] - values[i]) / d[j] * kernel.
                 secondDerivative(dist);
15       }
16
17       return sum;
18   }
```

The corresponding equation is:

$$\nabla^2 \phi(\mathbf{x}) = m \sum_j \left(\frac{\phi_j - \phi_i}{\rho_j} \right) \nabla^2 W(\mathbf{x} - \mathbf{x}_j) \qquad (2.7)$$

2.3.1.5.3   *Special Kernels for Operators*

So far we have been using Gaussian-like kernel function to compute the interpolation and field operators. Within the code, we compute the gradient or Laplacian of the kernel itself (Equations 2.5 and 2.7). Figure 2.8a plots the gradient and Laplacian of the kernel function. Notice that although the kernel function itself drops monotonically as the distance from the center increases, the gradient and Laplacian oscillate. As some of you might have guessed already, the gradient operator will be used for evaluating the pressure gradient which pushes particles apart when they become too close. (We will cover this in Section 2.3.2.) However, the graph shown in Figure 2.8a suggests that at some point the pressure force will drop even though the particles are getting closer. The Laplacian operator is even showing negative profile when the particles are closer than certain threshold.

To resolve this issue, Mueller and his colleagues suggested a new kernel function [89]. This function has a spiky shape which is plotted in Figure 2.8b. As you can see in the graph, this gradient and Laplacian of this kernel function drop monotonically as the distance increases. The kernel function itself can be written as below:

$$W_{spiky}(r) = \frac{15}{\pi h^3} \begin{cases} (1 - \frac{r}{h})^3 & 0 \le r \le h \\ 0 & \text{otherwise} \end{cases} \qquad (2.8)$$

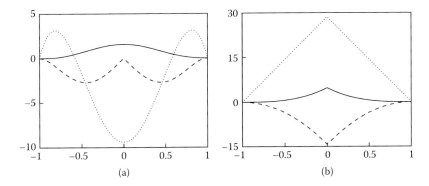

FIGURE 2.8

(a) The standard SPH kernel and (b) the spiky kernel. The solid, dashed, and dotted lines show the original function, its first derivative, and the second derivative, respectively.

The corresponding code can be written as:

```
1   struct SphSpikyKernel3 {
2       double h, h2, h3, h4, h5;
3
4       SphSpikyKernel3();
5
6       explicit SphSpikyKernel3(double kernelRadius);
7
8       double operator()(double distance) const;
9
10      double firstDerivative(double distance) const;
11
12      Vector3D gradient(double distance, const Vector3D& direction) const;
13
14      double secondDerivative(double distance) const;
15  };
16
17  inline SphSpikyKernel3::SphSpikyKernel3()
18      : h(0), h2(0), h3(0), h4(0), h5(0) {}
19
20  inline SphSpikyKernel3::SphSpikyKernel3(double h_)
21      : h(h_), h2(h * h), h3(h2 * h), h4(h2 * h2), h5(h3 * h2) {}
22
23  inline double SphSpikyKernel3::operator()(double distance) const {
24      if (distance >= h) {
25          return 0.0;
26      } else {
27          double x = 1.0 - distance / h;
```

```
28            return 15.0 / (kPiD * h3) * x * x * x;
29        }
30    }
31
32    inline double SphSpikyKernel3::firstDerivative(double distance) const {
33        if (distance >= h) {
34            return 0.0;
35        } else {
36            double x = 1.0 - distance / h;
37            return -45.0 / (kPiD * h4) * x * x;
38        }
39    }
40
41    inline Vector3D SphSpikyKernel3::gradient(
42        double distance,
43        const Vector3D& directionToCenter) const {
44        return -firstDerivative(distance) * directionToCenter;
45    }
46
47    inline double SphSpikyKernel3::secondDerivative(double distance) const {
48        if (distance >= h) {
49            return 0.0;
50        } else {
51            double x = 1.0 - distance / h;
52            return 90.0 / (kPiD * h5) * x;
53        }
54    }
```

As mentioned earlier, we can use any kernel function that meets Equation 2.2. Thus, using the spiky kernel in SPH computation is valid. But since the standard kernel, SphStdKernel3, gives the smoother profile for interpolation, we will use the spiky kernel only for the gradient and Laplacian calculation.

2.3.2   Dynamics

As we discussed in Section 1.7, the pressure gradient, viscosity, and gravity forces are the key components for implementing a fluid solver. Again, the pressure gradient force results in fluid flow from higher to lower pressure area, and the viscosity defines how thick the fluid is. In addition to these three forces, we will also incorporate the air-drag force from our previous examples in Sections 1.6.2 and 2.2.2. Similar to those examples, the SPH simulator also takes the following steps:

1. Measure the density with particles' current locations

2. Compute the pressure based on the density

3. Compute the pressure gradient force

4. Compute the viscosity force

5. Compute the gravity and other extra forces

6. Perform time integration

Some part of these steps are already covered, and we are going to extend the existing particle system solver, `ParticleSystemSolver3`. We know how to compute the density field in Section 2.3.1.4 which will clear the first step, and we are also going to use the external force and time integration parts from the particle system code. Let's find out how we can implement the rest of these steps and put everything together to build an SPH fluid solver.

2.3.2.1 Solver Overview

To define the logic behind the SPH-based fluid solver, we are going to leverage what we already have implemented in `ParticleSystemSolver3` from Section 2.2.2. Consider the following code:

```
1   class SphSystemSolver3 : public ParticleSystemSolver3 {
2    public:
3       SphSystemSolver3();
4
5       virtual ~SphSystemSolver3();
6
7       ...
8
9    protected:
10       void accumulateForces(double timeStepInSeconds) override;
11
12       void onBeginAdvanceTimeStep() override;
13
14       void onEndAdvanceTimeStep() override;
15
16       virtual void accumulateNonPressureForces(double timeStepInSeconds);
17
18       virtual void accumulatePressureForce(double timeStepInSeconds);
19
20       void computePressure();
21
22       void accumulateViscosityForce();
23
24       void computePseudoViscosity();
25
26       ...
27   };
```

As you can see, we are overriding three functions: `accumulateForces`, `onBeginAdvanceTimeStep`, and `onEndAdvanceTimeStep`. This implies that the new solver will accumulate different types of forces for the particles, and there will be additional pre- and postprocessing steps. This naturally leads to the next functions which compute the pressure, pressure gradient force, viscosity, and pseudo-viscosity during the process. Since the super class `ParticleSystemSolver3` will take care of everything including the collision handling and time integration, this class focuses only on the force computations.

Starting from the higher-level function, `accumulateForces`, the code looks as follows:

```
1   void SphSystemSolver3::accumulateForces(double timeStepInSeconds) {
2       accumulateNonPressureForces(timeStepInSeconds);
3       accumulatePressureForce(timeStepInSeconds);
4   }
5
6   void SphSystemSolver3::accumulateNonPressureForces(double
        timeStepInSeconds) {
7       ParticleSystemSolver3::accumulateForces(timeStepInSeconds);
8       accumulateViscosityForce();
9   }
10
11  void SphSystemSolver3::accumulatePressureForce(double timeStepInSeconds)
        {
12      auto particles = sphSystemData();
13      auto x = particles->positions();
14      auto d = particles->densities();
15      auto p = particles->pressures();
16      auto f = particles->forces();
17
18      computePressure();
19      accumulatePressureForce(x, d, p, f);
20  }
```

Note that we are adding the pressure and viscosity forces only, because `ParticleSystemSolver3::accumulateForces` takes care of the gravity and air-drag forces. The code also separates pressure and nonpressure forces for future use. For the preprocessing, remember that we need to update density prior to any SPH operations. Thus, `onBeginAdvanceTimeStep` can be implemented as shown below:

```
1   void SphSystemSolver3::onBeginAdvanceTimeStep() {
2       auto particles = sphSystemData();
3       particles->buildNeighborSearcher();
4       particles->buildNeighborLists();
5       particles->updateDensities();
6   }
```

The getter function `sphSystemData()` returns the shared pointer to `SphSystemData3` that we create in the constructor.

For the postprocessing, we will add a pseudo-physical velocity filtering which dampens any noticeable noises. The function `onEndAdvanceTimeStep` can be written as:

```
1   void SphSystemSolver3::onEndAdvanceTimeStep() {
2       computePseudoViscosity();
3   }
```

We now have a higher-level implementation of the solver by calling force accumulation functions. From the following sections, let's dive into the details of these subroutines.

2.3.2.2   Pressure Gradient Force

To compute the pressure gradient force, we need to evaluate the pressure. Pressure is highly related to the density – higher density generates higher pressure. Using the density calculation discussed in Section 2.3.1.4, let's find out how we can calculate pressure.

2.3.2.2.1   *Equation-of-State*

The Equation-of-State, or EOS, describes the relationship between state variables. In this case, we map density to pressure. Consider the code below:

```
1    double computePressureFromEos(
2        double density,
3        double targetDensity,
4        double eosScale,
5        double eosExponent) {
6        double p = eosScale / eosExponent
7            * (std::pow((density / targetDensity), eosExponent) - 1.0);
8
9        return p;
10   }
```

The function `computePressureFromEos` takes the current density (`density`), the desired target density of a fluid (`targetDensity`), some scaling factors (`eosScale`), and finally an exponent that controls the exaggeration of the mapping (`eosExponent`). The equivalent mathematical expression can be written as follows:

$$p = \frac{\kappa}{\gamma} \left(\frac{\rho}{\rho_0} - 1 \right)^{\gamma} \tag{2.9}$$

Here, p is pressure, κ is `eosScale`, γ is `eosExponent`, ρ is `density`, and ρ_0 is `targetDensity`.

To assign the pressure for each particle, we simply iterate over the list by:

```
1  void SphSystemSolver3::computePressure() {
2      auto particles = sphSystemData();
3      size_t numberOfParticles = particles->numberOfParticles();
4      auto d = particles->densities();
5      auto p = particles->pressures();
6
7      const double targetDensity = particles->targetDensity();
8      const double eosScale
9          = targetDensity * square(_speedOfSound) / _eosExponent;
10
11     parallelFor(
12         zeroSize,
13         numberOfParticles,
14         [&](size_t i) {
15             p[i] = computePressureFromEos(
16                 d[i],
17                 targetDensity,
18                 eosScale,
19                 eosExponent());
20         });
21 }
```

Note that the code above is calculating `eosScale` by

$$\kappa = \rho_0 \frac{c_s}{\gamma} \tag{2.10}$$

where c_s is the speed of sound in the fluid. This method is suggested by Becker and Teschner [15].

Now, if you look closely to `computePressureFromEos`, it can introduce negative pressure if the density is lower than the target density. This can cause unintended behavior near the surface due to the low number of neighboring particles. Take a look at Figure 2.9 which describes the situation near the surface more visually. It shows that the particles near the surface may experience clumping artifact because the SPH solver will try to make the density

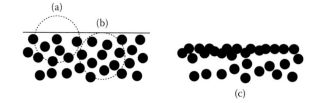

FIGURE 2.9
Particle near the surface can measure low density even with nearly uniform distribution. For instance, point (a) will evaluate lower density than point (b). This will cause the clumping of the particles near the surface (c).

distribution constant even though the spacing between particles is close to the target spacing. This can be viewed as a surface tension effect, but it is not an intended effect nor physically accurate. The solution to this problem is to clamp the negative pressure as shown below:

```
1  double computePressureFromEos(
2      double density,
3      double targetDensity,
4      double eosScale,
5      double eosExponent,
6      double negativePressureScale) {
7
8      double p = eosScale / eosExponent
9          * (std::pow((density / targetDensity), eosExponent) - 1.0);
10
11     // Negative pressure scaling
12     if (p < 0) {
13         p *= negativePressureScale;
14     }
15
16     return p;
17  }
```

From the code above, if `negativePressureScale` is zero, it will clamp the negative pressure to zero.[*] Otherwise, it will scale the negative pressure with the desired scaling factor.

The next step is to generate the pressure force so that it pushes such concentrating particles away.

2.3.2.2.2 Computing Pressure Gradient

Again, the gradient operator tells you what is the steepest direction and slope at given location. If you apply that to the pressure field, it gives you a vector that points the highest pressure region nearby where its magnitude corresponds to the slope of the pressure field at given location.

To compute the pressure gradient, we can use the symmetric version of the gradient in Equation 2.6. From the following pressure gradient equation in Section 1.7.2,

$$\mathbf{f}_p = -m\frac{\nabla p}{\rho} \tag{2.11}$$

we can apply the symmetric gradient operator to get

$$\mathbf{f}_p = -m^2 \sum_j \left(\frac{p_i}{\rho_i^2} + \frac{p_j}{\rho_j^2} \right) \nabla W(\mathbf{x} - \mathbf{x}_j) \tag{2.12}$$

---

[*]This solution is still heuristic, and more physically accurate method has been discussed in Macklin et al. [80].

Similarly, the code can be written as:

```
1   void SphSystemSolver3::accumulatePressureForce(double timeStepInSeconds) {
2       auto particles = sphSystemData();
3       auto x = particles->positions();
4       auto d = particles->densities();
5       auto p = particles->pressures();
6       auto f = particles->forces();
7
8       computePressureForce(x, d, p, f);
9   }
10
11  void SphSystemSolver3::accumulatePressureForce(
12      const ConstArrayAccessor1<Vector3D>& positions,
13      const ConstArrayAccessor1<Vector3D>& densities,
14      const ConstArrayAccessor1<Vector3D>& pressures,
15      ArrayAccessor1<Vector3D> pressureForces) {
16      auto particles = sphSystemData();
17      size_t numberOfParticles = particles->numberOfParticles();
18
19      const double massSquared = square(particles->mass());
20      const SphSpikyKernel3 kernel(particles->kernelRadius());
21
22      parallelFor(
23          zeroSize,
24          numberOfParticles,
25          [&](size_t i) {
26              const auto& neighbors = particles->neighborLists()[i];
27              for (size_t j : neighbors) {
28                  double dist = positions[i].distanceTo(positions[j]);
29
30                  if (dist > 0.0) {
31                      Vector3D dir = (positions[j] - positions[i]) / dist;
32                      pressureForces[i] -= massSquared
33                          * (pressures[i] / (densities[i] * densities[i])
34                          + pressures[j] / (densities[j] * densities[j]))
35                          * kernel.gradient(dist, dir);
36                  }
37              }
38          });
39  }
```

Note that we have added an additional function accumulatePressureForce which accepts input positions and outputs pressure forces array. The new function is introduced so that the subclasses can use the function to compute pressure forces for custom positions and stores the result to an arbitrary array. One of the use cases will appear in Section 2.4.

2.3.2.3 Viscosity

If you are familiar with the Laplacian operator in Section 2.3.1.5, computing the viscosity is also straight forward as the pressure gradient. First of all, the equation for the viscosity force can be written as:

$$\mathbf{f}_v = m\mu\nabla^2\mathbf{u} \tag{2.13}$$

This is identical to Equation 1.82 in Section 1.7.3, but only the unit in force instead of acceleration (which means it is multiplied by mass m). Based on the Laplacian operator in Section 2.3.1.5, the equation above can be rewritten as:

$$\mathbf{f}_v(\mathbf{x}) = m\sum_j \left(\frac{\mathbf{u}_j - \mathbf{u}_i}{\rho_j}\right)\nabla^2 W(\mathbf{x} - \mathbf{x}_j) \tag{2.14}$$

Implementing the equation above gives the code shown below:

```
1   void SphSystemSolver3::accumulateViscosityForce() {
2       auto particles = sphSystemData();
3       size_t numberOfParticles = particles->numberOfParticles();
4       auto x = particles->positions();
5       auto v = particles->velocities();
6       auto d = particles->densities();
7       auto f = particles->forces();
8
9       const double massSquared = square(particles->mass());
10      const SphSpikyKernel3 kernel(particles->kernelRadius());
11
12      parallelFor(
13          zeroSize,
14          numberOfParticles,
15          [&](size_t i) {
16              const auto& neighbors = particles->neighborLists()[i];
17              for (size_t j : neighbors) {
18                  double dist = x[i].distanceTo(x[j]);
19
20                  f[i] += viscosityCoefficient() * massSquared
21                      * (v[j] - v[i]) / d[j]
22                      * kernel.secondDerivative(dist);
23              }
24          });
```

2.3.2.4 Gravity and Drag Forces

For the gravity and drag forces, we are going to reuse what we have implemented in the particle system solver in Section 2.2.2. See the class `ParticleSystemSolver3` from the example code and the function `accumulateExternalForces`.

2.3.3   Results and Limitations

So far we have written `SphSystemSolver3`, which implements the SPH-based fluid simulator. Note that we haven't implemented that much from what we already had. Based on the existing class `ParticleSystemSolver3`, which simply holds basic data structures and time integration, we extended the class to `SphSystemSolver3` by adding and overriding several functions to have a fully functional fluid dynamics engine. You can see the sample 2D simulation results in Figure 2.10.

Now, let's discuss the limitation of the SPH simulation. To keep the fluid density (nearly) constant, SPH introduced EOS that maps the density to the pressure field (Equations 2.9 and 2.10). The equations introduce a number of parameters, especially the exponent part of the EOS (γ) and the speed of sound in the medium (c_s). You may probably wonder why the speed of sound is a parameter, not a constant. Also, why having such parameters can be a problem? These are all related to the time-step and compressibility of the simulation, and poorly tuning those parameters ends up having either too small time-step or unnatural compression/instability that are all undesirable in practice.

To have better understanding of the problem, take a look at Figure 2.11. This figure illustrates how the pressure propagates inside the fluid volume when a particle drops into a pool of particles. For each time-step, the information about the impact propagates only within the kernel radius h. So if some information should propagate with speed c, the maximum time-step size would be h/c. In a real-world situation, this information propagates with the speed of sound so that the impact of a water drop is notified to the entire fluid volume almost instantly. Thus, the ideal time-step should be at most h/c_s, where c_s is the speed of sound. Based on this, the literatures such

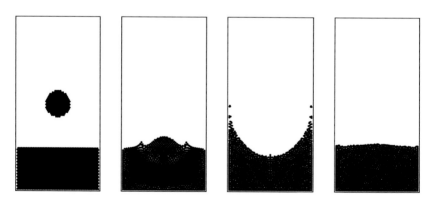

FIGURE 2.10
Results from the SPH solver in 2D.

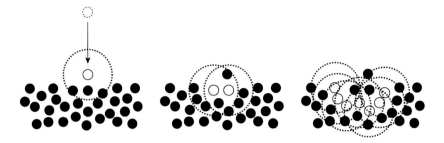

FIGURE 2.11
Propagation of the information in SPH. The white dots are informed particles about the collision and dotted circle line indicates the kernel radius. It takes multiple iterations to spread out the event completely.

as Becker and Teschner [15] and Goswami and Batty [45] suggest to limit the time-step by:

$$\Delta t_v = \frac{\lambda_v h}{c_s}$$

$$\Delta t_f = \lambda_f \sqrt{\frac{hm}{F_{max}}}$$

$$\Delta t \leq \min(\Delta t_v, \Delta t_f)$$

Here, coefficients λ_v and λ_f are scalars, which are tuned around 0.4 and 0.25, h is the kernel radius, m is the mass, and F_{max} is the maximum magnitude of the force vectors. This means the time-step size may vary every time-step.

To get an idea how small the time-step will be, let's assume that we have a kernel radius of 0.1 m, the mass is 0.001 kg, the speed of sound is 1482 m/sec^2, and only the gravity is acting on the system. From the equation above, Δt_v will be 0.00002699055331, and Δt_f will be 0.0007985957062. Thus, the maximum time-step will be 0.00002699055331, which means more than 618 substeps are required to advance a single 60 FPS frame. This is a really small time-step which will require lots of computational costs to generate even a short clip of animation.

To avoid extremely small time-steps, Becker and Teschner [15] used much smaller *pseudo* speed of sound by evaluating the maximum possible particle velocity in a simulation. But as pointed out by Solenthaler and Pajarola [109], Becker and Teschner method may introduce lots of parameter tuning since, in practice, it is hard to anticipate what would be the maximum velocity of the scene, especially for the software users.

Another way of allowing larger time-step is to tune the exponent part, κ, of the EOS. The suggested value in Becker and Teschner [15] for κ is 7 which is quite stiff. Stiffer κ means it will apply higher pressure for the same density offset, and this requires smaller time-step because otherwise, it may cause the simulation to diverge. The particles will explode because larger time-step can make particles too close to each other and stiff EOS will assign high pressure which leads to the divergence. Other studies such as Desbrun and Cani [34] or Müller et al. [89] used less-stiffer EOS by using 1 for κ. This approach, however, will introduce oscillations to the system because less-stiffer EOS allows a certain degree of compression.

To solve the problem more fundamentally, Solenthaler and Pajarola [109] suggested a predictor–corrector model which eliminates the dependency to the speed of sound and accelerate the information propagation while keeping the density constant without compression. Let's find out how to extend the original SPH method and build this model from the following section.

2.4 Incompressible SPH with Larger Time-Step

As discussed in the previous section, one of the major problems with the conventional SPH solver is the time-step limitation. In the original SPH, we first compute density from the current setting, calculate pressure using EOS, apply pressure gradient, and then run the time integration. This procedure means a certain amount of compression is needed to trigger the pressure force only inside the kernel radius which delays the computation. As a result, we need to use smaller time-step (meaning more iterations) which can be computationally expensive. Alternatively, we may use less-stiffer EOS. This solution, however, might introduce spring-like oscillations. Finely tuning the parameters such as the speed of sound (c_s) or the viscosity (to dampen out the overshoots that may be caused by stiff κ) can help avoiding such problems. However, it is not a fundamental solution and also impractical for the users. In this section, we will find out how we can tackle the problem by introducing a predictor–corrector concept to the SPH simulator.

2.4.1 Predict and Correct

In SPH, a local compression does not spread out fast enough to its neighbors. Hence, we should either use small time-step or allow compression. To solve this problem, Selenthaler and Pajarola proposed a new method in 2009 which is called Predictive-Corrective Incompressible SPH (PCISPH) [109]. As the name suggests, it is an error correction algorithm, which assumes that the difference between the measured and the desired density is the error.

The method first "predicts" the future density profile with candidate position and velocity, but still keeping the original state. After measuring the expected density, it calculates the "correction" force that will reduce any density error. Then, the algorithm rolls back the position and velocity to the original state and accumulates the correction force. After repeating this process multiple times, the method finds what is the optimal correction force to minimize the density error, and then use the accumulated force to proceed to the next time-step. Thus, the iterative nature of this method allows the system to propagate the density and pressure information further. Also, instead of taking multiple SPH steps which don't guarantee that the final state won't have any compressions, accumulating the correction force almost ensures that the resulting state will be in (or very close to) the incompressible state.

2.4.2   Implementation

Now we got a rough idea how PCISPH works. Let's see how we can implement it. As described above, the core algorithm is all about finding the right correction force. The correction force is, in fact, the pressure gradient force. So from the predictive-corrective iteration, our goal is to find the optimal pressure that drives the particles to the new positions which minimize the density error. To get start with, here's our skeleton code:

```
1   class PciSphSystemSolver3 : public SphSystemSolver3 {
2    public:
3       PciSphSystemSolver3();
4
5       virtual ~PciSphSystemSolver3();
6
7       ...
8
9    protected:
10      void accumulatePressureForce(double timeIntervalInSeconds) override;
11
12      ...
13
14   private:
15      double _maxDensityErrorRatio = 0.01;
16      unsigned int _maxNumberOfIterations = 5;
17
18      ...
19   };
20
21   void PciSphSystemSolver3::accumulatePressureForce(
22       double timeIntervalInSeconds) {
23       auto particles = sphSystemData();
24       const size_t numberOfParticles = particles->numberOfParticles();
25       const double targetDensity = particles->targetDensity();
26
27       // Initialize other variables
28       ...
29
```

```
30      for (unsigned int k = 0; k < _maxNumberOfIterations; ++k) {
31          // Predict velocity and position
32          ...
33
34          // Resolve collisions
35          ...
36
37          // Compute pressure from density error
38          ...
39
40          // Compute pressure gradient force
41          ...
42
43          // Compute max density error
44          double maxDensityError = /* compute error here */
45          double densityErrorRatio = maxDensityError / targetDensity;
46
47          if (std::fabs(densityErrorRatio) < _maxDensityErrorRatio) {
48              break;
49          }
50      }
51
52      // Accumulate pressure force
53      ...
54  }
```

Here, we are introducing a new class for the PCISPH simulation,
PciSphSystemSolver3. This class will add a couple of more functions to
SphSystemSolver3, but the function accumulatePressureForce is the core part
of the class. This is the function that is called from accumulateForces function in SphSystemSolver3, right after accumulateNonPressureForces call. Thus,
when accumulatePressureForce is called, all the nonpressure type forces are
accumulated in the force array.

At a first glance, you can notice that there is a loop that iterates until it
reaches to the max defined number of iterations. Also, the loop can terminate
if the density error is lower than the specified limit. Inside the loop, there are
several steps that reduce the density error by predicting and correcting it. The
first step within the loop is to predict the velocity and position by performing
the time integration with the current position, velocity, and accumulated force.
Then, the following step will resolve any collisions from the predicted state.
After the collision resolution, the pressure that will correct the density error
is computed based on the predicted position. Once the pressure is computed,
the gradient force is calculated to update the accumulated force state. This
force will be used for the next round of the iteration. The code repeats this
process until the error reaches the given threshold.

Now let's take a look at each step. First, the prediction step can be written as follows:

```
1   class PciSphSystemSolver3 : public SphSystemSolver3 {
2       ...
3
4   private:
5       ...
6
7       ParticleSystemData3::VectorData _tempPositions;
8       ParticleSystemData3::VectorData _tempVelocities;
9       ParticleSystemData3::VectorData _pressureForces;
10
11      ...
12  };
13
14  void PciSphSystemSolver3::accumulatePressureForce(
15      double timeIntervalInSeconds) {
16      auto particles = sphSystemData();
17      const size_t numberOfParticles = particles->numberOfParticles();
18      const double targetDensity = particles->targetDensity();
19      const double mass = particles->mass();
20
21      auto p = particles->pressures();
22      auto x = particles->positions();
23      auto v = particles->velocities();
24
25      ...
26
27      // Initialize buffers
28      parallelFor(
29          kZeroSize,
30          numberOfParticles,
31          [&] (size_t i) {
32              p[i] = 0.0;
33              _pressureForces[i] = Vector3D();
34          });
35
36      for (unsigned int k = 0; k < _maxNumberOfIterations; ++k) {
37          // Predict velocity and position
38          parallelFor(
39              kZeroSize,
40              numberOfParticles,
41              [&] (size_t i) {
42                  _tempVelocities[i]
43                      = v[i]
44                      + timeIntervalInSeconds / mass
45                      * (f[i] + _pressureForces[i]);
```

```
46                    _tempPositions[i]
47                        = x[i] + timeIntervalInSeconds * _tempVelocities[i];
48                });
49
50            ...
51        }
52
53        ...
54    }
```

The code is simply performing time integration from the current state to the temporary state, _tempPositions and _tempVelocities. Those are new arrays introduced in PciSphSystemSolver3 class. Note that the force accumulated before accumulatePressureForce call is stored in the variable f, and the pressure force is stored separately in _pressureForces, which is also a new array defined from the class PciSphSystemSolver3. At the first iteration, k = 0, _pressureForces and the pressure array p are zero vectors.

The next part is the collision resolution. This is even simpler since we can reuse the function from ParticleSystemSolver3 as shown below:

```
1    void PciSphSystemSolver3::accumulatePressureForce(
2        double timeIntervalInSeconds) {
3        ...
4
5        for (unsigned int k = 0; k < _maxNumberOfIterations; ++k) {
6            // Predict velocity and position
7            ...
8
9            // Resolve collisions
10           resolveCollision(
11               _tempPositions,
12               _tempVelocities,
13               _tempPositions,
14               _tempVelocities);
15
16           ...
17        }
18
19        ...
20   }
```

Now let's take a look at the density error measurement and pressure calculation which will correct the error.

```
1    void PciSphSystemSolver3::accumulatePressureForce(
2        double timeIntervalInSeconds) {
3        ...
```

```
4
5        const double delta = computeDelta(timeIntervalInSeconds);
6
7        // Predicted density ds
8        Array1<double> ds(numberOfParticles, 0.0);
9
10       SphStdKernel3 kernel(particles->kernelRadius());
11
12       // Initialize buffers
13       ...
14
15       for (unsigned int k = 0; k < _maxNumberOfIterations; ++k) {
16           // Predict velocity and position
17           ...
18
19           // Resolve collisions
20           ...
21
22           // Compute pressure from density error
23           parallelFor(
24               kZeroSize,
25               numberOfParticles,
26               [&] (size_t i) {
27                   double weightSum = 0.0;
28                   const auto& neighbors = particles->neighborLists()[i];
29
30                   for (size_t j : neighbors) {
31                       double dist
32                           = _tempPositions[j].distanceTo(_tempPositions[i]);
33                       weightSum += kernel(dist);
34                   }
35                   weightSum += kernel(0);
36
37                   double density = mass * weightSum;
38                   double densityError = (density - targetDensity);
39                   double pressure = delta * densityError;
40
41                   if (pressure < 0.0) {
42                       pressure *= negativePressureScale();
43                       densityError *= negativePressureScale();
44                   }
45
46                   p[i] += pressure;
47                   ds[i] = density;
48                   _densityErrors[i] = densityError;
49               });
50
51           ...
52       }
```

```
53
54       ...
55    }
```

This is not a short code, but let's focus from Line 27 to 48. The first step computes density error by measuring the density from the prediced position, _tempPositions. (If this is not straightforward, revisit Section 2.3.1.4.) The density error is then scaled with a scalar value delta to get pressure, such that:

$$\tilde{p}_i = \delta \rho^*_{err,i} \qquad (2.15)$$

where $\rho^*_{err,i}$ is the predicted density error and $\tilde{p}_i$ the correction pressure. As discussed in Section 2.3.2.2, this pressure is clamped with negativePressureScale(), which is likely to be zero, to avoid clustering near the surface due to the negative pressure.

Now the remaining unknown variable from the code above is delta, δ. This magical scalar variable, calculated by calling computeDelta, maps density error to pressure. I won't go into too many details on how to compute that variable here, but in short, the scalar maps the density to the optimal pressure that cancels out the density error. If interested, take a look at Appendix B.2 for the derivation and implementation.

After computing the pressure, the remaining job is to compute the gradient force and accumulate the final force to the original force array as shown below:

```
1    void PciSphSystemSolver3::accumulatePressureForce(
2        double timeIntervalInSeconds) {
3        ...
4
5
6        // Initialize buffers
7        ...
8
9        for (unsigned int k = 0; k < _maxNumberOfIterations; ++k) {
10           // Predict velocity and position
11           ...
12
13           // Resolve collisions
14           ...
15
16           // Compute pressure from density error
17           ...
18
19           // Compute pressure gradient force
20           _pressureForces.set(Vector3D());
21           SphSystemSolver3::accumulatePressureForce(
22               x, ds.constAccessor(), p, _pressureForces.accessor());
23
24           // Compute max density error
```

```
25          double maxDensityError = 0.0;
26          for (size_t i = 0; i < numberOfParticles; ++i) {
27              maxDensityError = absmax(maxDensityError, _densityErrors[i]);
28          }
29
30          double densityErrorRatio = maxDensityError / targetDensity;
31
32          if (std::fabs(densityErrorRatio) < _maxDensityErrorRatio) {
33              break;
34          }
35      }
36
37      ...
38  }
39
40  // Accumulate pressure force
41  parallelFor(
42      zeroSize,
43      numberOfParticles,
44      [&](size_t i) {
45          f[i] += _pressureForces[i];
46      });
```

Now, we have implemented the core implementation of the PCISPH solver.

2.4.3   Results

So far we have written `SphSystemSolver3` which implements an SPH-based fluid simulator. Note that we haven't implemented that much from what we already had. Based on `ParticleSystemSolver3`, which simply holds basic data structures and time integration, we extended the class to `SphSystemSolver3` by adding and overriding several functions to have a fully functional fluid dynamics engine. You can see the sample 2D simulation results in Figure 2.12. This example uses the same configuration we used for the similar SPH result (Figure 2.10). However, the PCISPH simulation used five times larger time-step to produce almost the same result.

Figure 2.13 shows more interesting result using a 3D PCISPH simulator. This simulation is one of the variations of the "dam-breaking" experiment which starts from one or more standing water columns as if they were inside imaginary dams. Assuming that the imaginary dams disappeared as soon as the simulation begins, the water columns collapse and generate splashes as they interact with the obstacles. The surface was extracted by taking the iso-surface from the SPH density field. If the fluid's density is ρ, $\rho/2$ is taken for the isosurface. It is then converted into the triangle mesh using the marching cubes algorithm (see Section 1.4.3) and rendered to the sequence of images using a path-tracing renderer. In this example, Mitsuba renderer was used [59].

FIGURE 2.12
Results from the PCISPH solver in 2D.

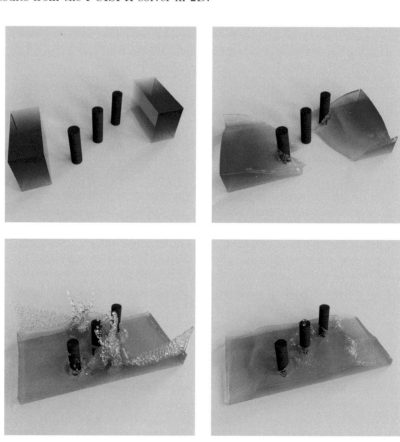

FIGURE 2.13
Image showing the results from the PCISPH solver in 3D. The simulation is generated using 839k particles.

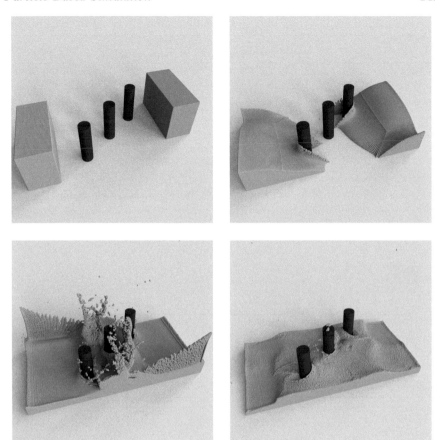

FIGURE 2.14
Visualization of particles from a PCISPH simulation. The same animation sequence in Figure 2.13 is rendered differently by displaying the particles as spheres.

Figure 2.14 shows the same simulation result but rendered differently by visualizing particles as spheres.

2.5 Collision Handling

This chapter introduces two types of collisions: particle-to-particle and particle-to-object. The former type is handled by computing SPH or PCISPH solvers, specifically by calculating the pressure and its gradient force. The latter collision problem focuses on the interaction between particles and solid objects in a scene, such as a floor, container, or even a moving character.

In this section, we will cover how to handle the particle-to-object collision problem.

The solvers we have implemented so far (`ParticleSystemSolver3`, `SphSystemSolver3`, and `PciSphSystemSolver3`) assumed that the collision can be resolved by calling the function `resolveCollision` in the class `ParticleSystemSolver3` which we treated as a blackbox solver. In this section, the actual implementation details will be discussed.

2.5.1 Defining Colliders

A solid object that fluid parcels can collide is called collider. To get started with the implementation, let's define the collider class that represents the solid object interacting with particles. Below is the starter code for the new class, `Collider3`.

```
1   class Collider3 {
2   public:
3       Collider3();
4
5       virtual ~Collider3();
6
7       void resolveCollision(
8           const Vector3D& currentPosition,
9           const Vector3D& currentVelocity,
10          double radius,
11          double restitutionCoefficient,
12          Vector3D* newPosition,
13          Vector3D* newVelocity);
14
15      ...
16  };
```

As shown above, `resolveCollision` is the key function that takes the current state (position and velocity) and particle properties (radius and restitution coefficient), and then returns a resolved state. But before we get into the implementation of the function, let's take a look at the overview of how the collider solves the collision event in Figure 2.15. There are many different approaches to resolve the particle-to-object collision, but we will take the simplest and most straightforward approach.[*]

The process starts by examining whether the new position of the particle is penetrating, or too close, to the surface. If not penetrating, we don't have to proceed further and can quit the function. If penetrating, as shown in Figure 2.15b, we push the particle outside of the surface.

---

[*]For more in-depth discussion about the collision handling, take a look at Baraff and Witkin [10], Bridson et al. [23] or Ericson [40].

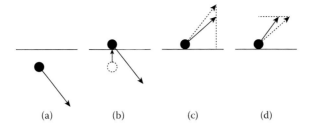

(a) (b) (c) (d)

FIGURE 2.15
Simple collision resolution. When a particle is penetrating the surface (a), it is pushed to the closest point (b). Then, the normal component of the velocity is scaled down based on the restitution coefficient (c). Then, the tangential velocity is also scaled according to the friction force (d).

Now let's take a look at the core function, `resolveCollision`, which takes the current state of the particle and returns a collision-free state. The first and second parameters of the function are the current position and velocity of a particle. The parameter `radius` defines the size of the particle. The parameter `restitutionCoefficient` determines the amount of the rebound. If this parameter is zero, it means there is no bouncing at all, meaning that the particle will stick to the surface. If the parameter is set to one, then it represents perfectly elastic collision; the particle will bounce back with the same magnitude of the velocity it collided. Finally, the parameters `newPosition` and `newVelocity` are the new states of the particle.

To implement the function, let's start with the skeleton code below:

```
1  void Collider3::resolveCollision(
2      double radius,
3      double restitutionCoefficient,
4      Vector3D* newPosition,
5      Vector3D* newVelocity) {
6      ColliderQueryResult3 colliderPoint;
7
8      ...
9
10     // Check if the new position is penetrating the surface
11     if (isPenetrating(colliderPoint, *newPosition, radius)) {
12         ...
13
14         // Check if the velocity is facing opposite direction of the
15         // surface normal
16         if (...) {
17             // Apply restitution coefficient to the surface normal
18             // component of the velocity
```

```
19                    ...
20
21                    // Apply friction to the tangential component of the velocity
22                    ...
23
24                    // Reassemble the components
25                    *newVelocity = /* normal vel */ + /* tangential vel */;
26                }
27
28                // Geometric fix
29                *newPosition = /* closest point on the surface */;
30            }
31    }
```

As shown in the above code, we first want to determine whether the particle is penetrating the surface. If so, we check whether the particle keeps penetrating the surface or is in the middle of escaping. This state can be evaluated by taking a dot product between the particle's velocity and the surface normal, $\mathbf{v} \cdot \mathbf{n}$. If the dot product is negative, meaning that the particle is going to continue the penetration, we reflect the normal component of the velocity and apply the restitution coefficient, such that:

$$v_n^{new} = -Rv_n \qquad (2.16)$$

Here, v_n is the surface normal component of the velocity and R is the restitution coefficient. This process is similar to applying the impulse to the particle. Note that the velocity change in the normal direction is $\Delta v_n = v_n^{new} - v_n = (-R-1)v_n$. This procedure corresponds to Figure 2.15c.

In physics, if an object is in contact with other surface and there is a normal force that pushes the object to the surface, friction force $F_f = \mu F_n$ can occur. The velocity change in the surface tangential direction due to this friction is $\Delta v_t = a_t \Delta t = F_f/m \Delta t = \mu F_n/m \Delta t$. Since we know the velocity change in the normal direction, Δv_n, which can be rewritten as $\Delta v_n = a_n \Delta t = F_n/m \Delta t$, we can say that Δv_t is $\mu \Delta v_n$. Of course, the friction only can slow down the speed but cannot make a particle to accelerate. Thus, the velocity change in the tangential direction, Δv_t, should be smaller than v_t. In conclusion, the tangential component of the velocity v_t can be calculated as follows:

$$\Delta v_t = \min(\mu \Delta v_n, v_t) \qquad (2.17)$$

and

$$v_t^{new} = \max(1 - \mu \frac{|\Delta v_n|}{|v_t|}, 0) \cdot v_t \qquad (2.18)$$

This step is illustrated in Figure 2.15d. For more details, see Bridson et al. [23].

So far we have computed the normal and tangential component of the new velocity state, v_n^{new} and v_t^{new}. Once we reassemble them, we can complete the collision resolution by assigning the closest point on the surface from the particle to `newPosition`. Below is the full implementation of the algorithm we have covered based on the skeleton code above. Note that additional member functions, `getClosestPoint` and `isPenetrating`, are added. Also, a simple struct, `ColliderQueryResult3`, is introduced to store a point on the collider surface that are queried from `getClosestPoint`. Finally, the code is assuming that the collider itself is also moving. (The velocity of a point on the collider surface can be accessed by `Collider3::velocityAt` function.) Due to this fact, the relative velocity between the particle and the collider is used for the velocity-related computation.

```cpp
void Collider3::resolveCollision(
    double radius,
    double restitutionCoefficient,
    Vector3D* newPosition,
    Vector3D* newVelocity) {
    ColliderQueryResult3 colliderPoint;

    getClosestPoint(_surface, *newPosition, &colliderPoint);

    // Check if the new position is penetrating the surface
    if (isPenetrating(colliderPoint, *newPosition, radius)) {
        // Target point is the closest non-penetrating position from the
        // current position.
        Vector3D targetNormal = colliderPoint.normal;
        Vector3D targetPoint = colliderPoint.point + radius *
            targetNormal;
        Vector3D colliderVelAtTargetPoint = colliderPoint.velocity;

        // Get new candidate relative velocity from the target point.
        Vector3D relativeVel = *newVelocity - colliderVelAtTargetPoint;
        double normalDotRelativeVel = targetNormal.dot(relativeVel);
        Vector3D relativeVelN = normalDotRelativeVel * targetNormal;
        Vector3D relativeVelT = relativeVel - relativeVelN;

        // Check if the velocity is facing opposite direction of the
        // surface normal
        if (normalDotRelativeVel < 0.0) {
            // Apply restitution coefficient to the surface normal
            // component of the velocity
            Vector3D deltaRelativeVelN
                = (-restitutionCoefficient - 1.0) * relativeVelN;
            relativeVelN *= -restitutionCoefficient;

            // Apply friction to the tangential component of the velocity
            if (relativeVelT.lengthSquared() > 0.0) {
                double frictionScale
                    = std::max(
```

```
37                              1.0
38                                 - _frictionCoeffient
39                                     * deltaRelativeVelN.length()
40                                     / relativeVelT.length(), 0.0);
41                      relativeVelT *= frictionScale;
42                  }
43
44              // Reassemble the components
45              *newVelocity
46                  = relativeVelN + relativeVelT + colliderVelAtTargetPoint;
47          }
48
49          // Geometric fix
50          *newPosition = targetPoint;
51      }
52  }
53
54  void Collider3::getClosestPoint(
55      const Surface3Ptr& surface,
56      const Vector3D& queryPoint,
57      ColliderQueryResult3* result) const {
58      result->distance = surface->closestDistance(queryPoint);
59      result->point = surface->closestPoint(queryPoint);
60      result->normal = surface->closestNormal(queryPoint);
61      result->velocity = velocityAt(queryPoint);
62  }
63
64  bool Collider3::isPenetrating(
65      const ColliderQueryResult3& colliderPoint,
66      const Vector3D& position,
67      double radius) {
68      // If the new candidate position of the particle is on the other side
69      // of the surface OR the new distance to the surface is less than the
70      // particle's radius, this particle is in colliding state.
71      return
72          (position - colliderPoint.point).dot(colliderPoint.normal) < 0.0
73          || colliderPoint.distance < radius;
74  }
```

The collider we just implemented above can be applied to both SPH and non-SPH simulators. Also, this approach works for most of the surfaces if it is possible to query the closest point on the surface from a given location. Thus, the code is flexible and can be applied to multiple applications without many restrictions. Sample results are shown in Figure 2.16.

It is also possible to model the collider with SPH particles. Such approaches do not have to handle the collision explicitly, but let the dynamics solver to embrace everything. See Ihmsen et al. [56] to find out more sophisticated collision handling techniques for SPH.

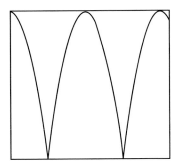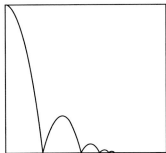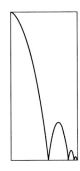

FIGURE 2.16
Particle trajectories from different collider settings. The left-most image shows a perfect bouncing of the free-falling particle (restitution coefficient = 1). The middle image shows the result for the restitution coefficient less than 1. The right-most image uses the same restitution coefficient, but with nonzero friction coefficient.

2.6 Discussion and Further Reading

The particle-based method is one of the approaches in the Lagrangian framework which track the fluid parcel along the flow by moving the particles. Among the methods using particles, SPH is one of the frequently used techniques which models fluid volume with particles with smoothed density distribution. The pressure is calculated from the density field using EOS which constrains the density to be almost constant. This solution, however, requires smaller time-step to conserve the volume. With larger time-step, the method will exhibit compressions and oscillations that often lead to instability. Such shortcoming of the conventional SPH is improved by introducing the predictive–corrective approach which iterates several times within a single time-step to find an optimal pressure that preserves the constant density.

The particle-based method is also called "meshfree method" since there is no fixed structure of the particle distribution. The connectivity of the neighbor list always changes and the numerical operations do not assume any predefined structures like grids. This feature gives the method flexibility; the particles can adapt to any kind of geometries or domains. For example, the particles can form different kinds of shapes ranging from sprays to breaking waves. Also, the particles can interact with various types of colliders with little restrictions.

As a Lagrangian method, the particle-based method also has strength in conserving physical quantities that are carried by the particles. Mass and velocity are good examples. Since those measures do not get redistributed to other discretization points, which we will observe from grid-based methods, at least there is a less numerical loss when translating the particles.

On the other hand, the random distribution of the particles can make the result noisy. The interpolation is based on the weighted average, and we can easily observe blobbyness from the outcome. Some studies discuss improving the reconstructed surface quality [122,127], but those are mostly focusing on the visualization issues. Methods with higher accuracy also exist, such as moving least squares, but the computational cost increases [7,35].

The two SPH-type methods we implemented in this chapter are frequently referred algorithms, but there are many other approaches worth mentioning. While PCISPH shows better performance on making the fluid incompressible, a similar but alternative approach called "position-based dynamics" (PBD) is also an active research area [80,90]. According to Macklin et al. [80], it shows better incompressibility compared to PCISPH. The PBD method is also part of the recent version of RealFlow software package [4]. Another approach for solving the incompressible flow is to use a linear system [32]. This method is very similar to what we will see from the grid-based framework in the next chapter, but with SPH formulation. Also, some studies extend the idea of SPH to the wider range of phenomena such as the interaction of multiple types of fluids (such as water–oil) [85,92] or with deformable objects [91].

From Chapter 3, we will learn a different aspect of simulating fluid dynamics using grids. The grid-based methods have their strength and weakness. Those characteristics make the framework not just an alternative solution to the particles, but set up their own domain of simulation. So let's find out what we can create with grids and why we need them.

3

Grid-Based Simulation

3.1 Pixelating the World

Grid is a multidimensional structure to store data in an organized way. It is a network of data points, and we often call it "mesh" as well. For example, a bitmap image is the simplest grid structure that stores color for each pixel. As shown in Figure 3.1, however, the grid doesn't necessarily have to be rectangular. It can have arbitrary shapes like arcs or triangles. Grids with aligned structure, such as the ones shown in Figure 3.1a or b, are called "regular" or "structured" grids. The other types of grids, such as the ones shown in Figure 3.1c, are called "irregular" or "unstructured" grid [26].

Simulating with a grid is quite different from the particle-based framework. The grid is like an array of fixed windows. For each point in time, data are recorded through the windows. You can also think of it as a digital camera that records a scene with a pixelated image. From a fixed point of view, physical quantities are captured at each grid point. As mentioned in Section 2.1, such a way of discretizing the world is called Eulerian framework, whereas the particle-based simulation is one of the Lagrangian methods. Note that there are methods in which grids move like particles. Those methods are either Lagrangian or Lagrangian–Eulerian hybrid, and they often use triangular or tetrahedral meshes [12,111]. In this chapter, we will only consider fixed grids.

In this chapter, we will learn how to develop a grid-based simulator. In the next section, the data structure design will be covered first. Similar to the particles, we will then extend the code to handle differential operators, which will be the foundation for the grid-based fluid solver. The first version of the solver will be a base simulator that encompasses the core dynamics: gravity, viscosity, and pressure. Also, a new step called advection will be introduced. Due to the nature of the Eulerian framework, the collision handling will be revisited as well. After building the base solver, we will conclude the chapter by implementing the smoke and liquid simulation engines.

3.2 Data Structures

In this book, we will define grid classes using an axis-aligned multidimensional array. It is not only like a bitmap image in two dimensions but also has

157

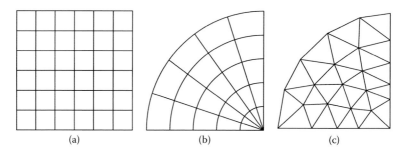

FIGURE 3.1
Image (a) shows rectangular regular grid, (b) curvilinear regular grid, and
(c) triangular irregular grid.

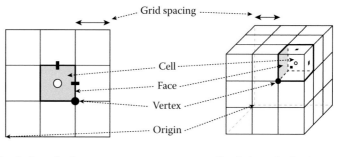

FIGURE 3.2
Illustration of 2D and 3D grids. Black dots indicate vertex, white dots indicate
cell-center, and black rectangles indicate face-center locations.

axis-aligned bounding box that defines the size and the location of the grid
in space, as shown in Figure 3.2. As can be seen in the figure, a "cell" is the
small rectangle piece of the grid, and grid spacing is the length of each edge.
Each cell has "vertex" on every corner, and "face" between two cells. We will
also use "resolution" to indicate a number of grid cells per direction. Also,
the origin of this grid is at the lower-left corner of the box. As can be seen,
this grid structure is perfectly aligned with the axes in Cartesian coordinate
system, and we will call it a Cartesian grid. As mentioned earlier, there are
other types of grids that are not aligned, such as the curvilinear grid shown in
Figure 3.1b. Such grids are used when we try to adapt the data structure to
the problem space [116], although this book will focus on Cartesian grids only.
    To implement a Cartesian grid, consider the following code:

```
1  class Grid3 {
2    public:
```

```
3      typedef std::function<Vector3D(size_t, size_t, size_t)>
           DataPositionFunc;

4

5      Grid3();

6

7      virtual ~Grid3();

8

9      const Size3& resolution() const;

10

11     const Vector3D& origin() const;

12

13     const Vector3D& gridSpacing() const;

14

15     const BoundingBox3D& boundingBox() const;

16

17     DataPositionFunc cellCenterPosition() const;

18

19     ...

20 };
```

As we can see, this simple class has a set of read-only properties including resolution, origin, gridSpacing, and boundingBox. These properties define not only the dimension of the 3D array but also the spatial mapping from a grid cell to a physical location. Note that function gridSpacing returns 3D vector, not a scalar. It means the grid can have different grid spacing per axis. Also note that the class only defines the very basic parameters but does not implement any data storage. In fact, there are different types of grids depending on how we would like to store the data. We can store values on vertices, cell centers, or faces. In the following sections, let us find out more details on the data storage design.

3.2.1 Types of Grids

In this book, we classify the grids according to the hierarchy shown in Figure 3.3. Let's not try to understand every type, but focus on the top level. From the hierarchy, we first categorize the grids into two major groups based on the type of data it stores: scalar and vector. As their names suggest, the scalar and vector grids are the numerical representation of the scalar and vector fields by discretizing the fields with a finite number of grid points. (See Section 1.3.5 to recall the concept of fields.) Thus, we can write a subclass of ScalarField3, VectorField3, and Grid3 to define the scalar and vector grids as follows:

```
1  class ScalarGrid3 : public ScalarField3, public Grid3 {
2  public:
3      ScalarGrid3();

4
```

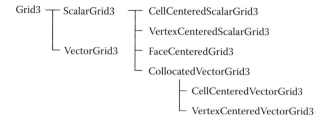

FIGURE 3.3
Hierarchy of the grids used in this book.

```
 5      virtual ~ScalarGrid3();
 6
 7      virtual Size3 dataSize() const = 0;
 8
 9      virtual Vector3D dataOrigin() const = 0;
10
11      void resize(
12          const Size3& resolution,
13          const Vector3D& gridSpacing = Vector3D(1, 1, 1),
14          const Vector3D& origin = Vector3D(),
15          double initialValue = 0.0);
16
17      const double& operator()(size_t i, size_t j, size_t k) const;
18
19      double& operator()(size_t i, size_t j, size_t k);
20
21      ...
22
23  private:
24      Array3<double> _data;
25      ...
26  };
```

and

```
 1  class VectorGrid3 : public VectorField3, public Grid3 {
 2  public:
 3      VectorGrid3();
 4
 5      virtual ~VectorGrid3();
 6
 7      void resize(
 8          const Size3& resolution,
 9          const Vector3D& gridSpacing = Vector3D(1, 1, 1),
10          const Vector3D& origin = Vector3D(),
11          const Vector3D& initialValue = Vector3D());
```

```
12
13   protected:
14      virtual void onResize(
15          const Size3& resolution,
16          const Vector3D& gridSpacing,
17          const Vector3D& origin,
18          const Vector3D& initialValue) = 0;
19   };
```

The full version of the class declaration can be found at include/jet/
scalar_grid3.h and include/jet/vector_grid3.h. Note that ScalarGrid3 contains purely virtual functions, dataSize and dataOrigin. Although we know
the type of the data we store, still the location of the data points is unknown;
it can be the vertex-, cell-, or face-center. So the class is postponing the actual
data positioning to their subclasses. These two functions may sound similar
to Grid3::resolution and Grid3::origin, but the key difference is that the
Grid3 functions return the grid cell resolution and the corner of the bounding box, whereas the ScalarGrid3 functions return the data point resolution
and the location of the data point at $(0, 0, 0)$. For example, $3 \times 4 \times 5$ resolution cell-centered grid with grid origin at $(0, 0, 0)$ and grid spacing $(1, 11)$ will
return $(0.5, 0.5, 0.5)$ from dataOrigin and $3 \times 4 \times 5$ for dataSize. In case of
vertex-centered grid, the functions will return $(0, 0, 0)$ and $4 \times 5 \times 6$, respectively. Note that VectorGrid3 doesn't have dataSize and dataOrigin funcions,
but has onResize callback. This is because the resolution and the location of
the data point may vary depending on the axis, especially in the case of face-
centered grid. Due to this reason, there is a new callback function onResize
which will be invoked from function resize and allocate subclass-specific data
points.

Going back to the hierarchy shown in Figure 3.3, let's take a look
at the subclasses of ScalarGrid3. The hierarchy tree shows two children:
CellCenteredScalarGrid3 and VertexCenteredScalarGrid3. These two subclasses define the data points either on the vertex of the grid or at the center
of a grid cell. Both implement the virtual functions, dataSize and dataOrigin,
from its parent class. For example, the cell-centered grid can be implemented
as follows:

```
1    class CellCenteredScalarGrid3 final : public ScalarGrid3 {
2    public:
3       CellCenteredScalarGrid3();
4
5       CellCenteredScalarGrid3(
6           const Size3& resolution,
7           const Vector3D& gridSpacing = Vector3D(1.0, 1.0, 1.0),
8           const Vector3D& origin = Vector3D(),
9           double initialValue = 0.0);
10
11      Size3 dataSize() const override;
```

```
12
13      Vector3D dataOrigin() const override;
14   };
15
16   Size3 CellCenteredScalarGrid3::dataSize() const {
17       return resolution();
18   }
19
20   Vector3D CellCenteredScalarGrid3::dataOrigin() const {
21       return origin() + 0.5 * gridSpacing();
22   }
```

Note that `dataSize` returns exactly the same value as `Grid3::resolution` because the number of cells per dimension is the number of cell centers per dimension. Also, `dataOrigin` returns a point with an offset of half of the grid spacing from the origin of the grid since that is cell center. Figure 3.4 illustrates the data layout of a cell-centered grid more clearly.

Similarly, we can also implement a vertex-centered grid as follows:

```
1    class VertexCenteredScalarGrid3 final : public ScalarGrid3 {
2    public:
3        VertexCenteredScalarGrid3();
4
5        VertexCenteredScalarGrid3(
6            const Size3& resolution,
7            const Vector3D& gridSpacing = Vector3D(1.0, 1.0, 1.0),
8            const Vector3D& origin = Vector3D(),
9            double initialValue = 0.0);
10
11       Size3 dataSize() const override;
12
```

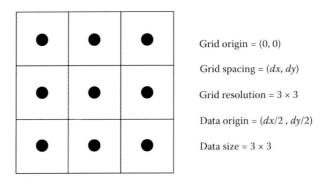

Grid origin = $(0, 0)$

Grid spacing = (dx, dy)

Grid resolution = 3×3

Data origin = $(dx/2, dy/2)$

Data size = 3×3

FIGURE 3.4
Data layout of a cell-centered grid in 2D is shown. The black dots represent the data positions.

```
13    virtual Vector3D dataOrigin() const override;
14  };
15
16  Size3 VertexCenteredScalarGrid3::dataSize() const {
17      return resolution() + Size3(1, 1, 1);
18  }
19
20  Vector3D VertexCenteredScalarGrid3::dataOrigin() const {
21      return origin();
22  }
```

The data layout of a vertex-centered grid is shown in Figure 3.5.

Now let's move on to the vector grids from the chart (Figure 3.3). In vector grids, data points for x, y, and z components of the vector field can be defined at the same location or at different locations. When defined at the same location, we call such grids as "collocated" grids. If the x, y, and z components do not collocate, it is called "staggered" grid. In this book, you will see two collocated grids: cell-centered and vertex-centered vector grids. For the staggered grid, we will use face-centered grids only. The collocated grid is quite similar to `ScalarGrid3`, which can be written as:

```
1   class CollocatedVectorGrid3 : public VectorGrid3 {
2    public:
3      CollocatedVectorGrid3();
4
5      virtual ~CollocatedVectorGrid3();
6
7      virtual Size3 dataSize() const = 0;
8
9      virtual Vector3D dataOrigin() const = 0;
10
```

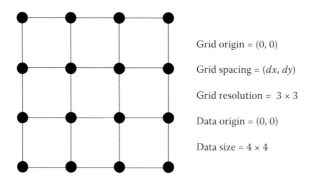

Grid origin = $(0, 0)$

Grid spacing = (dx, dy)

Grid resolution = 3×3

Data origin = $(0, 0)$

Data size = 4×4

FIGURE 3.5
Data layout of a vertex-centered grid in 2D is shown. The black dots represent the data positions.

```
11      const Vector3D& operator()(size_t i, size_t j, size_t k) const;
12
13      Vector3D& operator()(size_t i, size_t j, size_t k);
14      ...
15
16   private:
17      Array3<Vector3D> _data;
18
19      ...
20   };
```

As an underlying data storage, the class has 3D array of `Vector3D`. Note that we have two virtual functions that we have already seen from `ScalarGrid3`. These functions are overriden by the subclasses as follows:

```
1   class CellCenteredVectorGrid3 final : public CollocatedVectorGrid3 {
2    public:
3       CellCenteredVectorGrid3();
4
5       ...
6
7       Size3 dataSize() const override;
8
9       Vector3D dataOrigin() const override;
10
11      ...
12   };
13
14   Size3 CellCenteredVectorGrid3::dataSize() const {
15      return resolution();
16   }
17
18   Vector3D CellCenteredVectorGrid3::dataOrigin() const {
19      return origin() + 0.5 * gridSpacing();
20   }
```

and

```
1   class VertexCenteredVectorGrid3 final : public CollocatedVectorGrid3 {
2    public:
3       VertexCenteredVectorGrid3();
4
5       ...
6
7       Size3 dataSize() const override;
8
9       Vector3D dataOrigin() const override;
10
11      ...
```

```
12   };
13
14   Size3 VertexCenteredVectorGrid3::dataSize() const {
15       return resolution() + Size3(1, 1, 1);
16   }
17
18   Vector3D VertexCenteredVectorGrid3::dataOrigin() const {
19       return origin();
20   }
```

The data layout of these two grids is identical to their scalar version (see Figures 3.4 and 3.5).

Finally, we will see how the face-centered grid can be implemented. In this book, the face-centered grid is treated as a vector field since the grid cell faces can represent u, v, and w components of the vector field. Thus, the code can be written by inheriting the vector grid class as follows:

```
1    class FaceCenteredGrid3 final : public VectorGrid3 {
2     public:
3        FaceCenteredGrid3();
4
5        virtual ~FaceCenteredGrid3();
6
7        double& u(size_t i, size_t j, size_t k);
8
9        const double& u(size_t i, size_t j, size_t k) const;
10
11       double& v(size_t i, size_t j, size_t k);
12
13       const double& v(size_t i, size_t j, size_t k) const;
14
15       double& w(size_t i, size_t j, size_t k);
16
17       const double& w(size_t i, size_t j, size_t k) const;
18
19       ...
20
21     protected:
22        void onResize(
23            const Size3& resolution,
24            const Vector3D& gridSpacing,
25            const Vector3D& origin,
26            const Vector3D& initialValue) override;
27
28     private:
29        Array3<double> _dataU;
30        Array3<double> _dataV;
31        Array3<double> _dataW;
```

```
32      Vector3D _dataOriginU;
33      Vector3D _dataOriginV;
34      Vector3D _dataOriginW;
35
36      ...
37  };
38
39  void FaceCenteredGrid3::onResize(
40      const Size3& resolution,
41      const Vector3D& gridSpacing,
42      const Vector3D& origin,
43      const Vector3D& initialValue) {
44      _dataU.resize(resolution + Size3(1, 0, 0), initialValue.x);
45      _dataV.resize(resolution + Size3(0, 1, 0), initialValue.y);
46      _dataW.resize(resolution + Size3(0, 0, 1), initialValue.z);
47      _dataOriginU
48          = origin + 0.5 * Vector3D(0.0, gridSpacing.y, gridSpacing.z);
49      _dataOriginV
50          = origin + 0.5 * Vector3D(gridSpacing.x, 0.0, gridSpacing.z);
51      _dataOriginW
52          = origin + 0.5 * Vector3D(gridSpacing.x, gridSpacing.y, 0.0);
53
54      ...
55  }
```

You can see from the above code that we have separate data store for each vector component. Also, the size of each data array has one more extra grid along the direction it faces. Finally, the code is giving half-grid size offsets to each data origin from function onResize, except for the facing direction. This layout is illustrated in Figure 3.6.

The face-centered grid is often called the marker-and-cell (MAC) grid. MAC is the name of a computational fluid dynamics technique that solves fluid flow by marking each grid cell with different tags, such as fluid and air [48,83]. The same thought will be inherent in the methods we will discuss in this chapter, and we will use the face-centered grid to store velocity field for that reason. To learn more about the MAC method, read the review of McKee et al. [83].

3.2.2   Grid System Data

Similar to ParticleSystemData3 which supports arbitrary attribute channels, the equivalent data structure can be defined for the grid-based framework as well. Consider the following code:

```
1  class GridSystemData3 {
2  public:
3      GridSystemData3();
```

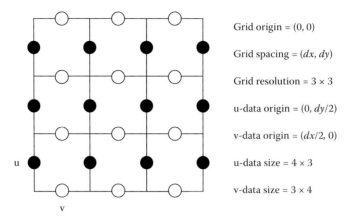

FIGURE 3.6
Data layout of a face-centered grid in 2D is shown. The black dots represent the u-face data positions and the white dots represent the v-faces.

```
 4
 5        virtual ~GridSystemData3();
 6
 7        void resize(
 8            const Size3& resolution,
 9            const Vector3D& gridSpacing,
10            const Vector3D& origin);
11
12        Size3 resolution() const;
13
14        Vector3D gridSpacing() const;
15
16        Vector3D origin() const;
17
18        BoundingBox3D boundingBox() const;
19
20        size_t addScalarData(
21            const ScalarGridBuilder3Ptr& builder,
22            double initialVal = 0.0);
23
24        size_t addVectorData(
25            const VectorGridBuilder3Ptr& builder,
26            const Vector3D& initialVal = Vector3D());
27
28        const FaceCenteredGrid3Ptr& velocity() const;
29
30        const ScalarGrid3Ptr& scalarDataAt(size_t idx) const;
31
32        const VectorGrid3Ptr& vectorDataAt(size_t idx) const;
33
```

```
34      size_t numberOfScalarData() const;

35

36      size_t numberOfVectorData() const;

37

38    private:
39      FaceCenteredGrid3Ptr _velocity;
40      std::vector<ScalarGrid3Ptr> _scalarDataList;
41      std::vector<VectorGrid3Ptr> _vectorDataList;
42  };
```

It looks similar, isn't it? The code has very similar interface to `ParticleSystemData3`. However, we can't find the position and force attributes in this class. The position attribute is not there because the grid has fixed-point locations and it can be computed on the fly. Also, the force is omitted because of the way the grid-based solvers compute the dynamics. It will become clearer when we move on to the details in Section 3.4, but in brief, the grid-based engine can apply force directly to the velocity field, just like a filtering. Thus, we can keep the velocity field only as a default attribute channel, and let the actual solvers determine whether they want to add force channel or not.

Another difference, other than the fact that we don't have the position and force attributes here, is the grid builders from the input parameters of `addScalarData` and `addVectorData`. The role of two functions is to create and append application-specific grid channel to the system, such as colors, densities, and vorticities, and the builders are used to create the grid instances inside the functions. We introduce such builder pattern because we can have different grid point layouts, such as cell-centered versus face-centered, unlike particles. The builder classes are derived from `ScalarGridBuilder3` and `VectorGridBuilder3` as follows:

```
1   class ScalarGridBuilder3 {
2   public:
3       ScalarGridBuilder3();

4

5       virtual ~ScalarGridBuilder3();

6

7       virtual ScalarGrid3Ptr build(
8           const Size3& resolution,
9           const Vector3D& gridSpacing,
10          const Vector3D& gridOrigin,
11          double initialVal) const = 0;
12  };
```

and

```
1   class VectorGridBuilder3 {
2   public:
3       VectorGridBuilder3();
```

```
 4
 5      virtual ~VectorGridBuilder3();
 6
 7      virtual VectorGrid3Ptr build(
 8          const Size3& resolution,
 9          const Vector3D& gridSpacing,
10          const Vector3D& gridOrigin,
11          const Vector3D& initialVal) const = 0;
12   };
```

An example of the actual builder implementation is shown in the following:

```
 1   class CellCenteredScalarGridBuilder3 final : public ScalarGridBuilder3 {
 2    public:
 3      CellCenteredScalarGridBuilder3();
 4
 5      ScalarGrid3Ptr build(
 6          const Size3& resolution,
 7          const Vector3D& gridSpacing,
 8          const Vector3D& gridOrigin,
 9          double initialVal) const override;
10   };
11
12   ScalarGrid3Ptr CellCenteredScalarGridBuilder3::build(
13          const Size3& resolution,
14          const Vector3D& gridSpacing,
15          const Vector3D& gridOrigin,
16          double initialVal) const {
17      return std::make_shared<CellCenteredScalarGrid3>(
18          resolution,
19          gridSpacing,
20          gridOrigin,
21          initialVal);
22   }
```

We now have a data collection class which will be our data model for the grid-based fluid simulator. In the following section, let's find out how we can define differential operators on grids.

3.3 Differential Operators

So far, we have seen how to store data into the grid data structures. As mentioned earlier, the grids are a numerical representation of scalar or vector fields. Thus, the vector differential operators, such as gradient, divergent, Laplacian, and curl differential operators, can be defined from the grids as well.

Those operators will then become the building blocks for computing fluid dynamics, similar to the SPH solver in Section 2.3.

3.3.1 Finite Difference

If you recall the differential operators from Section 1.3.5, the key ingredient that forms the operators is the partial derivative. So how can we calculate the partial derivatives, $\partial/\partial x$, on grids? In Section 1.3.5.1, we defined the partial derivative as the slope of a field along the given axis. Since we have grid points that are aligned to the axes, we can simply measure the slope by taking the difference between two grid points as follows:

$$\frac{\partial f}{\partial x} \approx \frac{f^{i+1,j,k} - f^{i,j,k}}{\Delta x} \tag{3.1}$$

where i, j, and k are the indices of a grid point, and $f^{i,j,k}$ is the value at grid point (i, j, k). Also, Δx is the grid spacing in the x-direction. Thus, the above equation measures the slope in the x-direction between two data points, $(i+1, j, k)$ and (i, j, k). The same process can be applied to the y- and z-axes as well. Similarly, the slope between $(i-1, j, k)$ and (i, j, k) can be written as:

$$\frac{\partial f}{\partial x} \approx \frac{f^{i,j,k} - f^{i-1,j,k}}{\Delta x}. \tag{3.2}$$

If we average these two slopes, we will get the approximated slope at the center point, (i, j, k), which is:

$$\frac{\partial f}{\partial x} \approx \frac{f^{i+1,j,k} - f^{i-1,j,k}}{2\Delta x} \tag{3.3}$$

The first equation (3.1) that measures the slope in the $+x$-direction is called forward difference. The second equation (3.2) that evaluates the derivative in the opposite direction is called backward difference. The last equation (3.3) that averages these two slopes is called, without surprise, central difference. Figure 3.7 illustrates these three methods. Such a technique, approximating a quantity by measuring the difference between grid points, is called the finite difference method (FDM) [30]. Most of the grid-based differential operator implementations in this book will use this FDM approach.

Note that these are all approximations for measuring the derivative, which means that there can be errors. Among these three methods, the central difference method gives the best answer in general. But depending on the application, the forward or the backward method can be a better fit. For instance, in the case of a wave propagation problem where the information behind the wave front is more valid, backward differencing can be preferred to the other two types. Also, there are even more accurate methods which involve more grid points. Note that we use only two grid points to measure the derivative here. But one can use three or more points to construct a spline

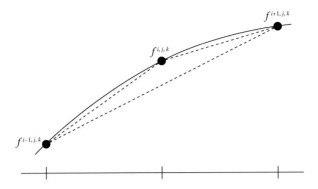

FIGURE 3.7
Forward, backward, and central differences are shown as dotted lines.

(such as the Catmull–Rom spline from Section 1.3.6.3), which could give better results [30]. Regarding accuracy, if we use smaller grid size, the accuracy obviously will go up because of denser information. However, some numerical methods converge to zero error faster than other methods. For example, the approximation error of the forward or backward difference is proportional to the grid size, hence $O(\Delta x)$. On the other hand, the central difference's error is a quadratic function, $O(\Delta x^2)$. Therefore, if we reduce the grid spacing by half, the error from the forward or backward difference becomes half of the original error, while the central difference can reduce it by a quarter.

We now understand how to approximate *first*-order partial derivatives. How about the second-order operators such as Laplacian? Extending the idea to the higher order is actually quite straightforward; we can simply apply the same derivative approximation to the first-order results. From the point (i, j, k) where we want to calculate the derivative, we can say

$$g^{i+\frac{1}{2},j,k} = \frac{f^{i+1,j,k} - f^{i,j,k}}{\Delta x}$$
$$g^{i-\frac{1}{2},j,k} = \frac{f^{i,j,k} - f^{i-1,j,k}}{\Delta x} \qquad (3.4)$$

where $g \approx \partial f / \partial x$. Thus, these two equations are forward and backward differences. Then, we can apply another central differencing to g to get the second-order derivative $h \approx \partial g / \partial x \approx \partial^2 f / \partial x^2$. The final equation can be written as:

$$\frac{\partial^2 f}{\partial x^2} \approx \frac{g^{i+\frac{1}{2},j,k} - g^{i-\frac{1}{2},j,k}}{\Delta x}$$
$$= \frac{f^{i+1,j,k} - 2f^{i,j,k} + f^{i-1,j,k}}{\Delta x^2} \qquad (3.5)$$

We now have a basic understanding on evaluating partial derivative using grid points. Let's find out how to define differential operators on grids.

3.3.2   Gradient

Among the four operators, let's start with the gradient first. As we covered in Section 1.3.5.2, the gradient operator measures the rate and the direction of change in a scalar field. This property can be expressed mathematically as shown in Equation 1.43:

$$\nabla f(\mathbf{x}) = \left(\frac{\partial f}{\partial x}(\mathbf{x}), \frac{\partial f}{\partial y}(\mathbf{x}), \frac{\partial f}{\partial z}(\mathbf{x}) \right) \qquad (3.6)$$

If we apply the central difference (Equation 3.3), this equation becomes:

$$\nabla f(\mathbf{x}) = \left(\frac{f^{i+1,j,k} - f^{i-1,j,k}}{2\Delta x}, \frac{f^{i,j+1,k} - f^{i,j-1,k}}{2\Delta y}, \frac{f^{i,j,k+1} - f^{i,j,k-1}}{2\Delta z} \right) \qquad (3.7)$$

The central difference equation given above can be written in a code form as follows:

```
1   Vector3D ScalarGrid3::gradientAtDataPoint(
2       size_t i, size_t j, size_t k) const {
3       double left = _data(i - 1, j, k);
4       double right = _data((i + 1, j, k);
5       double down = _data(i, j - 1, k);
6       double up = _data(i, j + 1, k);
7       double back = _data(i, j, k - 1);
8       double front = _data(i, j, k + 1);
9
10      return 0.5 * Vector3D(right - left, up - down, front - back)
11          / gridSpacing();
12  }
```

One problem with the above code is that the function can try accessing out-of-bound grid points if (i, j, k) is at the boundary. In such cases, we cannot perform central difference because there are no data outside the grid. One of the solutions to this problem is to define "imaginary" value outside the boundary by extrapolating the inner values. For instance, if $i = 0$ so that $i - 1$ is not available, we can simply say that value at $i - 1$ is equal to i. Using such approximation, the revised code that handles the boundary case is shown below:

```
1   Vector3D ScalarGrid3::gradientAtDataPoint(
2       size_t i, size_t j, size_t k) const {
3       const Size3 ds = _data.size();
4
5       double left = _data((i > 0) ? i - 1 : i, j, k);
```

```
6      double right = _data((i + 1 < ds.x) ? i + 1 : i, j, k);
7      double down = _data(i, (j > 0) ? j - 1 : j, k);
8      double up = _data(i, (j + 1 < ds.y) ? j + 1 : j, k);
9      double back = _data(i, j, (k > 0) ? k - 1 : k);
10     double front = _data(i, j, (k + 1 < ds.z) ? k + 1 : k);
11
12     return 0.5 * Vector3D(right - left, up - down, front - back)
13         / gridSpacing();
14  }
```

This function can evaluate the gradient at a given grid point index (i, j, k). If we want to measure the gradient at random location (x, y, z), the simplest approach is to interpolate the gradient near the query location. Take a look at the code below:

```
1   Vector3D ScalarGrid3::gradient(const Vector3D& x) const {
2       std::array<Point3UI, 8> indices;
3       std::array<double, 8> weights;
4       _linearSampler.getCoordinatesAndWeights(x, &indices, &weights);
5
6       Vector3D result;
7
8       for (int i = 0; i < 8; ++i) {
9           result += weights[i] * gradientAtDataPoint(
10              indices[i].x, indices[i].y, indices[i].z);
11      }
12
13      return result;
14  }
```

Member variable `_linearSampler` is an instance of a helper class `LinearArraySampler3<double, double>` which contains trilinear interpolation-related operations.[*] The function, `getCoordinatesAndWeights`, returns grid point indices (i, j, k) and trilinear interpolation weights. Then the function uses the indices and weights to interpolate gradient values from the eight surrounding grid points. Note that the function `ScalarGrid3::gradient` is overriding the virtual function from `ScalarField3` class.

3.3.3 Divergence

The second operator is the divergence. The divergence operator measures the sink or source of a vector field at a given point. If we repeat the equation from Section 1.3.5, it can be written as:

$$\nabla \cdot \mathbf{F}(\mathbf{x}) = \frac{\partial F_x}{\partial x} + \frac{\partial F_y}{\partial y} + \frac{\partial F_z}{\partial z} \tag{3.8}$$

---

[*]See Section 1.3.6 for the interpolations.

Applying the central difference, we get:

$$\nabla \cdot \mathbf{F}(\mathbf{x}) \approx \frac{F_x^{i+1,j,k} - F_x^{i-1,j,k}}{2\Delta x}$$
$$+ \frac{F_y^{i,j+1,k} - F_y^{i,j-1,k}}{2\Delta y}$$
$$+ \frac{F_z^{i,j,k+1} - F_z^{i,j,k-1}}{2\Delta z} \tag{3.9}$$

Similar to the gradient, we can write the code as follows:

```
Vector3D CollocatedVectorGrid3::divergenceAtDataPoint(
    size_t i, size_t j, size_t k) const {
    const Vector3D& gs = gridSpacing();

    double left = _data(i - 1, j, k);
    double right = _data((i + 1, j, k);
    double down = _data(i, j - 1, k);
    double up = _data(i, j + 1, k);
    double back = _data(i, j, k - 1);
    double front = _data(i, j, k + 1);

    return (right - left) / (2.0 * gs.x)
        + (up - down) / (2.0 * gs.y)
        + (front - back) / (2.0 * gs.z);
}
```

Again, we encounter a problem of accessing out-of-bound values. Taking the same extrapolation approach as the gradient implementation, the code can be rewritten as follows:

```
Vector3D CollocatedVectorGrid3::divergenceAtDataPoint(
    size_t i, size_t j, size_t k) const {
    const Vector3D center = _data(i, j, k);
    const Size3 ds = _data.size();
    const Vector3D& gs = gridSpacing();

    double left = _data((i > 0) ? i - 1 : i, j, k).x;
    double right = _data((i + 1 < ds.x) ? i + 1 : i, j, k).x;
    double down = _data(i, (j > 0) ? j - 1 : j, k).y;
    double up = _data(i, (j + 1 < ds.y) ? j + 1 : j, k).y;
    double back = _data(i, j, (k > 0) ? k - 1 : k).z;
    double front = _data(i, j, (k + 1 < ds.z) ? k + 1 : k).z;

    return 0.5 * (right - left) / gs.x
        + 0.5 * (up - down) / gs.y
        + 0.5 * (front - back) / gs.z;
}
```

Note that we have implemented this operation in `CollocatedVectorGrid3` instead of `VectorGrid3` which is the parent class. This is simply because we don't know where the vector components are located from the `VectorGrid3` level (see Section 3.2.1). From `CollocatedVectorGrid3`, we know that at least the x, y, and z components are collocated. Hence, we can write the divergence code as shown above. But what about `FaceCenteredGrid3`? How can we compute divergence on such a staggered grid?

For `FaceCenteredGrid3`, we move our center point to the cell center, not where the data points lie. Based on the fact that the central difference only requires the data points from the neighbors, not the center point itself, we can modify Equation 3.9 to

$$\nabla \cdot \mathbf{F}(\mathbf{x}) \approx \frac{F_x^{i+\frac{1}{2},j,k} - F_x^{i-\frac{1}{2},j,k}}{\Delta x}$$
$$+ \frac{F_y^{i,j+\frac{1}{2},k} - F_y^{i,j-\frac{1}{2},k}}{\Delta y}$$
$$+ \frac{F_z^{i,j,k+\frac{1}{2}} - F_z^{i,j,k-\frac{1}{2}}}{\Delta z}. \tag{3.10}$$

Note that the equation takes half of the grid spacing for the differencing. Figure 3.8 compares these two equations, one for the cell-centered grid and the other for the face-centered grid.

The face-centered version of the divergence can be implemented as follows:

```
double FaceCenteredGrid3::divergenceAtCellCenter(
    size_t i, size_t j, size_t k) const {
    const Vector3D& gs = gridSpacing();

    double leftU = _dataU(i, j, k);
```

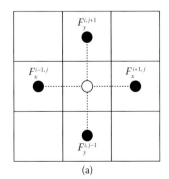 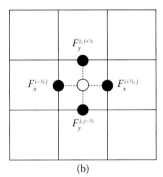

(a) (b)

FIGURE 3.8
Computing divergence using (a) cell-centered grid and (b) face-centered grid in 2D.

```
6        double rightU = _dataU(i + 1, j, k);
7        double bottomV = _dataV(i, j, k);
8        double topV = _dataV(i, j + 1, k);
9        double backW = _dataW(i, j, k);
10       double frontW = _dataW(i, j, k + 1);
11
12       return (rightU - leftU) / gs.x
13            + (topV - bottomV) / gs.y
14            + (frontW - backW) / gs.z;
15   }
```

For given cell index (i, j, k), the values at $(i + \frac{1}{2})$ and $(i - \frac{1}{2})$ faces can be read by accessing `_dataU(i, j, k)` and `_dataU(i + 1, j, k)` due to the layout of the grid points (see Figure 3.6). The same rule also applies to other faces. Note that the divergence code became even simpler than the one from the collocated grid. We don't even have a boundary-case handling. Moreover, this has an effect of having smaller grid size, meaning that the accuracy can be increased. Thus, if there is an application with many divergence operators involved, a face-centered grid is a good option to store vector field data. Evaluation of the divergence from arbitrary locations can be done by trilinear interpolation of the divergence values from surrounding grid points, similar to `ScalarGrid3::gradient`.

3.3.4 Curl

The third operator is the curl, which measures the rotational component of a vector field. The equation of the curl operator is

$$\nabla \times \mathbf{F}(\mathbf{x}) = \left(\frac{\partial}{\partial x}, \frac{\partial}{\partial y}, \frac{\partial}{\partial z} \right) \times \mathbf{F}(\mathbf{x}). \tag{3.11}$$

Again, by applying the central difference, we get

$$\nabla \times \mathbf{F}(\mathbf{x}) \approx \left(\frac{F_z^{i,j+1,k} - F_z^{i,j-1,k}}{\Delta y} - \frac{F_y^{i,j,k+1} - F_y^{i,j,k-1}}{\Delta z} \right) \mathbf{i}$$

$$+ \left(\frac{F_x^{i,j,k+1} - F_x^{i,j,k-1}}{\Delta z} - \frac{F_z^{i+1,j,k} - F_z^{i-1,j,k}}{\Delta x} \right) \mathbf{j}$$

$$+ \left(\frac{F_y^{i+1,j,k} - F_y^{i-1,j,k}}{\Delta x} - \frac{F_x^{i,j+1,k} - F_x^{i,j-1,k}}{\Delta y} \right) \mathbf{k}. \tag{3.12}$$

It seems a bit complicated, but it is nothing but a collection of six central differencing. For the collocated grid, we can write the code as follows:

```
1    Vector3D CollocatedVectorGrid3::curlAtDataPoint(
2        size_t i, size_t j, size_t k) const {
3        const Size3 ds = _data.size();
```

```
4       const Vector3D& gs = gridSpacing();
5
6       Vector3D left = _data((i > 0) ? i - 1 : i, j, k);
7       Vector3D right = _data((i + 1 < ds.x) ? i + 1 : i, j, k);
8       Vector3D down = _data(i, (j > 0) ? j - 1 : j, k);
9       Vector3D up = _data(i, (j + 1 < ds.y) ? j + 1 : j, k);
10      Vector3D back = _data(i, j, (k > 0) ? k - 1 : k);
11      Vector3D front = _data(i, j, (k + 1 < ds.z) ? k + 1 : k);
12
13      double Fx_ym = down.x;
14      double Fx_yp = up.x;
15      double Fx_zm = back.x;
16      double Fx_zp = front.x;
17
18      double Fy_xm = left.y;
19      double Fy_xp = right.y;
20      double Fy_zm = back.y;
21      double Fy_zp = front.y;
22
23      double Fz_xm = left.z;
24      double Fz_xp = right.z;
25      double Fz_ym = down.z;
26      double Fz_yp = up.z;
27
28      return Vector3D(
29          0.5 * (Fz_yp - Fz_ym) / gs.y - 0.5 * (Fy_zp - Fy_zm) / gs.z,
30          0.5 * (Fx_zp - Fx_zm) / gs.z - 0.5 * (Fz_xp - Fz_xm) / gs.x,
31          0.5 * (Fy_xp - Fy_xm) / gs.x - 0.5 * (Fx_yp - Fx_ym) / gs.y);
32  }
```

It looks quite verbose, but it is very similar to the divergence operator code, only longer. Variable Fx_ym corresponds to $F_x^{i,j-1,k}$, Fx_yp is $F_x^{i,j+1,k}$, and so on.

Calculating curl from a face-centered grid can be difficult, because of the staggered grid structure. But if we can first define neighbor values, such as $F_x^{i,j-1,k}$, the calculation should be exactly the same as the collocated grids. First, consider the function below.

```
1   Vector3D FaceCenteredGrid3::valueAtCellCenter(
2       size_t i, size_t j, size_t k) const {
3       return 0.5 * Vector3D(
4           _dataU(i, j, k) + _dataU(i + 1, j, k),
5           _dataV(i, j, k) + _dataV(i, j + 1, k),
6           _dataW(i, j, k) + _dataW(i, j, k + 1));
7   }
```

This function fetches interpolated value at cell center from a face-centered grid. Using this function, we can write the similar curl operation for face-centered grids as follows:

```cpp
Vector3D FaceCenteredGrid3::curlAtCellCenter(
    size_t i, size_t j, size_t k) const {
    const Size3& res = resolution();
    const Vector3D& gs = gridSpacing();

    Vector3D left = valueAtCellCenter((i > 0) ? i - 1 : i, j, k);
    Vector3D right = valueAtCellCenter((i + 1 < res.x) ? i + 1 : i, j, k);
    Vector3D down = valueAtCellCenter(i, (j > 0) ? j - 1 : j, k);
    Vector3D up = valueAtCellCenter(i, (j + 1 < res.y) ? j + 1 : j, k);
    Vector3D back = valueAtCellCenter(i, j, (k > 0) ? k - 1 : k);
    Vector3D front = valueAtCellCenter(i, j, (k + 1 < res.z) ? k + 1 : k);

    double Fx_ym = down.x;
    double Fx_yp = up.x;
    double Fx_zm = back.x;
    double Fx_zp = front.x;

    double Fy_xm = left.y;
    double Fy_xp = right.y;
    double Fy_zm = back.y;
    double Fy_zp = front.y;

    double Fz_xm = left.z;
    double Fz_xp = right.z;
    double Fz_ym = down.z;
    double Fz_yp = up.z;

    return Vector3D(
        0.5 * (Fz_yp - Fz_ym) / gs.y - 0.5 * (Fy_zp - Fy_zm) / gs.z,
        0.5 * (Fx_zp - Fx_zm) / gs.z - 0.5 * (Fz_xp - Fz_xm) / gs.x,
        0.5 * (Fy_xp - Fy_xm) / gs.x - 0.5 * (Fx_yp - Fx_ym) / gs.y);
}
```

3.3.5   Laplacian

Now let's move on to our final operator, the Laplacian operator. The Laplacian operator measures the bumpiness or curvature of the field. From Section 1.3.5, the equation can be written as

$$\nabla^2 f(\mathbf{x}) \approx \nabla \cdot \nabla f(\mathbf{x}) = \frac{\partial^2 f(\mathbf{x})}{\partial x^2} + \frac{\partial^2 f(\mathbf{x})}{\partial y^2} + \frac{\partial^2 f(\mathbf{x})}{\partial z^2}. \tag{3.13}$$

The central difference version of the equation can be written as

$$\nabla^2 f(\mathbf{x}) \approx \frac{f^{i+1,j,k} - 2f^{i,j,k} + f^{i-1,j,k}}{\Delta x^2}$$
$$+ \frac{f^{i,j+1,k} - 2f^{i,j,k} + f^{i,j-1,k}}{\Delta y^2}$$
$$+ \frac{f^{i,j,k+1} - 2f^{i,j,k} + f^{i,j,k-1}}{\Delta z^2}. \tag{3.14}$$

Taking the same pattern we have been using so far, the corresponding code can be written as follows:

```cpp
double ScalarGrid3::laplacianAtDataPoint(
    size_t i, size_t j, size_t k) const {
    const double center = _data(i, j, k);
    const Size3 ds = _data.size();
    const Vector3D gs = gridSpacing();

    double dleft = 0.0;
    double dright = 0.0;
    double ddown = 0.0;
    double dup = 0.0;
    double dback = 0.0;
    double dfront = 0.0;

    if (i > 0) {
        dleft = center - _data(i - 1, j, k);
    }
    if (i + 1 < ds.x) {
        dright = _data(i + 1, j, k) - center;
    }

    if (j > 0) {
        ddown = center - _data(i, j - 1, k);
    }
    if (j + 1 < ds.y) {
        dup = _data(i, j + 1, k) - center;
    }

    if (k > 0) {
        dback = center - _data(i, j, k - 1);
    }
    if (k + 1 < ds.z) {
        dfront = _data(i, j, k + 1) - center;
    }

    return (dright - dleft) / square(gs.x)
        + (dup - ddown) / square(gs.y)
```

```
37        + (dfront - dback) / square(gs.z);
38    }
```

We now have seen the most basic operators for the grid-based computation. In the following section, we will find out how to build a grid-based fluid simulation upon the foundation we have explored so far.

3.4 Fluid Simulation

So far, we have been focusing on the foundation. We covered how to store and lay out the grid points followed by the mathematical operators to evaluate scalar and vector fields. In this section, we will finally build our first grid-based fluid simulator. Figure 3.9 shows some examples from the grid-based solvers. To simplify the problem, we will start from a single-phase fluid, meaning that there will be only a single kind of fluid in the system.

As stated in Section 1.7, the three key components that drive the fluid flow are the external forces, viscosity, and pressure gradient. In the case of the particle-based simulation, we computed external forces including the gravity

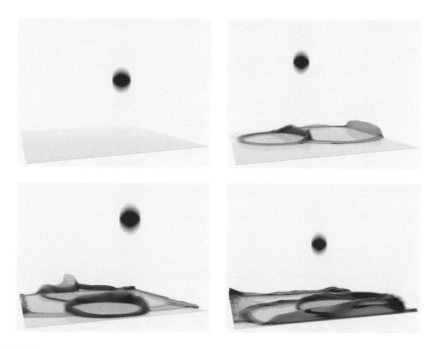

FIGURE 3.9
Sample results from the grid-based fluid simulators from Kim and Ko [65]. Randomly generated water balls are dropped into the tank.

and drag forces. For the viscosity force, the Laplacian operator is applied to the velocity field which is then scaled before being added to the force vector. To incorporate the pressure gradient force, we calculated the density, converted into the pressure field, and then accumulated the gradient of the field to the force. Grid-based methods share most of the processes, except that we need one more—the advection. The advection will be explained in Section 3.4.2, but in brief, it is the process that transfers quantities or materials along the fluid flow.

In grid-based simulations, these four steps are applied like filters. Each step takes a velocity field as an input and then outputs the velocity field with modifications. This filtering-based approach can be considered as simulating a single component at a time with the same time interval instead of applying every force at once. This is obviously an approximation since the real-world fluid flow does not time-split the effect for the forces, but the divide-and-conquer approach helps to solve each of the forces, especially the pressure, more effectively. One such technique used in this book to solve pressure is called fractional-step or pressure correction/projection method [29,70], which is widely adopted by the graphics community from Stam's famous 1999 paper "Stable Fluids" [112]. To implement this higher-level logic, a base solver class is defined below.

```
 1   class GridFluidSolver3 : public PhysicsAnimation {
 2   public:
 3       GridFluidSolver3();
 4
 5       virtual ~GridFluidSolver3();
 6
 7       ...
 8
 9   protected:
10       void onAdvanceTimeStep(double timeIntervalInSeconds) override;
11
12       virtual void computeExternalForces(double timeIntervalInSeconds);
13
14       virtual void computeViscosity(double timeIntervalInSeconds);
15
16       virtual void computePressure(double timeIntervalInSeconds);
17
18       virtual void computeAdvection(double timeIntervalInSeconds);
19
20       ...
21
22   private:
23       ...
24
25       void beginAdvanceTimeStep(double timeIntervalInSeconds);
26
```

```
27        void endAdvanceTimeStep(double timeIntervalInSeconds);
28    };
29
30    void GridFluidSolver3::onAdvanceTimeStep(double timeIntervalInSeconds) {
31        beginAdvanceTimeStep(timeIntervalInSeconds);
32
33        computeExternalForces(timeIntervalInSeconds);
34        computeViscosity(timeIntervalInSeconds);
35        computePressure(timeIntervalInSeconds);
36        computeAdvection(timeIntervalInSeconds);
37
38        endAdvanceTimeStep(timeIntervalInSeconds);
39    }
```

The above code shows the base class that implements the fundamental features from the grid-based fluid simulation algorithm. The new class inherits `PhysicsAnimation` class and overrides the main virtual function, `onAdvanceTimeStep`, to implement the fractional step method. As seen from `ParticleSystemSolver3`, `GridSystemSolver3` also implements the computational logic only, but puts all the data model to `GridSystemData3`. Note that `onAdvanceTimeStep` calls four subroutines sequentially. Let's find out more details on each of these functions in the rest of this chapter.

3.4.1 Collision Handling

When simulating fluids with particles, the collision is handled after the time-integration by detecting the particles that penetrate the collider surface and relocating them to the nonpenetrating positions (see Section 2.5). For grids, the process to constrain the fluid flow is similar to the particle's approach. It is a filter-like technique that fixes the flow that tries to penetrate the collider.

3.4.1.1 Collider to Signed-Distance Field

From Section 2.5, the class `Collider3` is defined to represent a solid obstacle that prevents the fluid flow from the penetration. The grid-based framework also takes the same class instance as an input. But internally, it is convenient to convert the collider surface into a signed-distance field. This conversion becomes handy because the inside/outside testing and closest distance measuring can be cached into a grid, which will accelerate the collider queries. Now let us consider the following code:

```
1    CellCenteredScalarGrid3 colliderSdf;
2
3    ...
4
5    Surface3Ptr surface = collider()->surface();
6    ImplicitSurface3Ptr implicitSurface
```

```
7        = std::dynamic_pointer_cast<ImplicitSurface3>(surface);
8
9    if (implicitSurface == nullptr) {
10        implicitSurface = std::make_shared<SurfaceToImplicit3>(surface);
11    }
12
13    colliderSdf.fill([&](const Vector3D& pt) {
14        return implicitSurface->signedDistance(pt);
15    });
```

At the beginning of the time-step, the above code determines whether the input collider has implicit surface or not. If it is an implicit surface type, then the function assigns the signed-distance value directly from the surface object to the signed-distance field cache (`colliderSdf`). If it is a nonimplicit surface type, the code measures the closest point and normal to the surface and then evaluates the signed-distance geometrically using class `SurfaceToImplicit3`. See Section 1.4.3 for more details.

3.4.1.2 Boundary Conditions

The set of conditions that constrains fluid flow near the collider boundary is called the boundary conditions. Based on the signed-distance field that we generated from the collider, we will apply the boundary conditions to the velocity field as well as to other scalar or vector fields that are associated with the flow. Let's find out what kinds of boundary conditions we need to know and how we can apply the constraints to the fields.

3.4.1.2.1 No-flux Condition

First, the nonpenetration constraint is called the no-flux boundary condition. It means that the velocity at the collider surface cannot have surface normal component, but only should be parallel. Mathematically, this condition can be written as follows:

$$\mathbf{u} \cdot \mathbf{n} = 0 \tag{3.15}$$

where $\mathbf{u}$ is the velocity field of the fluid at the boundary and $\mathbf{n}$ is the surface normal at the same location.

Now, since the collider can move, we can incorporate the velocity at the boundary to the equation, which becomes

$$(\mathbf{u} - \mathbf{u}_c) \cdot \mathbf{n} = \mathbf{u}_{rel} \cdot \mathbf{n} = 0 \tag{3.16}$$

where $\mathbf{u}_c$ is the velocity of the collider and $\mathbf{u}_{rel} = \mathbf{u} - \mathbf{u}_c$ is the relative velocity between the fluid and the collider. Now by recalling the vector projection from Section 1.3.2

$$\mathbf{v}^* = \mathbf{v} - (\mathbf{v} \cdot \mathbf{n})\mathbf{n}, \tag{3.17}$$

we can project $\mathbf{u}_{rel}$ onto the surface so that it satisfies the no-flux condition as follows:

$$\mathbf{u}_{rel}^* = \mathbf{u}_{rel} - (\mathbf{u}_{rel} \cdot \mathbf{n})\mathbf{n}$$
$$\mathbf{u}^* = \mathbf{u}_{rel}^* + \mathbf{u}_c \tag{3.18}$$

where $\mathbf{u}_{rel}^*$ is the projected relative velocity and $\mathbf{u}^*$ is the final fluid velocity.

To apply this boundary condition to the velocity field, we have to iterate every grid point and then apply the projection equation (3.18) to the velocity field if the point is at the collider boundary. Since the grid points are often not perfectly aligned with the surface of the collider, we project the velocity inside the collider.

In the case of the face-centered grid, the code can be written as follows:

```
auto u = velocity->uAccessor();
auto uPos = velocity->uPosition();

velocity->parallelForEachU([&](size_t i, size_t j, size_t k) {
    Vector3D pt = uPos(i, j, k);
    if (colliderSdf.sample(pt) <= 0.0) {
        Vector3D colliderVel = collider()->velocityAt(pt);
        Vector3D vel = velocity->sample(pt);
        Vector3D g = colliderSdf.gradient(pt);
        if (g.lengthSquared() > 0.0) {
            Vector3D n = g.normalized();
            Vector3D velp
                = (vel - colliderVel).projected(n) + colliderVel;
            u(i, j, k) = velp.x;
        } else {
            u(i, j, k) = colliderVel.x;
        }
    }
});
```

For the sake of simplicity, only the projection of u-component is shown. Repeating this to v- and w-components is straightforward.

Note that the implementation we have so far is simply a filter. It takes the velocity from a grid point and modifies it based on the boundary shape at the point location. It is a local process that only focuses on the local information. In many cases, however, the velocity field where the collider occupies ($SDF < 0$) is not well defined and often omitted from the computation. Thus, it is necessary first to fill in the velocity field inside the collider boundary with fictional values and then run the filtering. Note that this is "not" the velocity of the collider, but an imaginary velocity that is going to be used for computing fluid velocity near the boundary. The most common way of filling in this region is to extrapolate fluid velocity field to the boundary area in the opposite direction of the boundary surface normal. Adopting the implementation from Batty et al. [14], the extrapolation code can be written as follows:

```cpp
template <typename T>
void extrapolateToRegion(
    const ConstArrayAccessor3<T>& input,
    const ConstArrayAccessor3<char>& valid,
    unsigned int numberOfIterations,
    ArrayAccessor3<T> output) {
    const Size3 size = input.size();
    Array3<char> valid0(size);
    Array3<char> valid1(size);

    valid0.parallelForEachIndex([&](size_t i, size_t j, size_t k) {
        valid0(i, j, k) = valid(i, j, k);
        output(i, j, k) = input(i, j, k);
    });

    for (unsigned int iter = 0; iter < numberOfIterations; ++iter) {
        valid0.forEachIndex([&](size_t i, size_t j, size_t k) {
            T sum = 0;
            unsigned int count = 0;

            if (!valid0(i, j, k)) {
                if (i + 1 < size.x && valid0(i + 1, j, k)) {
                    sum += output(i + 1, j, k);
                    ++count;
                }

                if (i > 0 && valid0(i - 1, j, k)) {
                    sum += output(i - 1, j, k);
                    ++count;
                }

                if (j + 1 < size.y && valid0(i, j + 1, k)) {
                    sum += output(i, j + 1, k);
                    ++count;
                }

                if (j > 0 && valid0(i, j - 1, k)) {
                    sum += output(i, j - 1, k);
                    ++count;
                }

                if (k + 1 < size.z && valid0(i, j, k + 1)) {
                    sum += output(i, j, k + 1);
                    ++count;
                }

                if (k > 0 && valid0(i, j, k - 1)) {
```

```
48                    sum += output(i, j, k - 1);
49                    ++count;
50                }
51
52                if (count > 0) {
53                    output(i, j, k)
54                        = sum / (T)count;
55                    valid1(i, j, k) = 1;
56                }
57            } else {
58                valid1(i, j, k) = 1;
59            }
60        });
61
62        valid0.swap(valid1);
63    }
64 }
```

Calling this function before the projection will ensure that the velocity everywhere conforms to the no-flux boundary condition.

3.4.1.2.2 Slip and No-Slip Conditions

If the no-flux boundary condition were constraining the flow in a surface normal direction, the free-slip and no-slip conditions would describe the behavior of the tangential component of the fluid velocity. The free-slip condition allows the flow to move freely in the tangential directions on the surface, whereas the no-slip condition assumes that the velocity at the fluid–solid interface is zero. To apply the free-slip condition, there is nothing to do after the extrapolation and projection. To implement the no-slip condition, we can assign collider's velocity to the grid points at and within the collider boundary. But what about the case in between the free-slip and no-slip?

Similar to the way we handled the particle–collider friction in Section 2.5, we can apply the friction effect to the slip condition as well. Rewriting Equation 2.18, the friction filtering can be written as

$$\mathbf{u}_t = \max\left(1 - \mu \frac{\max(-\mathbf{u} \cdot \mathbf{n}, 0)}{|\mathbf{u}_t|}, 0\right) \mathbf{u}_t, \qquad (3.19)$$

which can also be found in Zhu and Bridson [127]. The equivalent code can be written by modifying the projection code:

```
1  auto u = velocity->uAccessor();
2  auto uPos = velocity->uPosition();
3
4  velocity->parallelForEachU([&](size_t i, size_t j, size_t k) {
5      Vector3D pt = uPos(i, j, k);
6      if (colliderSdf.sample(pt) <= 0.0) {
```

```
7        Vector3D colliderVel = collider()->velocityAt(pt);
8        Vector3D vel = velocity->sample(pt);
9        Vector3D g = colliderSdf.gradient(pt);
10       if (g.lengthSquared() > 0.0) {
11           Vector3D n = g.normalized();
12           Vector3D velr = vel - colliderVel;
13           Vector3D velt = velr.projected(n);
14           if (velt.lengthSquared() > 0) {
15               double veln = std::max(-velr.dot(n), 0.0);
16               double mu = collider()->frictionCoefficient();
17               velt *= std::max(1 - mu * veln / velt.length(), 0.0);
18           }
19
20           Vector3D velp = velt + colliderVel;
21           u(i, j, k) = velp.x;
22       } else {
23           u(i, j, k) = colliderVel.x;
24       }
25   }
26 });
```

Again, only the projection of u-component is shown for the sake of simplicity.

3.4.1.2.3 Neumann and Dirichlet

So far, we have covered boundary conditions for velocity fields. To generalize the constraints to other fields, let's consider two higher-level boundary conditions: Neumann and Dirichlet conditions.

For a given field f, the Neumann boundary condition constrains the derivative of f at the boundary, such that

$$\frac{\partial f}{\partial n} = c \tag{3.20}$$

where n is the surface normal of the boundary. For example, if c is zero, it means that f does not change across the boundary. Therefore, the no-flux boundary condition can be a subset of the Neumann boundary condition.

The Dirichlet boundary condition, on the other hand, constrains the f itself at the boundary, such that:

$$f = c \tag{3.21}$$

If c is zero and applied to the velocity field, then it is equivalent to no-slip condition.

3.4.2 Advection

In fluid dynamics, the term "advection" means transferring matters along the flow. For instance, if massless particles are sprinkled over a stream of water, they will passively flow along the stream. The advection problem is automatically solved in particle-based solvers because the particles carry the data with themselves. The grid, on the other hand, is fixed in space.[*] It just observes the flow. So when the simulation evolves, the data should be transferred from one grid point to another.

3.4.2.1   Semi-Lagrangian Method

To solve the advection problem, we need one little trick. In the particles world, remember that we simply shoot particles to relocate physical quantities. Let's say that the existing grid points are actually the result of the particle-shooting from the past. They must have started from some locations, but happen to land perfectly on an aligned grid structure. Therefore, the trick is to trace backward and examine what the values were before by linearly interpolating the nearby grid values. This concept is illustrated in Figure 3.10. This method can also be written as follows:

$$f(\mathbf{x})^{n+1} = \widetilde{f}(\mathbf{x} - \Delta t\mathbf{u})^n \tag{3.22}$$

where f represents the quantity that we want to transfer along the flow, and $\widetilde{f}$ is the linearly interpolated value at a given location. The vector field $\mathbf{u}$ is the flow that carries f, the superscript n denotes the nth time-step, and Δt is the time-step size. Thus, the equation is assigning interpolated f^n at back-traced location, $\mathbf{x} - \Delta t\mathbf{u}$, to f^{n+1}.

This technique is called the semi-Lagrangian method. The reason is that we often call the particle-based approach as "Lagrangian" framework, and the method is somewhere in the middle of the particle- and grid-based methods. (The grid-based approach is also often called "Eulerian" framework.)

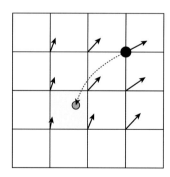

FIGURE 3.10
A particle from a given grid point is back-traced by following the underlying velocity field. Then, it samples the value from the back-trace location (gray dot) and assigns it to the grid point (black dot).

---

[*]There are methods in which the grids can also move in space [60], but those are for effective grid placement and do not allow individual grid points to follow the flow separately.

This method first became popular for simulating atmospheric models [113], and then was introduced to computer graphics domain by Jos Stam [112].

The semi-Lagrangian method is one of the most popular methods to solve the advection problem in the graphics field due to two characteristics. First, the new field is always guaranteed to be bounded between the min and the max value from the previous field since it maps the new field from the old field by linear interpolation. This is an important feature because otherwise the field may continue to oscillate or diverge which will eventually "blow-up" the simulation. Second, the method can take arbitrary time-step without, again, making the system diverge.

Unlike the semi-Lagrangian, other FDM-based methods often have time-step restrictions because of the way they approximate the advection equation. To understand this in more detail, let's consider the upwind method, the most typical FDM method to solve advection problem, as our example.

First the original, nonapproximated version of the advection equation is given below:

$$\frac{\partial f}{\partial t} + \mathbf{u} \cdot \nabla f = 0 \tag{3.23}$$

This is not a trivial equation to understand at the first glance, but once we convert into discretized version, it will become more understandable. For the sake of simplicity, let's bring the equation down to a 1D problem.

$$\frac{\partial f}{\partial t} + u \frac{\partial f}{\partial x} = 0 \tag{3.24}$$

The identical equation can be written as:

$$\frac{\partial f}{\partial t} = -u \frac{\partial f}{\partial x} \tag{3.25}$$

The idea of the upwind method is to apply one-way differencing to the derivative $\frac{\partial f}{\partial x}$. So the above equation turns into:

$$\frac{\partial f}{\partial t} = \begin{cases} -u \frac{f_i - f_{i-1}}{\Delta x}, & \text{if } u > 0 \\ -u \frac{f_{i+1} - f_i}{\Delta x}, & \text{otherwise} \end{cases} \tag{3.26}$$

Note that we measure the derivative $\frac{\partial f}{\partial x}$ by taking f from upwind direction. If u is positive, we take the derivative from $i - 1$ direction, and if it is negative, we get f from $i + 1$. For the sake of simplicity, let's assume that u is positive. We can also apply the Euler method to approximate $\frac{\partial f}{\partial t}$ such that:

$$f_i^{t+\Delta t} = f_i^t - \Delta t u \frac{f_i^t - f_{i-1}^t}{\Delta x} \tag{3.27}$$

The visual explanation of this equation can be found in Figure 3.11. Note that in 1D, the upwind method is identical to the semi-Lagrangian method *if* $u\Delta t$ is smaller than the grid spacing Δx. If it exceeds, this means that the back-traced point (gray dot in the figure) will be outside the $i-1$ boundary. In the case of semi-Lagrangian, it is not a problem because it will then perform the linear interpolation between two nearby grid points. The upwind method, however, will still use the derivative $\frac{f_i^t - f_{i-1}^t}{\Delta x}$, which can cause out-of-bound interpolation as shown in Figure 3.12. Thus, we can say that the upwind method is stable only when $u\Delta t/\Delta x < 1$. This metric, $u\Delta t/\Delta x$, is called Courant number, and the condition is called Courant–Friedrichs–Lewy (CFL) condition. We often call the Courant number the CFL number too. This is a universal metric for numerical algorithms, and in the case of the upwind

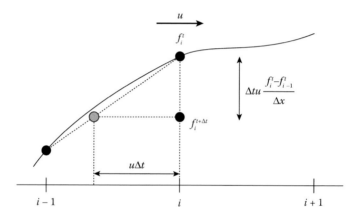

FIGURE 3.11
Illustration of the upwind method in 1D.

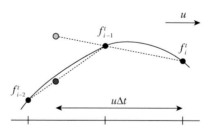

FIGURE 3.12
Comparing upwind and semi-Lagrangian methods when $u\Delta t$ is greater than the grid spacing Δx. The light gray dot represents the interpolated value from the upwind method, while the dark gray dot represents the semi-Lagrangian method.

scheme, we say the CFL limit is 1. On the other hand, the semi-Lagrangian method is unconditionally stable (although the accuracy is a different story).

To implement the semi-Lagrangian method, let's first define the base class for advection solvers.

```
1   class AdvectionSolver3 {
2    public:
3       AdvectionSolver3();
4
5       virtual ~AdvectionSolver3();
6
7       virtual void advect(
8           const FaceCenteredGrid3& input,
9           const VectorField3& flow,
10          double dt,
11          FaceCenteredGrid3* output);
12   };
```

The class has a single method that takes input and output grid, as well as the flow field that carries the input field. Note that the method can take arbitrary vector field for the background flow, and it doesn't have to be a grid.

To implement the semi-Lagrangian solver, consider the following code:

```
1   class SemiLagrangian3 : public AdvectionSolver3 {
2    public:
3       SemiLagrangian3();
4
5       virtual ~SemiLagrangian3();
6
7       void advect(
8           const FaceCenteredGrid3& input,
9           const VectorField3& flow,
10          double dt,
11          FaceCenteredGrid3* output) final;
12
13   protected:
14      Vector3D backTrace(
15          const VectorField3& flow,
16          double dt,
17          double h,
18          const Vector3D& pt0);
19   };
20
21  void SemiLagrangian3::advect(
22      const FaceCenteredGrid3& input,
23      const VectorField3& flow,
24      double dt,
25      FaceCenteredGrid3* output,
```

```
26      const ScalarField3& boundarySdf) {
27          auto inputSamplerFunc = input.sampler();
28
29          double h = std::max(output->gridSpacing().x, output->gridSpacing().y);
30
31          auto uTargetDataPos = output->uPosition();
32          auto uTargetDataAcc = output->uAccessor();
33          auto uSourceDataPos = input.uPosition();
34
35          output->parallelForEachU([&](size_t i, size_t j, size_t k) {
36              Vector3D pt = backTrace(
37                  flow, dt, h, uTargetDataPos(i, j, k));
38              uTargetDataAcc(i, j, k) = inputSamplerFunc(pt).x;
39          });
40
41          // Advect v and w
42          ...
43      }
```

For the sake of simplicity, the code only shows advection of the u-component only. For scalar or collocated grids, a single loop will complete the advection step, but face-centered grid requires three loops. In any case, in the code given above, `inputSamplerFunc` is a function object that calls trilinear interpolation function (from Section 1.3.6) for the grid `input` internally. Also the function `uPosition` returns a function object that returns u-data position at given grid index (i, j, k), and `uAccessor` returns 3D array pointer wrapper that can get and set data at (i, j, k). Finally, the function `backTrace` returns the back-traced location that can be implemented as shown below:

```
1   Vector3D SemiLagrangian3::backTrace(
2       const VectorField3& flow,
3       double dt,
4       const Vector3D& startPt) {
5       // Euler step
6       return pt0 - dt * flow.sample(pt0);
7   }
```

The above implementation uses the simple Euler method for the time integration (Section 1.6.2.4) to back-trace the imaginary particle.

We now have completed the basic implementation of the semi-Lagrangian method. The following section covers how we can further improve the performance of the method.

3.4.2.2   Improving Back-Tracing Accuracy

First, our focus is on the back-tracing part. The idea of back-tracing makes the semi-Lagrangian robust in terms of time-step. But this does not guarantee that the solution is accurate. For example, imagine a circular flow field as

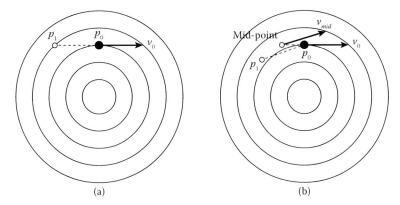

(a)   (b)

FIGURE 3.13
Comparison between (a) the Euler method and (b) the mid-point rule.

shown in Figure 3.13. If we use the Euler time integration method to back-trace along the flow, it will sample from the incorrect location because of the linear approximation of the method. Since most of the flows are nonlinear, the back-tracing also should be able to adapt to the nonlinear, curved streamline of the flow.

There are many different approaches to improve the time integration accuracy [30], and one of them is the mid-point rule. When the Euler method evaluates the derivative of time from the current location, the mid-point method measures it at the middle point between the current location and the new location. The modified code is shown below.

```
1   Vector3D SemiLagrangian3::backTrace(
2       const VectorField3& flow,
3       double dt,
4       double h,
5       const Vector3D& startPt,
6       const ScalarField3& boundarySdf) {
7       // Mid-point rule
8       Vector3D midPt = startPt - 0.5 * dt * vel0;
9       Vector3D midVel = flow.sample(midPt);
10      pt1 = startPt - dt * midVel;
11
12      return pt1;
13  }
```

As you can see, it first performs conventional Euler method with half of the time-step to evaluate the velocity at the mid-point. Then, the mid-point velocity is measured and used for taking the final Euler step. Figure 3.13 illustrates the process. By simply performing two cascaded Euler steps, the result can be improved significantly.

3.4.2.3   Improving Interpolation Accuracy

As described in the previous section, the semi-Lagrangian method utilizes linear interpolation for sampling the field value at an arbitrary location. The linear approach will work if the grid resolution is very high. But if it is not high enough, it will suffer from the approximation error just like the linear Euler time integration we discussed earlier. If the time integration error causes the solution to drift away from the flow, this approximation error makes the solution diffusive. Such an unintended diffusion due to the numerical error is called numerical diffusion. If applied to the density field advection, the numerical diffusion will make the field dissipate so that the original distribution spreads out and loses the local details as well as the net mass. In the case of the velocity field, the numerical diffusion will introduce additional viscosity. This will make the flow lose swirls or vortices and also make it too thick like oil. Thus, it is very clear that the error strongly impacts the final result.

There have been many different approaches to solve the numerical diffusion. One solution is to use a particle-based method which doesn't have the advection step at all. This topic will be discussed at the end of this chapter, but there are cases where the grid-based approaches fit better than the particle-based approach. Still, if the numerical diffusion is the key concern, it is worth considering the particle-based methods. Another solution is to go hybrid, use particles to solve advection problem, and apply grid-based methods for the rest of the steps. The hybrid methods will be covered in detail in Chapter 4, but in summary, they are good solutions and are actively used in the industrial software packages. Finally, there are purely grid-based solutions that focus on improving the accuracy of the advection solver; the remainder of this section explains this approach.

Among the grid-based solutions, there are techniques that replace the linear interpolation with higher order methods such as cubic polynomials [42,67,110]. Also similar to the idea of PCISPH, a predictive–corrective approach can also be used when solving the advection problem [64,102]. In addition, there are methods that focus on the velocity field and the vortices (the swirls), and try to resolve the subgrid details by adopting the turbulent theory [71,93] or by simply adding extra vortices back to the field [42].

In this section, the cubic interpolation approach will be implemented, which was proposed by Fedkiw et al. [42]. The basic idea of this method is to use series of Catmull–Rom interpolation instead of the trilinear interpolation (see Section 1.3.6 for Catmull–Rom). However, this higher order interpolation will break one of the key features of the original semi-Lagrangian method. The linear interpolation uses a linear function for the approximation, and that function is monotonic—the slope of the function is either negative or positive only. This allows the interpolation to return the bounded solution between the min and the max of the original field. However, the cubic polynomial is not monotonic, meaning that the solution is not bounded and make overshoots. Figure 3.14 (dashed line) illustrates an example case.

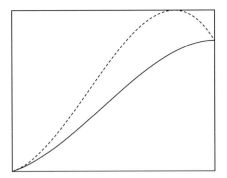

FIGURE 3.14
Original Catmull–Rom interpolation (dashed line) and its monotonic version (solid line).

To solve the monotonicity problem, Fedkiw et al. [42] proposed a clamping method which simply clamps the derivative at the end of the spline function to zero if it creates any overshoots. Figure 3.14 (solid line) shows how the clamping limits the spline function. The new Catmull–Rom interpolation code with the clamping is presented below:

```
template <typename T>
inline T monotonicCatmullRom(
    const T& f0,
    const T& f1,
    const T& f2,
    const T& f3,
    T f) {
    T d1 = (f2 - f0) / 2;
    T d2 = (f3 - f1) / 2;
    T D1 = f2 - f1;

    if (std::fabs(D1) < kEpsilonF) {
        d1 = d2 = 0;
    }

    if (sign(D1) != sign(d1)) {
        d1 = 0;
    }

    if (sign(D1) != sign(d2)) {
        d2 = 0;
    }

    T a3 = d1 + d2 - 2 * D1;
```

```
25        T a2 = 3 * D1 - 2 * d1 - d2;
26        T a1 = d1;
27        T a0 = f1;
28
29        return a3 * cubic(f) + a2 * square(f) + a1 * f + a0;
30    }
```

In the above code, d1 and d2 are the derivatives at the beginning and the end of the interpolation interval computed using the central differencing. Also, D1 represents the difference between the two end points as shown in Figure 3.14b. In order to be monotonic, the following condition should be met:

$$\begin{cases} sign(d1) = sign(d2) = sign(D1) & D1 \neq 0 \\ d1 = d2 = 0 & D1 = 0 \end{cases} \qquad (3.28)$$

The if-statements in the above code apply the clamping if the condition is not satisfied, and hence achieve the monotonicity. Similar to the trilinear interpolation, the multidimensional monotonic cubic interpolation can be done by cascading per-dimension interpolations. The 2D and 3D codes can be found at include/jet/detail/array_sampler2-inl.h and include/jet/detail/array_sampler3-inl.h.

In Figure 3.15, both linear and monotonic cubic versions of the semi-Lagrangian are shown to compare their accuracy in 2D. This experiment rotates a signed-distance field of a disk with a slot to see if the selected solver preserves the sharp features of the input shape after multiple revolutions.[*] Clearly, the cubic version shows better performance than the linear one.

3.4.2.4 Boundary Handling

During the back-tracing, it is possible that the end point is inside the boundary. In such cases, we simply clip the tracing line at the fluid–solid interface [42]

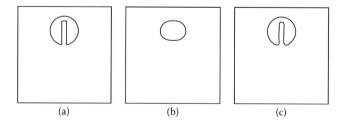

(a)   (b)   (c)

FIGURE 3.15
(a) The original Zalesak disk field, (b) the result after revolving twice with linear semi-Lagrangian, and (c) the result from monotonic cubic interpolation.

---

[*]This experiment is called Zalesak's disk test [39]. It is one of the classic experiments that are used for evaluating the performance of advection solvers.

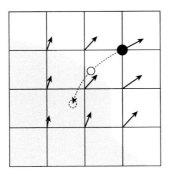

FIGURE 3.16
When a collider is found during the back-tracing, the trace is clamped at the collider boundary.

as shown in Figure 3.16. The corresponding code can be written as follows:

```
1   Vector3D SemiLagrangian3::backTrace(
2       const VectorField3& flow,
3       double dt,
4       double h,
5       const Vector3D& startPt,
6       const ScalarField3& boundarySdf) {
7
8       // Mid-point rule
9       Vector3D midPt = startPt - 0.5 * dt * vel0;
10      Vector3D midVel = flow.sample(midPt);
11      pt1 = startPt - dt * midVel;
12
13      // Boundary handling
14      double phi0 = boundarySdf.sample(startPt);
15      double phi1 = boundarySdf.sample(pt1);
16
17      if (phi0 * phi1 < 0.0) {
18          double w = std::fabs(phi1) / (std::fabs(phi0) + std::fabs(phi1));
19          pt1 = w * pt0 + (1.0 - w) * pt1;
20          break;
21      }
22
23      return pt1;
24  }
```

So far, we have been improving the semi-Lagrangian implementation in various aspects. The example code only showed solving the advection of a face-centered grid, but the same algorithm can easily be extended to the scalar and collocated vector grids as well. See the implementation from `include/jet/semi_lagrangian3.h` and `include/jet/semi_lagrangian3.cpp`.

Finally, the code below shows how the advection solver is called from
`GridFluidSolver3`.

```
1   void GridFluidSolver3::computeAdvection(double timeIntervalInSeconds) {
2       auto vel = velocity();
3       if (_advectionSolver != nullptr) {
4           // Solve velocity advection
5           auto vel0 = std::dynamic_pointer_cast<FaceCenteredGrid3>(vel->
                clone());
6           _advectionSolver->advect(
7               *vel0,
8               *vel0,
9               timeIntervalInSeconds,
10              vel.get(),
11              _colliderSdf);
12          applyBoundaryCondition();
13      }
14  }
```

Before the advection, the code first copies the current velocity field and
lets the advection solver write the new values to the original velocity grid.
Also note that the function `applyBoundaryCondition` is called after solving
the advection. This function applies the boundary conditions covered in
Section 3.4.1.

3.4.3   Gravity

Applying gravity to the grid-based solver is very straightforward. The model
we are trying to solve, however, is a constant-density, single-phase fluid, which
means that the effect of the gravity will be neutralized by the pressure field
(see Section 1.7), resulting in no interesting motion. But since the gravity
will take a dominant role as we move forward to other types of simulations
such as smoke and air–water simulations, the following code is implemented
in `GridFluidSolver3`:

```
1   void GridFluidSolver3::computeGravity(double timeIntervalInSeconds) {
2       if (_gravity.lengthSquared() > kEpsilonD) {
3           auto vel = _grids->velocity();
4           auto u = vel->uAccessor();
5           auto v = vel->vAccessor();
6           auto w = vel->wAccessor();
7
8           if (std::abs(_gravity.x) > kEpsilonD) {
9               vel->forEachU([&](size_t i, size_t j, size_t k) {
10                  u(i, j, k) += timeIntervalInSeconds * _gravity.x;
11              });
12          }
```

```
13
14        if (std::abs(_gravity.y) > kEpsilonD) {
15            vel->forEachV([&](size_t i, size_t j, size_t k) {
16                v(i, j, k) += timeIntervalInSeconds * _gravity.y;
17            });
18        }
19
20        if (std::abs(_gravity.z) > kEpsilonD) {
21            vel->forEachW([&](size_t i, size_t j, size_t k) {
22                w(i, j, k) += timeIntervalInSeconds * _gravity.z;
23            });
24        }
25
26        applyBoundaryCondition();
27    }
28 }
```

The code simply sees if each of the gravity components is nonzero, and then adds it to the velocity field.

3.4.4 Viscosity

As already covered in Section 1.7.3 and also in the SPH solver (Section 2.3.2.3), the viscosity is the force that makes a fluid thick and sticky. For the SPH, this was done by blurring out the velocity of a particle to its neighboring particles. The blurring process is called diffusion, and we can bring the same idea to the grid-based fluid simulations.

3.4.4.1 Solving Diffusion with Forward Euler

From Equation 1.82, the viscosity equation can be written as:

$$\mathbf{a}_v = \mu \nabla^2 \mathbf{u} \tag{3.29}$$

where $\mathbf{a}_v$ is the acceleration generated due to the viscosity force, μ is the viscosity coefficient, and $\mathbf{u}$ is the velocity. Using the Euler time integration method, we can break down the equation into:

$$\mathbf{u}^{n+1} = \mathbf{u}^n + \Delta t \mu \nabla^2 \mathbf{u}^n \tag{3.30}$$

where $\mathbf{u}^n$ is the velocity at nth frame and Δt is the time-step. This is a straightforward equation which can directly map into the code. To start the implementation, let's first define an abstract base class for the generic diffusion solver.

```
1 class GridDiffusionSolver3 {
2 public:
3     GridDiffusionSolver3();
```

```
4        virtual ~GridDiffusionSolver3();
5
6        virtual void solve(
7            const ScalarGrid3& source,
8            double diffusionCoefficient,
9            double timeIntervalInSeconds,
10           ScalarGrid3* dest) = 0;
11
12       ...
13   };
```

The virtual function `solve` takes the input grid, diffusion coefficient, and the output grid. To implement Equation 3.30, we can inherit this base class and use the central differencing from Section 3.3.5 to compute $\nabla^2 \mathbf{u}^n$ as shown below.

```
1    class GridFowardEulerDiffusionSolver3 final : public GridDiffusionSolver3
         {
2    public:
3        GridFowardEulerDiffusionSolver3();
4
5        void solve(
6            const ScalarGrid3& source,
7            double diffusionCoefficient,
8            double timeIntervalInSeconds,
9            ScalarGrid3* dest) override;
10
11       ...
12   };
13
14   void GridFowardEulerDiffusionSolver3::solve(
15       const ScalarGrid3& source,
16       double diffusionCoefficient,
17       double timeIntervalInSeconds,
18       ScalarGrid3* dest) {
19       Size3 size = source.dataSize();
20       source.forEachDataPoint(
21           [&](size_t i, size_t j, size_t k) {
22               (*dest)(i, j, k)
23                   = source(i, j, k)
24                   + diffusionCoefficient * timeIntervalInSeconds
25                   * source.laplacianAtDataPoint(i, j, k);
26           });
27   }
```

For the sake of simplicity, only the `solve` function with `ScalarGrid3` is shown. Also note that we named the class `GridFowardEulerDiffusionSolver3` because the Euler method we are using is called the forward Euler as it marches forward from the current state. The other functions can be easily extended. The solver then can be used from `GridFluidSolver3` as shown below.

```
1   void GridFluidSolver3::computeViscosity(
2       double timeIntervalInSeconds) {
3       if (_diffusionSolver != nullptr
4           && _viscosityCoefficient > kEpsilonD) {
5           auto vel = velocity();
6           auto vel0
7               = std::dynamic_pointer_cast<FaceCenteredGrid3>(vel->clone());
8
9           _diffusionSolver->solve(
10              *vel0,
11              _viscosityCoefficient,
12              timeIntervalInSeconds,
13              vel.get(),
14              _colliderSdf,
15              *fluidSdf());
16          applyBoundaryCondition();
17      }
18  }
```

3.4.4.2 Stability of Diffusion Solver

At the first glance, the forward Euler implementation seems good enough. However, the method is not robust enough for large time-steps. If a time-step greater than a certain threshold is used, it will break the field with nonphysical values. Let's find out the reason.

To help understand the problem in more detail, a simplified (from the forward Euler implementation we saw earlier) 1D code is shown below.

```
1   double invGridSpacingSqr = 1.0 / square(grid.gridSpacing());
2
3   for(...) {
4       dest[i] = source[i]
5           + diffusionCoefficient * timeIntervalInSeconds
6           * (source[i + 1] - 2.0 * source[i] + source[i - 1])
7           * invGridSpacingSqr;
8   }
```

This code can be reorganized as follows.

```
1   double invGridSpacingSqr = 1.0 / square(grid.gridSpacing());
2   double diffusionCoefficient = viscosityCoefficient *
        timeIntervalInSeconds;
3
4   for(...) {
```

```
5    double c = diffusionCoefficient * timeIntervalInSeconds *
         invGridSpacingSqr;
6    dest[i] = c * source[i + 1] + (1.0 - 2.0 * c) * source[i] + c *
         source[i - 1]);
7  }
```

Note that the diffusion code we wrote was in fact a triangle filter. Variable `c` is proportional to the width of the filter kernel; thus, higher `c` means more blurring. Figure 3.17a shows the shape of this kernel. Now `c` is the combination of the time-step `timeIntervalInSeconds`, diffusion coefficient `diffusionCoefficient`, and inverse square of the grid-spacing `invGridSpacingSqr`. This means that the kernel shape depends on these three parameters. The problem is that variable `c` has its limit. The lowest possible value is zero (Figure 3.17b) and the highest value is 0.5 (Figure 3.17c). Otherwise, the kernel will include the grid points that are not part of the central differencing, resulting in unintended calculations.[*] Therefore, the highest possible diffusion coefficient is limited by `0.25 * gridSpacingSquare / dt`. In the case of 2D and 3D, the limits are `gridSpacingSquare / dt / 8.0` and `gridSpacingSquare / dt / 12.0`.

This limit can be problematic if we want very viscous simulations, such as thick oil and honey. Also, if we increase the resolution, which will decrease the grid-spacing, the limit will drop quadratically. Figure 3.18 shows what would happen if `c` is greater than the limit.

As briefly mentioned earlier, the time integration we have been using is called the "forward" Euler method, and this stability problem is one of the known issues of the forward Euler. The predictor–corrector from PCISPH (Section 2.4) and the Runge–Kutta method (Section 3.4.2) are other kinds of forward time integration that have better performance than the forward Euler

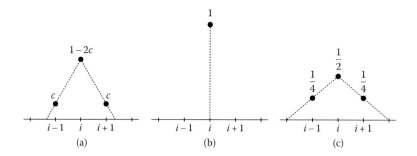

FIGURE 3.17
Diffusion filters in 1D: (a) general case $(1/2 < c < 1)$, (b) dirac delta $(c = 1)$, and (c) max width $(c = 1/2)$.

---

[*]You can also think of this as an information propagation problem that we observed in the SPH simulations.

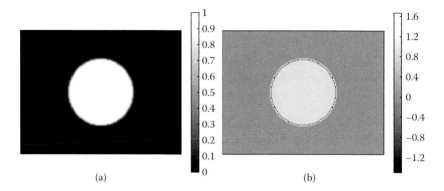

FIGURE 3.18
Stable (a) and unstable (b) diffusion results from higher c.

regarding both accuracy and stability. However, the methods are still forward methods and stable ranges for c are bounded.

3.4.4.3 Solving Diffusion with Backward Euler

To solve this problem, let's take a look at Equation 3.30 again:

$$f_{i,j,k}^{n+1} = f_{i,j,k}^n + \Delta t \mu L(f_{i,j,k}^n) \tag{3.31}$$

where L represents the central differencing. We learned that due to the small coverage of L, the propagation of the information is limited to the adjacent neighbors, and the diffusion of a single grid point cannot exceed more than two grid points. Now, one possible attempt would be increasing the size of the coverage of L. This approach won't scale, however, because if the viscosity coefficient is very high, it should eventually cover the entire domain, which means that computing L at a single grid point would take $O(N^2)$ in time if N is the number of grid points.

How can then we solve the information propagation problem? Let's think of the problem in a somewhat different way. The problem is that propagating the information is bounded. That is because we don't know what is going to happen after Δt, and we have to inform carefully the nearby grid points about what has changed from a grid point. But what if every grid point knows what is going to happen in the future? It might be a recursive statement, but if we know the solution, we may not have to worry about propagating the changes to all the grid points because they already know the change.

Assuming we know $f_{i,j,k}^{n+1}$, we can change Equation 3.31 to:

$$f_{i,j,k}^{n+1} = f_{i,j,k}^n + \Delta t \mu L(f_{i,j,k}^{n+1}). \tag{3.32}$$

Note that the second term in the right-hand side of the equation has changed from n to $n + 1$. This is still a valid approximation. You can think of it as going backward in time instead of the forward marching. Thus, such time-integrations are called backward Euler. This small change, however, makes a huge difference regarding the stability. Since we are updating the current state with the future state, there is no need to care about the propagation of the information, and the solution will be unconditionally stable. No matter what time-step or grid spacing is used, the question that still remains is, "how do we know the future sate?"

Let's simplify the backward Euler to 1D for now and see how we can solve the equation. By shuffling the position of each term in Equation 3.32, we get:

$$f_i^{n+1} - \Delta t \mu L(f_i^{n+1}) = f_i^n \tag{3.33}$$

All the terms in the left-hand side have f^{n+1}, the future state, while the right-hand side has only f^n. Although we pretended, we do not know the future state, and the goal here is to compute it. But since the whole equation is designed assuming that we know the future, it is still unconditionally stable. By expanding L from Equation 3.33, we get:

$$f_i^{n+1} - \Delta t \mu \frac{f_{i+1}^{n+1} - 2f_i^{n+1} + f_{i-1}^{n+1}}{\Delta x^2} = f_i^n \tag{3.34}$$

which is simply a central differencing from Section 3.3.5. Regrouping the terms, we get:

$$-\frac{\Delta t \mu}{\Delta x^2}(f_{i+1}^{n+1} - \left(2 + \frac{\Delta x^2}{\Delta t \mu}\right)f_i^{n+1} + f_{i-1}^{n+1}) = f_i^n \tag{3.35}$$

which can be further simplified as:

$$-cf_{i+1}^{n+1} + (2c+1)f_i^{n+1} - cf_{i-1}^{n+1}) = f_i^n \tag{3.36}$$

where $c = \Delta t \mu / \Delta x^2$. Again, f^{n+1} is an unknown. But everything else is known, and if we iterate for every i, we will get a set of linear equations. For example, if we have only three grid points in this 1D system and assume that $c = 1$, we get:

$$-f_0^{n+1} + 3f_1^{n+1} - f_2^{n+1} = f_1^n$$
$$-f_1^{n+1} + 3f_2^{n+1} - f_3^{n+1} = f_2^n$$
$$-f_2^{n+1} + 3f_3^{n+1} - f_4^{n+1} = f_3^n$$

Note that we don't have $i = 0$ or $i = 4$ in the system—they are out of bounds. Similar to the approach in Section 3.3.5, let's just extend the values at the edges to f_0 and f_4 access such that:

$$2f_1^{n+1} - f_2^{n+1} = f_1^n$$
$$-f_1^{n+1} + 3f_2^{n+1} - f_3^{n+1} = f_2^n$$
$$-f_2^{n+1} + 2f_3^{n+1} = f_3^n$$

We now have three unknowns (f_1^{n+1}, f_2^{n+1}, and f_3^{n+1}) with three linear equations. All f^ns on the right-hand side are known values. As shown in

Section 1.3.4, we can turn these equations into a matrix form as follows:

$$\begin{bmatrix} 2 & -1 & 0 \\ -1 & 3 & -1 \\ 0 & -1 & 2 \end{bmatrix} \cdot \begin{bmatrix} f_1^{n+1} \\ f_2^{n+1} \\ f_3^{n+1} \end{bmatrix} = \begin{bmatrix} f_1^n \\ f_2^n \\ f_3^n \end{bmatrix} \tag{3.37}$$

Note that the matrix on the left-hand side is symmetric. If we solve this system directly by using the inverse matrix, the solution will be:

$$\begin{bmatrix} f_1^{n+1} \\ f_2^{n+1} \\ f_3^{n+1} \end{bmatrix} = \frac{1}{8} \begin{bmatrix} 5 & 2 & 1 \\ 2 & 4 & 2 \\ 1 & 2 & 5 \end{bmatrix} \cdot \begin{bmatrix} f_1^n \\ f_2^n \\ f_3^n \end{bmatrix} \tag{3.38}$$

So what does this mean? Think about the case where the grid point in the middle, f_2^n, is set to 1 and everything else is zero. This will form a vector of $[0, 1, 0]$ for the right-hand side of the equation, and if we multiply it by the inverse matrix above, we get $[1/4, 1/2, 1/4]$, which means that the original field has spread out to its neighbors. If f_1^n, the edge value, was set to 1, we would get $[5/8, 1/4, 1/8]$—a diffused-out profile starting from the edge.

We can generalize this linear system to arbitrary number of 1D grid points and arbitrary c such that:

$$\begin{bmatrix} c+1 & -c & 0 & \dots & 0 & 0 \\ -c & 2c+1 & -c & \dots & 0 & 0 \\ \vdots & \vdots & \ddots & \vdots & \vdots \\ 0 & 0 & \dots & -c & c+1 \end{bmatrix} \cdot \mathbf{f}^{n+1} = \mathbf{f}^n \tag{3.39}$$

The diffusion problem with backward Euler now became a linear system problem:

$$\mathbf{A} \cdot \mathbf{x} = \mathbf{b} \tag{3.40}$$

Thus, we only need to focus on constructing the matrix $\mathbf{A}$ and solving the equation (Section 1.3.4).

Extending this idea to 2D and 3D is also straightforward. You only need to know how to unroll the multidimensional array into a vector $\mathbf{f}$, and the solution is quite simple: just iterate (i, j, k) grid points from i to k and append the value from the grid to the vector. Thus, f at grid point (i, j, k) is mapped to $i + width \cdot (j + height \cdot k)$th row of the vector. Then, a row of the matrix will have $-c$ for the off-diagonal columns that correspond to neighboring grid points and $kc + 1$ for the diagonal column where k is the number of non-out-of-bound neighbor points.

To find out how we can construct and solve the linear system for the diffusion problem, let's first create a class called `GridBackwardEulerDiffusion-Solver3`, which inherits `GridDiffusionSolver3`. Similar to `GridForwardEuler-DiffusionSolver3` class we saw earlier, the interface of the class looks as follows.

```
1  class GridBackwardEulerDiffusionSolver3 final : public
       GridDiffusionSolver3 {
2  public:
3      GridBackwardEulerDiffusionSolver3();
4
5      void solve(
6          const ScalarGrid3& source,
7          double diffusionCoefficient,
8          double timeIntervalInSeconds,
9          ScalarGrid3* dest) override;
10
11     ...
12
13 private:
14     FdmLinearSystem3 _system;
15     FdmLinearSystemSolver3Ptr _systemSolver;
16
17     void buildMatrix(
18         const Size3& size,
19         const Vector3D& c);
20
21     void buildVectors(const ConstArrayAccessor3<double>& f);
22 };
```

For the definition of the class `FdmLinearSystem3`, see Appendix C.1. In brief, it is consisted of the system matrix, the right-hand side vector ($\mathbf{f}^n$ in our case), and the solution vector ($\mathbf{f}^{n+1}$ in our case). The implementation of the member function `GridBackwardEulerDiffusionSolver3::solve` is shown below.

```
1  void GridBackwardEulerDiffusionSolver3::solve(
2      const ScalarGrid3& source,
3      double diffusionCoefficient,
4      double timeIntervalInSeconds,
5      ScalarGrid3* dest) {
6      Vector3D h = source.gridSpacing();
7      Vector3D c = timeIntervalInSeconds * diffusionCoefficient / (h * h);
8
9      buildMatrix(source.dataSize(), c);
10     buildVectors(source.constDataAccessor());
11
12     if (_systemSolver != nullptr) {
13         // Solve the system
14         _systemSolver->solve(&_system);
15
16         // Assign the solution
17         source.parallelForEachDataPoint(
```

```
18              [&](size_t i, size_t j, size_t k) {
19                  (*dest)(i, j, k) = _system.x(i, j, k);
20              });
21      }
22  }
```

Note that the source code includes other **solve** functions for collocated vector grids and face-centered grids. But only for the sake of simplicity, the function that takes a scalar grid is shown as an example. In any case, the above code first builds the matrix and vectors and then solves the linear system to compute new field with diffusion applied. To solve the system, any linear system solvers can be used. But if the diffusion coefficient and the time-step are high or the grid spacing is small, conjugate gradient-type of solvers would be preferred. Otherwise, Gauss–Seidel or even Jacobi methods may work. However, since the size of the matrix is quite big in practice,[*] to find out the details of these solvers, see Appendix C.

The system matrix and vector can be constructed as shown below.

```
1   void GridBackwardEulerDiffusionSolver3::buildMatrix(
2       const Size3& size,
3       const Vector3D& c) {
4       _system.A.resize(size);
5
6       // Build linear system
7       _system.A.parallelForEachIndex(
8           [&](size_t i, size_t j, size_t k) {
9               auto& row = _system.A(i, j, k);
10
11              // Initialize
12              row.center = 1.0;
13              row.right = row.up = row.front = 0.0;
14
15              if (i + 1 < size.x) {
16                  row.center += c.x;
17                  row.right -=  c.x;
18              }
19
20              if (i > 0) {
21                  row.center += c.x;
22              }
23
24              if (j + 1 < size.y) {
25                  row.center += c.y;
26                  row.up -=  c.y;
27              }
```

---

[*]The number of rows and columns is the number of grid points. Thus, if the grid resolution is $100 \times 100 \times 100$, the number of elements is 1,000,000.

```
28
29                 if (j > 0) {
30                     row.center += c.y;
31                 }
32
33                 if (k + 1 < size.z) {
34                     row.center += c.z;
35                     row.front -=  c.z;
36                 }
37
38                 if (k > 0) {
39                     row.center += c.z;
40                 }
41         });
42  }
43
44  void GridBackwardEulerDiffusionSolver3::buildVectors(
45      const ConstArrayAccessor3<double>& f) {
46      Size3 size = f.size();
47
48      _system.x.resize(size, 0.0);
49      _system.b.resize(size, 0.0);
50
51      // Build linear system
52      _system.x.parallelForEachIndex(
53          [&](size_t i, size_t j, size_t k) {
54              _system.b(i, j, k) = _system.x(i, j, k) = f(i, j, k);
55          });
56  }
```

The matrix is built row-by-row, and for each row, c is accumulated to be the diagonal component per neighbor if the point is within the grid range. For the off-diagonal columns, $-c$ is assigned. Note that the matrix is symmetric. Thus, we assign $-c$ to $+x$, $+y$, and $+z$ directions only.

We now have implemented unconditionally stable diffusion solver. This solver is efficient when solving highly viscous flow with higher grid resolution and large time-step (again, $\mu < \frac{\mu \Delta x^2}{12 \Delta t}$ for 3D). Otherwise, the overhead of constructing and solving the linear system can be dominant and using the forward Euler method can be sufficient.

3.4.4.4   Boundary Handling

When solving the diffusion equation, the boundary conditions also should be considered. See Section 3.4.1 for the boundary condition in general.

In the case of the forward Euler method, there is nothing much to change the previous code—just a single line to check if the grid point is inside the boundary or not as shown below.

```
1   void GridForwardEulerDiffusionSolver3::solve(
2       const ScalarGrid3& source,
3       double diffusionCoefficient,
4       double timeIntervalInSeconds,
5       ScalarGrid3* dest,
6       const ScalarField3& boundarySdf) {
7       auto pos = source.dataPosition();
8
9       source.parallelForEachDataPoint(
10          [&](size_t i, size_t j, size_t k) {
11              if (!isInsideSdf(boundarySdf.sample(pos(i, j, k)))) {
12                  (*dest)(i, j, k)
13                      = source(i, j, k)
14                      + diffusionCoefficient
15                      * timeIntervalInSeconds
16                      * source.laplacianAtDataPoint(i, j, k);
17              }
18          });
19  }
```

We first assume that the input field has properly set inside the object region by `applyBoundaryCondition` function (again, from Section 3.4.1) from the previous step. We then apply the solver to compute the new values for the fluid grid points. Finally, we apply the boundary condition by calling `applyBoundaryCondition` to set the field inside the objects. This is all managed in `GridFluidSolver3` level as we saw earlier from `GridFluidSolver3-::computeViscosity`.

Applying the boundary condition for the backward Euler method is a bit more complicated. Since the method constructs the matrix of unknown values, we need to encode the boundary condition into the matrix implicitly. To get into more details, let's bring back the 1D example:

$$
\begin{bmatrix} 2 & -1 & 0 \\ -1 & 3 & -1 \\ 0 & -1 & 2 \end{bmatrix} \cdot \begin{bmatrix} f_1^{n+1} \\ f_2^{n+1} \\ f_3^{n+1} \end{bmatrix} = \begin{bmatrix} f_1^n \\ f_2^n \\ f_3^n \end{bmatrix} \tag{3.41}
$$

Assume that the point number 3 is occupied by a solid object. If the boundary is of Neumann-type, we can extrapolate point 2 to 3 such that f_3^{n+1} is the same as f_2^{n+1}. This will take out -1 from $(1, 2)$ and 1 from $(1, 1)$. Also the third row and column are no longer needed because it is not part of the computation. Thus, the matrix can change to:

$$
\begin{bmatrix} 2 & -1 \\ -1 & 2 \end{bmatrix} \cdot \begin{bmatrix} f_1^{n+1} \\ f_2^{n+1} \end{bmatrix} = \begin{bmatrix} f_1^n \\ f_2^n \end{bmatrix} \tag{3.42}
$$

If the boundary condition is of Dirichlet-type, this means that we know the solution for f_3^{n+1}. Similar to the forward Euler, if we assume that applyBoundaryCondition is already called before solving the diffusion, the solution will be $f_3^{n+1} = f_3^n$. Thus, we can move f_3^{n+1} from the left-hand side to the right-hand side as shown below:

$$\begin{bmatrix} 2 & -1 \\ -1 & 3 \end{bmatrix} \cdot \begin{bmatrix} f_1^{n+1} \\ f_2^{n+1} + f_3^n \end{bmatrix} = \begin{bmatrix} f_1^n \\ f_2^n \end{bmatrix} \qquad (3.43)$$

Generalizing this idea to 3D and arbitrary c, the boundary conditions can be implemented as:

```
1    const char kFluid = 0;
2    const char kBoundary = 1;
3
4    GridBackwardEulerDiffusionSolver3::GridBackwardEulerDiffusionSolver3(
5        BoundaryType boundaryType) : _boundaryType(boundaryType) {
6        ...
7    }
8
9    void GridBackwardEulerDiffusionSolver3::buildMatrix(
10       const Size3& size,
11       const Vector3D& c) {
12       _system.A.resize(size);
13
14       bool isDirichlet = _boundaryType == Dirichlet;
15
16       // Build linear system
17       _system.A.parallelForEachIndex([&](size_t i, size_t j, size_t k) {
18           auto& row = _system.A(i, j, k);
19
20           // Initialize
21           row.center = 1.0;
22           row.right = row.up = row.front = 0.0;
23
24           if (_markers(i, j, k) == kFluid) {
25               if (i + 1 < size.x) {
26                   if (isDirichlet || _markers(i + 1, j, k) == kFluid) {
27                       row.center += c.x;
28                   }
29
30                   if (_markers(i + 1, j, k) == kFluid) {
31                       row.right -=  c.x;
32                   }
33               }
34
35               if (i > 0 && (isDirichlet || _markers(i - 1, j, k) == kFluid)
                   ) {
36                   row.center += c.x;
37               }
38
```

```
39            // Repeat the same process for j + 1, j - 1, k + 1, and k -
                 1.
40            ...
41         }
42      });
43   }
44   void GridBackwardEulerDiffusionSolver3::buildVectors(
45       const ConstArrayAccessor3<double>& f,
46       const Vector3D& c) {
47       Size3 size = f.size();
48
49       _system.x.resize(size, 0.0);
50       _system.b.resize(size, 0.0);
51
52       // Build linear system
53       _system.x.parallelForEachIndex([&](size_t i, size_t j, size_t k) {
54           _system.b(i, j, k) = _system.x(i, j, k) = f(i, j, k);
55
56           if (_boundaryType == Dirichlet && _markers(i, j, k) == kFluid) {
57               if (i + 1 < size.x && _markers(i + 1, j, k) == kBoundary) {
58                   _system.b(i, j, k) += c.x * f(i + 1, j, k);
59               }
60
61               if (i > 0 && _markers(i - 1, j, k) == kBoundary) {
62                   _system.b(i, j, k) += c.x * f(i - 1, j, k);
63               }
64
65               // Repeat the same process for j + 1, j - 1, k + 1, and k -
                     1.
66               ...
67           }
68       });
69   }
```

Here, the flag _boundaryType is either Neumann or Dirichlet. Also, _markers is a 3D array that is marked as kFluid if a point is not occupied by objects and kBoundary if the point is inside an object. As shown in Figure 3.19, Neumann boundary condition let the field diffuse out equaly even at the edge of the solid boundary. However, Dirichlet boundary condition makes the diffusion to experience friction, causing less spread-out near the interface.

3.4.5   Pressure and Incompressibility

Let's talk about the pressure and its gradient. As seen in Section 1.7.2 and particle-based fluid solvers from Chapter 2, the pressure gradient force is one of the core components of the fluid dynamics and is highly related to the density. When simulating fluids with SPH, for example, we computed pressure from

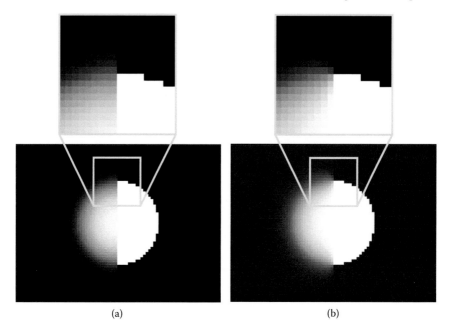

(a)   (b)

FIGURE 3.19
Initial field is set to white if inside the circle and black otherwise. Right-half
of the domain is set to a solid region. (a) Neumann boundary condition is
applied to the left and (b) Dirichlet boundary condition is for the right.

density profile. Then, the gradient force is applied to redistribute the density
move evenly.

We can also take the similar approach with the grids, that is, compute the
pressure from density and then apply the gradient. The approach, however, is
based on "forward" integration, just like the forward Euler diffusion solver in
Section 3.4.4. With the original SPH method, such an integration exposed the
compression/oscillation issue, and the predictor–corrector was introduced to
solve the problem. But the method is still a forward method and is definitely
not unconditionally oscillation-free. However, as we already covered in the
same section, would it be possible to formulate a backward-style approach for
solving the pressure?

Repeating the equation from Section 1.7.2, the acceleration caused by the
pressure gradient can be written as:

$$\mathbf{a}_p = -\frac{\nabla p}{\rho} \tag{3.44}$$

Applying the Euler method to the acceleration, we get:

$$\mathbf{u}^{n+1} = \mathbf{u}^n - \Delta t \frac{\nabla p}{\rho} \tag{3.45}$$

From Equation 3.45, let's assume that the density ρ is constant. Also, the time-step Δt is a constant value for every grid point. We can then simplify the equation to:

$$\mathbf{u}^{n+1} = \mathbf{u}^n - \nabla p^* \tag{3.46}$$

where $p^* = \Delta t \Delta p / \rho$. Similar to the backward Euler, we do not know the pressure p. The forward-style method would take the current density error to compute pressure. So, in backward sense, we would deduce the pressure by saying that this still-unknown pressure will make the density error to zero. The zero density error means that the density should remain constant, and that leads to Equation 1.85 from Section 1.7.4:

$$\nabla \cdot \mathbf{u}^{n+1} = 0 \tag{3.47}$$

We can think of $\mathbf{u}^n$ as an intermediate velocity field after advection, gravity, and diffusion. Therefore, $\nabla \cdot \mathbf{u}^n$ may not be zero. But $-\nabla p^*$ is the force that will project out the velocity that creates any divergence so that the final velocity field $\nabla \cdot \mathbf{u}^{n+1}$ is zero.

Based on this assumption, let's apply a divergence operator to Equation 3.46. This will turn the equation into:

$$\nabla \cdot \mathbf{u}^{n+1} = \nabla \cdot \mathbf{u}^n - \nabla \cdot \nabla p^* \tag{3.48}$$

By the assumption from Equation 3.47, the left-hand side becomes zero. Also, by the definition of Laplacian operator, which is $\nabla \cdot \nabla = \nabla^2$, the equation can be rewritten as:

$$\nabla^2 p^* = \nabla \cdot \mathbf{u}^n \tag{3.49}$$

The right-hand side is a known value while the left-hand side is unknown. Looks familiar? Yes, this is another linear system similar to that of the backward Euler diffusion solver. This new linear system is called pressure Poisson equation (PPE), and by solving the system, we get the right pressure to keep the velocity field divergence-free ($\nabla \cdot \mathbf{u} = 0$). For example, PPE for 1D using central differencing is shown below:

$$\frac{p^*_{i+1} - 2p^*_i + p^*_{i-1}}{\Delta x^2} = \frac{u^n_{i+1/2} - u^n_{i-1/2}}{\Delta x} \tag{3.50}$$

Note that p^*_{i-1} or p^*_{i+1} can be out-of-bounds. In such cases, we can extrapolate p^*_i to the neighbor so that the left-hand side would become $\frac{p^*_{i+1} - p^*_i}{\Delta x^2}$ if p^*_{i-1} is outside the boundary. This extrapolation especially makes sense for the pressure because it means that the difference between p^*_i and p^*_{i-1} is zero, and thus no pressure gradient is generated in the normal direction of the domain boundary. Unless explicitly modeled, it is always safe not to introduce any source from the domain boundary. However, note that the right-hand side is using half-side of the grid for the central differencing. This implies that we are going to use face-centered grid for velocity field, which allows us to have smaller grid spacing for such finite differencing ($2\Delta x$ versus Δx), meaning that we can achieve better accuracy. Rewriting the equation in a matrix form becomes:

$$\frac{1}{\Delta x^2} \begin{bmatrix} 1 & -1 & 0 & 0 & \cdots \\ -1 & 2 & -1 & 0 & \cdots \\ 0 & -1 & 2 & -1 & \cdots \\ \vdots & \vdots & \vdots & \vdots & \ddots \end{bmatrix} \begin{bmatrix} p_1^* \\ p_2^* \\ p_3^* \\ \vdots \end{bmatrix} = \frac{-1}{\Delta x} \begin{bmatrix} u_{3/2}^n - u_{1/2}^n \\ u_{5/2}^n - u_{3/2}^n \\ u_{7/2}^n - u_{5/2}^n \\ \vdots \end{bmatrix} \quad (3.51)$$

One more change to note here is that we flipped the sign of the matrix so that the diagonal elements can have positive signs. This is required if you use a system solver that assumes positive diagonal elements such as conjugate gradient.[*] Anyway, when generalized to 2D and 3D, the diagonal element will have the number of valid (not out-of-bounds or inside colliders) neighbors. The off-diagonal columns will have -1 if it is not valid.

3.4.5.1   Building Matrix

Now let's find out how we can implement the pressure solver. Similar to the diffusion solver, we will first build the matrix, solve the system, and then apply the solution. Thus, our starter code can be written as:

```
1   class GridPressureSolver3 {
2   public:
3       GridPressureSolver3();
4
5       virtual ~GridPressureSolver3();
6
7       virtual void solve(
8           const FaceCenteredGrid3& input,
9           double timeIntervalInSeconds,
10          FaceCenteredGrid3* output,
11          const ScalarField3& boundarySdf) = 0;
12
13      ...
14  };
15
16  class GridSinglePhasePressureSolver3 : public GridPressureSolver3 {
17  public:
```

---

[*]More specifically, the system matrix has to be a positive-definite matrix for conjugate gradient-type solvers. See Klein [72] for a better understanding of the positive-definite matrix.

```
18      GridSinglePhasePressureSolver3();
19
20      virtual ~GridSinglePhasePressureSolver3();
21
22      void solve(
23          const FaceCenteredGrid3& input,
24          double timeIntervalInSeconds,
25          FaceCenteredGrid3* output,
26          const ScalarField3& boundarySdf) override;
27
28      ...
29
30   protected:
31      FdmLinearSystem3 _system;
32      FdmLinearSystemSolver3Ptr _systemSolver;
33      Array3<char> _markers;
34
35      void buildMarkers(
36          const Size3& size,
37          const std::function<Vector3D(size_t, size_t, size_t)>& pos,
38          const ScalarField3& boundarySdf);
39
40      virtual void buildSystem(const FaceCenteredGrid3& input);
41
42      virtual void applyPressureGradient(
43          const FaceCenteredGrid3& input,
44          FaceCenteredGrid3* output);
45   };
46
47   void GridSinglePhasePressureSolver3::solve(
48      const FaceCenteredGrid3& input,
49      double timeIntervalInSeconds,
50      FaceCenteredGrid3* output,
51      const ScalarField3& boundarySdf) {
52      auto pos = input.cellCenterPosition();
53      buildMarkers(
54          input.resolution(),
55          pos,
56          boundarySdf);
57      buildSystem(input);
58
59      if (_systemSolver != nullptr) {
60          // Solve the system
61          _systemSolver->solve(&_system);
62
63          // Apply pressure gradient
64          applyPressureGradient(input, output);
65      }
66   }
```

Again, this is quite similar to the backward Euler diffusion solver. The main function, `solve`, starts with marking the grid points to classify whether the point falls into the collider or not. Then, we build the PPE matrix and divergence vector as shown below.

```
1   const char kFluid = 0;
2   const char kBoundary = 1;
3
4   ...
5
6   void GridSinglePhasePressureSolver3::buildSystem(
7       const FaceCenteredGrid3& input) {
8       Size3 size = input.resolution();
9       _system.A.resize(size);
10      _system.x.resize(size);
11      _system.b.resize(size);
12
13      Vector3D invH = 1.0 / input.gridSpacing();
14      Vector3D invHSqr = invH * invH;
15
16      // Build linear system
17      _system.A.parallelForEachIndex([&](size_t i, size_t j, size_t k) {
18          auto& row = _system.A(i, j, k);
19
20          // Initialize
21          row.center = row.right = row.up = row.front = 0.0;
22          _system.b(i, j, k) = 0.0;
23
24          if (_markers(i, j, k) == kFluid) {
25              // Assign divergence to the RHS vector
26              _system.b(i, j, k) = input.divergenceAtCellCenter(i, j, k);
27
28              // If the neighbor at i + 1
29              if (i + 1 < size.x && _markers(i + 1, j, k) != kBoundary) {
30                  row.center += invHSqr.x;
31                  row.right -= invHSqr.x;
32              }
33
34              if (i > 0 && _markers(i - 1, j, k) != kBoundary) {
35                  row.center += invHSqr.x;
36              }
37
38              // Repeat the same process for j + 1, j - 1, k + 1, and k -
                   1.
39              ...
40
41          } else {
42              row.center = 1.0;
43          }
```

```
44        });
45    }
```

The code simply iterates all the neighbors of a grid point, and then accumulates the values to the diagonal and off-diagonal columns (row.center and others) if the point is tagged as kFluid. Similar to the backward Euler diffusion matrix, excluding the contribution from kBoundary-tagged grid points means that we are setting the same pressure for the center point and the tagged neighbor so that there is no gradient going in or out across the interface (which is the Neumann boundary condition). Also the matrix is symmetric and we assign values to the center, right, and up neighbors only.

After solving the system, we get the pressure. To complete the process, we compute the gradient of the pressure and apply it to the velocity field as shown below.

```
1    void GridSinglePhasePressureSolver3::applyPressureGradient(
2        const FaceCenteredGrid3& input,
3        FaceCenteredGrid3* output) {
4        Size3 size = input.resolution();
5        auto u = input.uConstAccessor();
6        auto v = input.vConstAccessor();
7        auto w = input.wConstAccessor();
8        auto u0 = output->uAccessor();
9        auto v0 = output->vAccessor();
10       auto w0 = output->wAccessor();
11
12       Vector3D invH = 1.0 / input.gridSpacing();
13
14       _system.x.parallelForEachIndex([&](size_t i, size_t j, size_t k) {
15           if (_markers(i, j, k) == kFluid) {
16               if (i + 1 < size.x && _markers(i + 1, j, k) != kBoundary) {
17                   u0(i + 1, j, k)
18                       = u(i + 1, j, k)
19                       + invH.x
20                       * (_system.x(i + 1, j, k) - _system.x(i, j, k));
21               }
22
23               // Repeat the same process for j + 1, j - 1, k + 1, and k -
                        1.
24               ...
25           }
26       });
27   }
```

Note that the encoding of the collider boundary relies on the markers. A marker is either true or false, thus interpreting the collider shape as a set of Lego blocks. This can cause an aliasing artifact and can be improved by using the fractions, not markers. For instance, if a solid occupies a half of a grid cell, we use 0.5 for the fraction. This fractional method was proposed by Batty et al. [13], and the implementation adopted from their study [14] is shown here.

```
1   class GridFractionalSinglePhasePressureSolver3
2       : public GridPressureSolver3 {
3    public:
4       ...
5
6       void solve(
7           const FaceCenteredGrid3& input,
8           double timeIntervalInSeconds,
9           FaceCenteredGrid3* output,
10          const ScalarField3& boundarySdf) override;
11
12      ...
13   };
14
15   template <typename T>
16   T isInsideSdf(T phi) {
17       return phi < 0;
18   }
19
20   template <typename T>
21   T fractionInsideSdf(T phi0, T phi1) {
22       if (isInsideSdf(phi0) && isInsideSdf(phi1)) {
23           return 1;
24       } else if (isInsideSdf(phi0) && !isInsideSdf(phi1)) {
25           return phi0 / (phi0 - phi1);
26       } else if (!isInsideSdf(phi0) && isInsideSdf(phi1)) {
27           return phi1 / (phi1 - phi0);
28       } else {
29           return 0;
30       }
31   }
32
33   void GridFractionalSinglePhasePressureSolver3::buildSystem(
34       const FaceCenteredGrid3& input) {
35       Size3 size = input.resolution();
36       _system.A.resize(size);
37       _system.x.resize(size);
38       _system.b.resize(size);
39
40       Vector3D invH = 1.0 / input.gridSpacing();
41       Vector3D invHSqr = invH * invH;
42
43       // Build linear system
44       _system.A.parallelForEachIndex([&](size_t i, size_t j, size_t k) {
45           auto& row = _system.A(i, j, k);
```

```
46
47          // initialize
48          row.center = row.right = row.up = row.front = 0.0;
49          _system.b(i, j, k) = 0.0;
50
51          double term;
52
53          if (i + 1 < size.x) {
54              term = _uWeights(i + 1, j, k) * invHSqr.x;
55              row.center += term;
56              row.right -= term;
57              _system.b(i, j, k)
58                  += _uWeights(i + 1, j, k)
59                  * input.u(i + 1, j, k) * invH.x;
60          } else {
61              _system.b(i, j, k) += input.u(i + 1, j, k) * invH.x;
62          }
63
64          if (i > 0) {
65              term = _uWeights(i, j, k) * invHSqr.x;
66              row.center += term;
67              _system.b(i, j, k)
68                  -= _uWeights(i, j, k)
69                  * input.u(i, j, k) * invH.x;
70          } else {
71              _system.b(i, j, k) -= input.u(i, j, k) * invH.x;
72          }
73
74          // Repeat the same process for j + 1, j - 1, k + 1, and k - 1.
75          ...
76      });
77 }
78
79 void GridFractionalSinglePhasePressureSolver3::applyPressureGradient(
80      const FaceCenteredGrid3& input,
81      FaceCenteredGrid3* output) {
82      Size3 size = input.resolution();
83      auto u = input.uConstAccessor();
84      auto v = input.vConstAccessor();
85      auto w = input.vConstAccessor();
86      auto u0 = output->uAccessor();
87      auto v0 = output->vAccessor();
88      auto w0 = output->vAccessor();
89
90      Vector3D invH = 1.0 / input.gridSpacing();
91
92      _system.x.parallelForEachIndex([&](size_t i, size_t j, size_t k) {
93          if (i + 1 < size.x && _uWeights(i + 1, j, k) > 0.0) {
94              u0(i + 1, j, k)
```

```
95              = u(i + 1, j, k)
96              + invH.x
97              * (_system.x(i + 1, j, k) - _system.x(i, j, k));
98        }
99
100       // Repeat the same process for j + 1, j - 1, k + 1, and k - 1.
101       ...
102   });
103 }
```

From the above code, 3D array _uWeights stores the fraction of the fluid versus collider. If the fluid occupies 100%, the array returns 1. See GridFractionalSinglePhasePressureSolver3 from the codebase for more details.

3.5   Smoke Simulation

The grid-based fluid simulator we have built so far implements most of the core fluid dynamics. This is going to be our foundation, and in the following sections, we will extend the solver to simulate more interesting phenomena.

One of the most simple extensions to the solver is the smoke simulator. Imagine a scene in a movie with burning fuel or massive explosion. The goal of the new solver is to simulate clouds of hot dark smoke coming out of the source. To build a smoke simulation engine, we just need to add a couple of extra pieces including the smoke density and temperature field, as well as the buoyancy force generated due to the temperature/density distribution. As a result, the simulator will be able to generate rising smoke that interacts with obstacles and generates interesting swirls. Figure 3.20 shows some expected outputs from the solver. The example images were rendered by using Mitsuba renderer [59].

To get started, let's add a new class that represents the smoke simulator which extends the generic grid-based simulator as follows:

```
1  class GridSmokeData3 : public GridSystemData3 {
2  public:
3      ...
4
5      ScalarGrid3Ptr smokeDensity() const;
6      ScalarGrid3Ptr temperature() const;
7
8      ...
9  }
10
11 class GridSmokeSolver3 : public GridFluidSolver3 {
```

```
12      ...
13
14   protected:
15      void computeBuoyancy(double timeIntervalInSeconds);
16
17      void computeSmokeAdvection(double timeIntervalInSeconds);
18   };
```

From the above code, note that we are also defining a data model to hold the smoke density and temperature field. Note also that there is a function to compute the buoyancy force that will drive the rising of the smoke. Finally, a function that will carry the density and temperature field along the velocity field, which is `computeSmokeAdvection`, is added to the class as well.

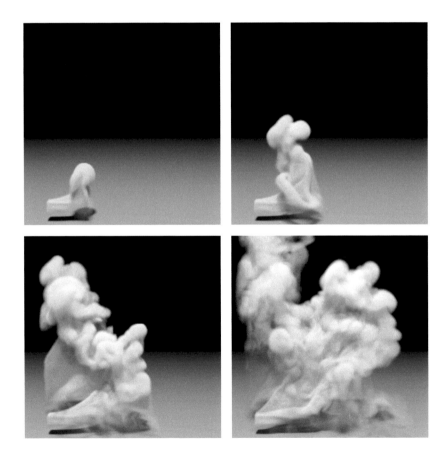

FIGURE 3.20
Sample animation sequence from the smoke simulation solver. The smoke emitted from the source rises due to the buoyancy force. The simulation is generated using a $150 \times 180 \times 75$ resolution grid.

3.5.1　Buoyancy Force

We are assuming that the smoke we simulate is produced by burning fuel or some explosion. Thus, the air around the smoke is hotter than the other area, and dark smoke aerosols are occupying the hot region. The relatively hot gas will then become lighter because the density drops, and it will experience a rising force. At the same time, the region where the smoke occupies will be relatively heavier than others which cause the down-force. This vertical force is called the buoyancy force. One way to compute the buoyancy forces is to encode such density distribution in the PPE. Since the density field is not a constant, the PPE from Section 3.4.5 will change to

$$\nabla \cdot \frac{\nabla p}{\rho} = c \frac{\nabla \cdot \mathbf{u}}{\Delta t} \tag{3.52}$$

where ρ is the density field. Such an approach is essential when the density difference is significant and computing the accurate solution is crucial, such as air versus water. In the case of simulating smoke, however, solving such a complex system matrix would be overkill. Phenomenologically, we know that the buoyancy force is dominant in the vertical direction. Thus, we can approximate the force by saying

$$\mathbf{f}_{buoy} = -\alpha \rho \mathbf{y} + \beta (T - T_{amb}) \mathbf{y} \tag{3.53}$$

where α and β are the scaling factors that map smoke density (ρ) and temperature (T) difference to the force. The smoke density is zero if the area is filled with the air only. Also, T_{amb} is the ambient temperature which can be calculated by taking the average temperature. Thus, the equation adds not only up-force if the temperature is hotter than the ambient area but also down-force if the smoke density is positive. This model was first introduced by Fedkiw et al. [42], and has been proven to be effective for simulating hot smokes.

Implementing the buoyancy equation is pretty straightforward. Take a look at the code below.

```
1   void GridSmokeData3::computeBuoyancy(double timeIntervalInSeconds) {
2       auto vel = _gridSet->velocity();
3       auto den = _gridSet->smokeDensity();
4       auto temp = _gridSet->temperature();
5       auto v = vel->v();
6       auto vPos = vel->vPosition();
7       Size3 numTempGridPoints = temp->dataSize().x * temp->dataSize().y *
            temp->dataSize().z;
8
9       double Tamb = 0.0;
10      temp->forEachDataPoint([&](size_t i, size_t j, size_t k) {
11          Tamb += temp(i, j, k);
12          });
13      Tamb /= static_cast<double>(numTempGridPoints);
14
```

```
15      velocity->forEachV([&](size_t i, size_t j, size_t k) {
16          Vector3D pt = vPos(i, j, k);
17          v(i, j, k)
18              += timeIntervalInSeconds
19                  * (_densityBuoyancyFactor * den->sample(pt)
20                  + _temperatureBuoyancyFactor * (temp->sample(pt) - Tamb))
                    ;
21          });
22  }
```

The first part of the code calculates the average temperature, and the second part of the code applies the buoyancy force.

3.5.2 Advection and Diffusion

The density and temperature fields are also carried by the velocity fields. This can be solved by reusing the advection solvers from Section 3.4.2. Both smoke aerosols and heat also experience diffusion. Thus, we can apply diffusion to the fields by using the same solver from Section 3.4.4.

3.6 Fluid with Surface

So far, we have seen how to build a generic grid-based fluid solver, and then we further extended the code base to a smoke simulator by modeling the smoke behavior with spatially varying temperature and density fields. In this section, we are going to cover how to extend the generic solver to simulate the motion of liquids, such as sloshing water in a tank.

The key of the realistic liquid animation lies in the proper handling of the fluid surface. Unlike the blurry smoke density field, we now have a clear boundary between the air and the liquid. This will raise many interesting problems. Let's find out how we can solve those.

3.6.1 Defining Surface on Grids

When simulating liquids with particles, we don't need to explicitly define the liquid–air interface. The region where the particles occupy is where the liquid is; thus, by looking up the nearby particles, we can determine whether the area is in or out of the liquid.

Using grids, the immediate attempt we can make is to color the grid where the liquid is occupying. For example, we can use binary expressions 0 and 1 to encode liquid on the grid.[*] This seems to be a very clear solution; however,

---

[*]This is very similar to modeling the smoke aerosols with a density field. To represent liquid volume and liquid–air interface, this method maps air density to 0 and liquid density to 1.

computing the finite difference on the binary field can be problematic. The field is discontinuous at the interface, and thus it is not differentiable. However, since the majority of dynamics happening at the interface such as surface tension or calculating normals require proper differencing, we need a smooth and continuous field to represent the surface.

One of the most popular approaches to overcome such a discontinuity problem is to use implicit surface, such as the signed-distance field [104] (see Section 1.4.2 for implicit surface). So far, we have been using signed-distance fields for representing the colliders or fluid sources only; however, we can also use the field to shape the liquid–air interface.

Echoing the definition of the signed-distance field from Section 1.4.2, it is a scalar field that maps a point to the distance to the closest point on the surface. Again, this field satisfies the equation

$$|\nabla \phi| = 1 \tag{3.54}$$

where ϕ is the signed-distance field. Also its sign is determined by knowing whether the point is in the volume or not. Thus, the zero isocontour implicitly defines the surface, and in our case, the interface between the liquid and the air. Figure 3.21 shows an example of a signed-distance field. As can be seen from the cross-sectional view, the signed-distance field is definitely continuous near the interface. This characteristic solves the issues with the binary field. Since it is continuous and smooth, it is differentiable near the surface.

Using the signed-distance field for modeling interface is called level set method [95,96]. By encoding the interface into a signed-distance function, the level set method can easily compute geometric properties near the interface without suffering from the discontinuity. Thus, when modeling any discontinuous features or phenomena, the level set method can be a good solution. Therefore, the level set method covers not only the fluid dynamic simulations

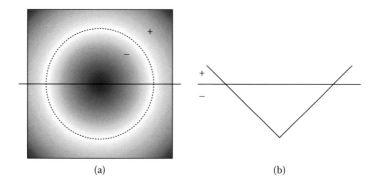

(a)   (b)

FIGURE 3.21
Signed-distance field of a circle (a) and its cross-sectional view (b). In (a), the red region has a positive sign while the blue area has a negative sign.

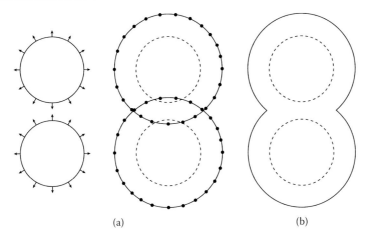

(a)   (b)

FIGURE 3.22
Expanding circle with mesh (a) and implicit (b) representations.

but also has a wide range of applications such as image segmentation and 3D model reconstruction.

Another key feature of the level set method is its ability to handle topological changes. Take a look at the example in Figure 3.22. The figure shows two expanding sphere-shaped fluid bodies with both explicit (mesh) and implicit surfaces. For explicit mesh surface, evolving the surface in normal direction can be done by moving each point along the normal direction. In the case with implicit mesh, the same operation can be performed by subtracting a constant value from the signed-distance field. As time passes, two spheres are going to collide each other, and the fun part begins.

First, let's think about what we can do with the explicit surface. If you think about two colliding water drops, they will merge each other and form a single body of water. So we are expecting to see the topological change when two surfaces collide. To make that happen with mesh, you have to find intersection points, figure out which part of the surface should be thrown away, and then fix the mesh structure properly. This is not a trivial task, and things can go wrong very easily since the geometry of fluid surface is often very complicated.

How about the implicit surface? Well, we don't need to do anything. If you keep updating the grid points even without knowing what is happening, the topological change is handled automatically. This is one of the key strengths of the level set method, and when applied to the fluid simulation, it really shines because merging and splitting (yes, splitting can be handled easily, too) happen very often for fluids.

To have the level set method implemented in our fluid solver, there are two major pieces that we have to build. The first one is the surface tracking module, which is simply an advection problem. The second component is called "reinitialization" that keeps the signed-distance field to satisfy Equation 3.54

after the advection which distorts the field and breaks the signed-distance property. Let's find out how these two modules can be implemented in a liquid simulation engine.

3.6.1.1   Tracking the Surface under the Flow

There is no difference between signed-distance field and other scalar fields when it comes to the advection. Just pass the signed-distance field to the advection solver, and that's it. But someone may wonder whether it is valid to apply advection solver to the signed-distance field because distance field is not a physical quantity. If you apply advection to the signed-distance field, will it still keep the signed-distance property? In fact, applying advection is valid only at the surface, the zero isocontours, but as you go further from the surface, it starts to show distortion.

Figure 3.23 shows a clear example. Under the vortex flow, the signed-distance field starts to stretch out, and its value no longer represents the closest distance to the surface. The sign, however, is still valid. Also, the amount of distortion becomes smaller as we get closer to the interface, and as mentioned just above, the solution of the advection is valid at the interface. Thus, we can restore the signed-distance property from the distorted field, which is explained in the following section.

3.6.1.2   Reinitializing Signed-Distance Field

After solving the advection, the signed-distance field no longer satisfies $|\nabla \phi| = 1$ due to the distortion. But as mentioned above, the sign is still preserved, and the field near the interface is still a valid distance function. To restore the signed-distance field for the entire domain, we can re-evaluate the closest distance for each grid point. However, iterating all the grid points and finding the closest point on the interface is not trivial and could be computationally cumbersome.

Instead of measuring the distance directly from the grid points, we take an opposite approach. For example, imagine a distorted signed-distance field in 1D (Figure 3.24). Since the field at the zero isocontour is valid, we can start from the grid point near the interface, traverse to the outer grid points, and add the traveled distance to the grid points. It is like propagating the wave from the interface to the farther region and accumulate the distance. After the propagation, we will have a reinitialized signed-distance field.

We can use the advection equation (Equation 3.23) with extra source term to model this propagation problem. This can be written as

$$\frac{\partial \phi}{\partial \tau} + \mathbf{u} \cdot \nabla \phi = 1. \tag{3.55}$$

Note that we are using pseudo-time τ because this is not a physics simulation but more like a geometric postprocessing. The difference between Equation 3.55 and Equation 3.23 is on the right-hand side. If the right-hand

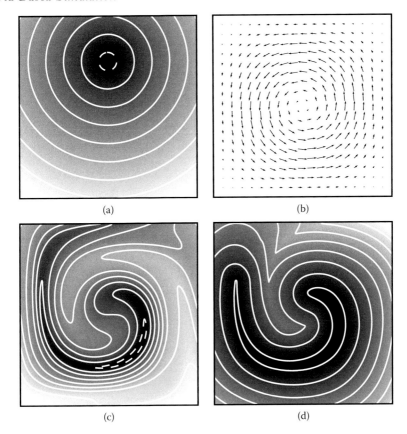

(a) (b)

(c) (d)

FIGURE 3.23
Starting from the initial signed-distance field (a), a vortex flow (b) rotates a distorted field (c). When reinitialization is applied, the signed-distance property is restored (d). White solid lines represent positive isocontour and white dashed lines indicate negative isocontour.

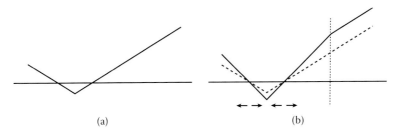

(a) (b)

FIGURE 3.24
Distorted signed-distance field (a) gets reinitialized. The intermediate results are shown in (b). The reinitialization is propagated from the zero-isocontour to the dotted line.

side is zero, it means ϕ is only carried by the vector field $\mathbf{u}$. If a constant c is assigned, it means c is added to ϕ when it travels one distance unit along $\mathbf{u}$. Thus, setting the right-hand side to 1 means we will assign the traveled distance to ϕ.

For the propagation velocity $\mathbf{u}$, we can use the surface normal. From Section 1.4.2, the normal of the implicit surface with signed-distance field is

$$\mathbf{n} = \frac{\nabla\phi(\mathbf{x})}{|\nabla\phi(\mathbf{x})|} \tag{3.56}$$

Note that this normal is inaccurate when the field is distorted. But let's accept the error for now and move on to the next step. We will discuss the issue in the end. In any case, replacing $\mathbf{u}$ with $\mathbf{n}$ leads to

$$\frac{\partial\phi}{\partial\tau} + \frac{\nabla\phi}{|\nabla\phi|} \cdot \nabla\phi = 1 \tag{3.57}$$

which can be further simplified to

$$\frac{\partial\phi}{\partial\tau} + (|\nabla\phi| - 1) = 0. \tag{3.58}$$

Note that this equation only applies to the positive signed-distance region. For the negative region, the same equation can be written as

$$\frac{\partial\phi}{\partial\tau} - (|\nabla\phi| - 1) = 0. \tag{3.59}$$

Combining the two equations, we can write the final equation as follows:

$$\frac{\partial\phi}{\partial\tau} + sign(\phi)(|\nabla\phi| - 1) = 0 \tag{3.60}$$

Before we implement the above equation, let's step back and try to understand its meaning. If we provide a perfect signed-distance field, the second term will be zero since $|\nabla\phi| = 1$. This means that ϕ is not going to change over time, and that is what is supposed to happen. If there is a distortion in the input field, the second term will be nonzero. If we think $|\nabla\phi| - 1$ as an error metric, the equation is trying to correct the error by subtracting it over (pseudo) time.

Now, let's start coding. Below is the core portion of the implementation.

```
1  class IterativeLevelSetSolver3 : public LevelSetSolver {
2      ...
3  };
4
5  void IterativeLevelSetSolver3::reinitialize(...) {
6      ...
7
```

```
 8      for (unsigned int n = 0; n < numberOfIterations; ++n) {
 9          input.parallelForEachDataPoint(
10              [&](size_t i, size_t j, size_t k) {
11                  double s = sign(input, i, j, k);
12
13                  std::array<double, 2> dx, dy, dz;
14
15                  getDerivatives(input, gridSpacing, i, j, k, &dx, &dy, &dz);
16
17                  output(i, j, k) = input(i, j, k)
18                      - dtau * std::max(s, 0.0)
19                          * (std::sqrt(square(std::max(dx[0], 0.0))
20                                      + square(std::min(dx[1], 0.0))
21                                      + square(std::max(dy[0], 0.0))
22                                      + square(std::min(dy[1], 0.0))
23                                      + square(std::max(dz[0], 0.0))
24                                      + square(std::min(dz[1], 0.0))) - 1.0)
25                      - dtau * std::min(s, 0.0)
26                          * (std::sqrt(square(std::min(dx[0], 0.0))
27                                      + square(std::max(dx[1], 0.0))
28                                      + square(std::min(dy[0], 0.0))
29                                      + square(std::max(dy[1], 0.0))
30                                      + square(std::min(dz[0], 0.0))
31                                      + square(std::max(dz[1], 0.0))) - 1.0);
32              });
33
34          std::swap(input, output);
35      }
36
37      ...
38  }
```

We start the code by defining a new class `IterativeLevelSetSolver3` to represent an iterative level set solver. For simplicity, only the gist of the code is shown here. In the function `reinitialize`, note that we have a for-loop that iterates the subcode block multiple times. Since we are solving an advection-like equation in pseudo-time space, this for-loop determines how far we want to propagate the wave from the interface. More iterations will move the wave further.

Inside the for-loop, we have another iteration for each grid point. For each point i, j, and k, we first compute the sign of the field by using function `sign`. Now, evaluating the sign of a field at point (i, j, k) should be trivial. But instead of incorporating such a discontinuous measure (either -1 or 1) to the computation, it is better to use *smoothed* sign function [98]

$$sign = \frac{\phi}{\sqrt{\phi^2 + h^2}} \tag{3.61}$$

where h is the grid spacing. After computing the sign using this equation, we compute $\nabla\phi$ by invoking `getDerivatives`. Note that this function returns two one-sided derivatives for each axis. For example, `dx[0]` has the derivative between $i-1$ and i while `dx[1]` has the derivative between i and $i+1$. We are not using central differencing, but instead calculate two one-sided derivatives and determine which one to use later on. This is the upwind scheme discussed in Section 3.4.2.

However, after computing the derivatives, we finally compute the Euler integration to solve

$$\phi = \phi_{old} - \Delta\tau \cdot sign(\phi)(|\nabla\phi| - 1) \qquad (3.62)$$

which is from Equation 3.60. All the min/max codes are the way of solving upwind-style methods. Again, see Section 3.4.2 for more details on the upwind method. The final code can be found at `src/jet/iterative_level_set_solver3.cpp`.

In this book, we classified `UpwindLevelSetSolver3` and `EnoLevelSetSolver3` as iterative level set solvers since they iteratively refine the solution by minimizing $|\nabla\phi| - 1$. Depending on the way of calculating the derivative from `getDerivatives`, the class `IterativeLevelSetSolver3` has subclasses such as `UpwindLevelSetSolver3` which is the first-order accurate level set solver and `EnoLevelSetSolver3` which is used as third-order essentially nonoscillatory (ENO) method [108]. There are other methods that directly solve $|\nabla\phi| = 1$ condition, such as the fast-marching method (FMM) and the fast-sweeping method (FSM). Interested readers can refer to Sethian [105] or Zhao [124,125].

3.6.2 Free-Surface Flow

When simulating fluid motion with grids, there are four key steps to solve: advection, gravity (and external forces), viscosity, and pressure. Since we now have two different fluids in the system, the underlying model is going to change, and these four steps should be revisited.

The fluid dynamics of multiple fluids in the system is called multiphase fluid flow, and typically it is simulated by incorporating different density and viscosity coefficients to the equations [50,62,110]. Solving multiphase fluid flow is required when the dynamics of both the fluids is important, such as a bubbly flow [50,69]. However, if one fluid is dominant in the scene, we can simplify the other fluid's dynamics. Especially when simulating a scene with the air where air is not the dominant fluid, we can approximate the air and give less consideration to its contribution to the water flow. This is called a free-surface fluid flow, and the model assumes that the air does not affect the motion of the liquid in terms of pressure and viscosity. Also, the air pressure is often approximated with a constant value. Among many different methods to model liquid motion, we are going to take this free-surface flow model because it is not only one of the most simple methods but also powerful enough to generate realistic fluid simulations.

To get started, let's see how our grid-based liquid simulator looks like from the higher level.

```
class LevelSetLiquidSolver3 : public GridFluidSolver3 {
 public:
    LevelSetLiquidSolver3();

    ...

 protected:
    void onEndAdvanceTimeStep(double timeIntervalInSeconds) override;

    void computePressure(double timeIntervalInSeconds) override;

 private:
    size_t _signedDistanceFieldId;
    LevelSetSolver3Ptr _levelSetSolver;
    double _maxReinitializeDistance = 1.0;

    void reinitialize();

    ...
};
```

As you can see, the class inherits `GridFluidSolver3` and adds the signed-distance field to represent the liquid–air interface. There is also the level set solver that has been discussed earlier. Note that we are overriding two virtual functions: `onEndAdvanceTimeStep` and `computePressure`. This indicates that we will add a postsimulation step as well as a custom pressure solver. Part of the implementation of these functions looks as follows.

```
LevelSetLiquidSolver3::LevelSetLiquidSolver3() {
    auto grids = gridSystemData();
    _signedDistanceFieldId = grids->addAdvectableScalarData(
        CellCenteredScalarGrid3::builder(), kMaxD);
    _levelSetSolver = std::make_shared<EnoLevelSetSolver3>();
}

...

void LevelSetLiquidSolver3::onEndAdvanceTimeStep(double
        timeIntervalInSeconds) {
    reinitialize();
    ...
}

void LevelSetLiquidSolver3::reinitialize() {
    if (_levelSetSolver != nullptr) {
```

```
17          auto sdf = signedDistanceField();
18          auto sdf0 = sdf->clone();
19
20          _levelSetSolver->reinitialize(
21              *sdf0, _maxReinitializeDistance, sdf.get());
22          extrapolateIntoCollider(sdf.get());
23      }
24  }
```

From the constructor, we are adding the signed-distance field as an advectable grid channel to the grid system. Thus, the advection of the field will be handled by the parent class. Also, we are setting `EnoLevelSetSolver3` as the default level set solver. In the postprocessing step (`onEndAdvanceTimeStep`), we call for `reinitialize` function to fix the distorted signed-distance field.

The above code mainly shows the integration of the level set solver into the grid-based fluid simulator. But what about the dynamics itself? As mentioned, we are introducing the free-surface model to simulate liquids. What does it mean to the advection, gravity, viscosity, and pressure?

First, let's start with the most simplest step, that is, the gravity. The gravity applies to the entire domain without exception, which means that the same constant acceleration is assigned for both the air and the liquid region. Therefore, we don't need to change the code, but only leave the implementation from the parent class, `GridFluidSolver3`.

Next, consider the advection. As described earlier, the advection of the surface itself can be solved by applying the advection solver followed by reinitialization. The underlying velocity field, however, needs a bit more thinking. The free-surface flow model does not define the dynamics of the air region. Thus, we do not have proper velocity field in the air. To make the advection solvers work, however, we need a velocity field at least near the liquid surface. Imagine a ball of liquid in the air as shown in Figure 3.25. Even if the velocity field is assigned inside the ball, applying the advection solver doesn't work because of the back-tracing nature of the advection solver. To solve the issue, we can extrapolate the liquid velocity at the surface to the air region by using the function `extrapolateToRegion` from Section 3.4.1. See the code below.

```
1  class LevelSetLiquidSolver3 : public GridFluidSolver3 {
2      ...
3
4      void extrapolateVelocityToAir();
5  };
6
7  void LevelSetLiquidSolver3::extrapolateVelocityToAir() {
8      if (_levelSetSolver != nullptr) {
9          auto sdf = signedDistanceField();
10         auto vel = gridSystemData()->velocity();
11
12         auto u = vel->uAccessor();
```

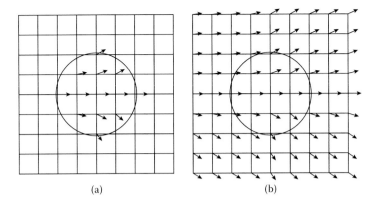

FIGURE 3.25
Velocity field defined only inside the surface (a) and extrapolated to the external region (b).

```
13        auto v = vel->vAccessor();
14        auto w = vel->wAccessor();
15        auto uPos = vel->uPosition();
16        auto vPos = vel->vPosition();
17        auto wPos = vel->wPosition();
18
19        Array3<char> uMarker(u.size());
20        Array3<char> vMarker(v.size());
21        Array3<char> wMarker(w.size());
22
23        uMarker.parallelForEachIndex([&](size_t i, size_t j, size_t k) {
24            if (isInsideSdf(sdf->sample(uPos(i, j, k)))) {
25                uMarker(i, j, k) = 1;
26            } else {
27                uMarker(i, j, k) = 0;
28            }
29        });
30
31        vMarker.parallelForEachIndex([&](size_t i, size_t j, size_t k) {
32            if (isInsideSdf(sdf->sample(vPos(i, j, k)))) {
33                vMarker(i, j, k) = 1;
34            } else {
35                vMarker(i, j, k) = 0;
36            }
37        });
38
39        wMarker.parallelForEachIndex([&](size_t i, size_t j, size_t k) {
40            if (isInsideSdf(sdf->sample(wPos(i, j, k)))) {
41                wMarker(i, j, k) = 1;
42            } else {
```

```
43                    wMarker(i, j, k) = 0;
44                }
45            });
46
47            unsigned int depth
48                = static_cast<unsigned int>(std::ceil(maxCfl()));
49            extrapolateToRegion(vel->uConstAccessor(), uMarker, depth, u);
50            extrapolateToRegion(vel->vConstAccessor(), vMarker, depth, v);
51            extrapolateToRegion(vel->wConstAccessor(), wMarker, depth, w);
52
53            applyBoundaryCondition();
54        }
55    }
```

The code itself is pretty straightforward. It first marks each grid point with 1 if the point is inside the liquid and sets 0 otherwise. Then, each of the u, v, and w components is extrapolated to the nonliquid region, which is the air. Similar to how we extrapolated fields into the colliders in Section 3.4.1, the maximum extrapolation distance is determined by the maximum CFL number.

This extrapolation process actually applies the Neumann boundary condition at the interface. The velocity does not change across the interface in the surface normal direction. So more formally, we can say

$$\frac{\partial v}{\partial n} = 0 \tag{3.63}$$

where v is the velocity and n is the surface normal. We just solved this boundary condition for the advection problem by extrapolating the velocity in the normal direction.

Now let's talk about the viscosity. Again, the free-surface model does not consider the interaction between the air and the liquid. Thus, we only need to solve the diffusion inside the liquid volume. This can be achieved by simply excluding the air region from the computation and applying the Neumann boundary condition when the adjacent grid point falls into the air region, just like treating the solid boundary condition as a Neumann. For example, the backward Euler implementation from Section 3.4.4 can be updated as follows:

```
1    const char kFluid = 0;
2    const char kAir = 1;
3    const char kBoundary = 2;
4
5    ...
6
7    void GridBackwardEulerDiffusionSolver2::buildMarkers(
8        const Size2& size,
9        const std::function<Vector2D(size_t, size_t)>& pos,
10       const ScalarField2& boundarySdf,
```

```
11        const ScalarField2& fluidSdf) {
12        _markers.resize(size);
13
14        _markers.parallelForEachIndex(
15            [&](size_t i, size_t j) {
16                if (isInsideSdf(boundarySdf.sample(pos(i, j)))) {
17                    _markers(i, j) = kBoundary;
18                } else if (isInsideSdf(fluidSdf.sample(pos(i, j)))) {
19                    _markers(i, j) = kFluid;
20                } else {
21                    _markers(i, j) = kAir;
22                }
23            });
24    }
25
26    void GridBackwardEulerDiffusionSolver3::buildMatrix(
27        const Size3& size,
28        const Vector3D& c) {
29        _system.A.resize(size);
30
31        bool isDirichlet = (_boundaryType == Dirichlet);
32
33        // Build linear system
34        _system.A.parallelForEachIndex([&](size_t i, size_t j, size_t k) {
35            auto& row = _system.A(i, j, k);
36
37            // Initialize
38            row.center = 1.0;
39            row.right = row.up = row.front = 0.0;
40
41            if (_markers(i, j, k) == kFluid) {
42                if (i + 1 < size.x) {
43                    if ((isDirichlet && _markers(i + 1, j, k) != kAir)
44                        || _markers(i + 1, j, k) == kFluid) {
45                        row.center += c.x;
46                    }
47
48                    if (_markers(i + 1, j, k) == kFluid) {
49                        row.right -=  c.x;
50                    }
51                }
52
53                if (i > 0
54                    && ((isDirichlet && _markers(i - 1, j, k) != kAir)
55                        || _markers(i - 1, j, k) == kFluid)) {
56                    row.center += c.x;
57                }
58
59                ...
```

```
60          }
61      });
62  }
```

Note that the signed-distance field that represents the liquid–air interface is added, and the air region is tagged separately as kAir. When building the matrix, the marker is checked to see if the neighboring grid point is in the air region. If true, its contribution is excluded from the matrix, which means that it is a Neumann condition. For more details about building the matrix, see Section 3.4.4.

Finally, there is the pressure element. The free-surface model assumes that the pressure of the air is constant. To make it simpler, let's assume that it is zero. This is a Dirichlet boundary condition, similar to the example in Section 3.4.4. The pressure equation in 1D from Section 3.4.5 can be written as:

$$\frac{p_{i+1}^* - 2p_i^* + p_{i-1}^*}{\Delta x^2} = \frac{u_{i+1/2}^n - u_{i-1/2}^n}{\Delta x} \tag{3.64}$$

Now imagine that point $i + 1$ is in the air region. Based on the assumption, which states that the pressure at $i + 1$ is zero, Equation 3.64 now becomes

$$\frac{-2p_i^* + p_{i-1}^*}{\Delta x^2} = \frac{u_{i+1/2}^n - u_{i-1/2}^n}{\Delta x}. \tag{3.65}$$

So by simply excluding the contribution of the off-diagonal matrix element, we can solve the pressure equation for the free-surface fluid flow. The code for building the matrix can be written as follows:

```cpp
1   const char kFluid = 0;
2   const char kAir = 1;
3   const char kBoundary = 2;
4
5   ...
6
7   void GridSinglePhasePressureSolver3::buildMarkers(
8       const Size3& size,
9       const std::function<Vector3D(size_t, size_t, size_t)>& pos,
10      const ScalarField3& fluidSdf,
11      const ScalarField3& boundarySdf) {
12      _markers.resize(size);
13      _markers.parallelForEachIndex([&](size_t i, size_t j, size_t k) {
14          Vector3D pt = pos(i, j, k);
15          if (isInsideSdf(boundarySdf.sample(pt))) {
16              _markers(i, j, k) = kBoundary;
17          } else if (isInsideSdf(fluidSdf.sample(pt))) {
18              _markers(i, j, k) = kFluid;
19          } else {
20              _markers(i, j, k) = kAir;
21          }
```

```
22            });
23      }
24
25      void GridSinglePhasePressureSolver3::buildSystem(
26          const FaceCenteredGrid3& input) {
27          ...
28
29          // Build linear system
30          _system.A.parallelForEachIndex([&](size_t i, size_t j, size_t k) {
31              auto& row = _system.A(i, j, k);
32
33              // initialize
34              row.center = row.right = row.up = row.front = 0.0;
35              _system.b(i, j, k) = 0.0;
36
37              if (_markers(i, j, k) == kFluid) {
38                  _system.b(i, j, k) = input.divergenceAtCellCenter(i, j, k);
39
40                  if (i + 1 < size.x && _markers(i + 1, j, k) != kBoundary) {
41                      row.center += invHSqr.x;
42                      if (_markers(i + 1, j, k) == kFluid) {
43                          row.right -= invHSqr.x;
44                      }
45                  }
46
47                  if (i > 0 && _markers(i - 1, j, k) != kBoundary) {
48                      row.center += invHSqr.x;
49                  }
50
51                  // Repeat the same process for j + 1, j - 1, k + 1, and k - 1.
52                  ...
53              }
54          }
55      }
```

Similar to the viscosity problem, we now classify the grid point into three categories: fluid, air, and boundary. When building the matrix, the off-diagonal element is excluded from the system by checking whether it is not marked as air (Line 42).

Now, similar to the Lego-block problem in Section 3.4.5, the interpretation of the liquid region by only looking up the sign from its signed-distance field can cause the aliasing effect. This artifact is even more serious than the collider boundary handling problem because the liquid surface is visible and the aliasing noise can impact the visual appearance. To solve this problem, Enright et al. [38] used the ghost fluid method (GFM) to solve free-surface flow. The GFM was invented for capturing such a subcell resolution phenomenon [43] and is very similar to the fractional approach for solving the Lego-boundary problem.

To apply the GFM, let's bring back the previous 1D example. Starting from Equation 3.64 again, assume that the interface is between i and $i+1$ grid points and the distance to the surface from i is $\theta\Delta x$, where $0 \leq \theta \leq 1$. Rewriting Equation 3.64 becomes

$$\frac{\frac{p^*_{i+1}-p^*_i}{\Delta x} - \frac{p^*_i-p^*_{i-1}}{\Delta x}}{\Delta x} = \frac{u^n_{i+1/2} - u^n_{i-1/2}}{\Delta x} \tag{3.66}$$

Now imagine that there is a grid point at the surface which is θ away from i. We can then say

$$\frac{\frac{p^*_\theta-p^*_i}{\theta\Delta x} - \frac{p^*_i-p^*_{i-1}}{\Delta x}}{\Delta x} = \frac{u^n_{i+1/2} - u^n_{i-1/2}}{\Delta x} \tag{3.67}$$

Since $p^*_\theta = 0$, the final equation can be written as:

$$\frac{-p^*_i}{\theta\Delta x^2} - \frac{p^*_i - p^*_{i-1}}{\Delta x^2} = \frac{u^n_{i+1/2} - u^n_{i-1/2}}{\Delta x} \tag{3.68}$$

Note that θ is in the denominator which can be problematic when $\theta = 0$. In such cases, we can clamp θ to a small value, such as 0.01.

In the codebase, the GFM is implemented together with the fractional boundary handling code as shown below.

```
1   void GridFractionalSinglePhasePressureSolver3::buildSystem(
2       const FaceCenteredGrid3& input) {
3       Size3 size = input.resolution();
4       _system.A.resize(size);
5       _system.x.resize(size);
6       _system.b.resize(size);
7
8       Vector3D invH = 1.0 / input.gridSpacing();
9       Vector3D invHSqr = invH * invH;
10
11      // Build linear system
12      _system.A.parallelForEachIndex([&](size_t i, size_t j, size_t k) {
13          auto& row = _system.A(i, j, k);
14
15          // initialize
16          row.center = row.right = row.up = row.front = 0.0;
17          _system.b(i, j, k) = 0.0;
18
19          double centerPhi = _fluidSdf(i, j, k);
20
21          if (isInsideSdf(centerPhi)) {
22              double term;
23
24              if (i + 1 < size.x) {
25                  term = _uWeights(i + 1, j, k) * invHSqr.x;
```

```
26              double rightPhi = _fluidSdf(i + 1, j, k);
27              if (isInsideSdf(rightPhi)) {
28                  row.center += term;
29                  row.right -= term;
30              } else {
31                  double theta = fractionInsideSdf(centerPhi, rightPhi);
32                  theta = std::max(theta, 0.01);
33                  row.center += term / theta;
34              }
35              _system.b(i, j, k)
36                  += _uWeights(i + 1, j, k)
37                  * input.u(i + 1, j, k) * invH.x;
38          } else {
39              _system.b(i, j, k) += input.u(i + 1, j, k) * invH.x;
40          }
41
42          if (i > 0) {
43              term = _uWeights(i, j, k) * invHSqr.x;
44              double leftPhi = _fluidSdf(i - 1, j, k);
45              if (isInsideSdf(leftPhi)) {
46                  row.center += term;
47              } else {
48                  double theta = fractionInsideSdf(centerPhi, leftPhi);
49                  theta = std::max(theta, 0.01);
50                  row.center += term / theta;
51              }
52              _system.b(i, j, k)
53                  -= _uWeights(i, j, k) * input.u(i, j, k) * invH.x;
54          } else {
55              _system.b(i, j, k) -= input.u(i, j, k) * invH.x;
56          }
57
58          // Repeat the same process for j + 1, j - 1, k + 1, and k - 1.
59          ...
60
61      } else {
62          row.center = 1.0;
63      }
64  });
65 }
66
67 void GridFractionalSinglePhasePressureSolver3::applyPressureGradient(
68     const FaceCenteredGrid3& input,
69     FaceCenteredGrid3* output) {
70     Size3 size = input.resolution();
71     auto u = input.uConstAccessor();
72     auto v = input.vConstAccessor();
73     auto w = input.wConstAccessor();
74     auto u0 = output->uAccessor();
```

```
75      auto v0 = output->vAccessor();
76      auto w0 = output->wAccessor();
77
78      Vector3D invH = 1.0 / input.gridSpacing();
79
80      _system.x.parallelForEachIndex([&](size_t i, size_t j, size_t k) {
81          double centerPhi = _fluidSdf(i, j, k);
82
83          if (i + 1 < size.x
84              && _uWeights(i + 1, j, k) > 0.0
85              && (isInsideSdf(centerPhi)
86                  || isInsideSdf(_fluidSdf(i + 1, j, k)))) {
87              double rightPhi = _fluidSdf(i + 1, j, k);
88              double theta = fractionInsideSdf(centerPhi, rightPhi);
89              theta = std::max(theta, 0.01);
90
91              u0(i + 1, j, k)
92                  = u(i + 1, j, k)
93                  + invH.x / theta
94                  * (_system.x(i + 1, j, k) - _system.x(i, j, k));
95          }
96
97          // Repeat the same process for j + 1, j - 1, k + 1, and k - 1.
98          ...
99      });
100 }
```

3.6.3 Results

Figure 3.26 shows an example from the liquid simulator. When a chunk of water volume is dropped into the tank, the level set–based free-surface flow simulator generates realistic waves and splashes. Using the same configuration, a different simulation result with higher viscosity is shown in Figure 3.27. The simulation was performed using the backward Euler diffusion solver from Section 3.4.4. Note that the initial shape tends to remain and the fluid looks like honey or glue. The example images were rendered by using Mitsuba renderer [59].

3.7 Discussion and Further Reading

In this chapter, we have covered the grid-based approach for simulating fluids including the submodules—advection, gravity, viscosity, and pressure. To enable larger time-stepping, we implemented the semi-Lagrangian advection scheme as well as the backward Euler diffusion solver. We also achieved the

FIGURE 3.26
Sample simulation results from the free-surface solver. A bunny-shaped water chunk is dropped into an invisible tank. The simulation is generated using a 150^3 resolution grid.

incompressibility by computing the PPE using linear system solvers. Based on this foundation, we extended the implementation to the smoke solver. Also, we combined the level set method and the base solver to build a free-surface liquid simulation.

The advantage of the grid-based fluid simulation mainly comes from the structured discretizations. The numerical operators are well defined, and the solution is smooth, compared to the particle-based methods. Also, it is easier to form a linear system that allows better numerical stability compared to other unstructured or meshfree methods.

The drawback of the grid-based approach includes numerical dissipation. Unlike particle-based methods, which carry the physical quantities using particles, the grid-based methods transfer from one grid point to another by

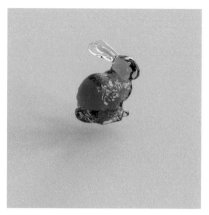 

FIGURE 3.27
Free-surface flow simulation using the same configuration as Figure 3.26, except for the higher viscosity.

explicitly solving the advection equation. During the process, we use interpolation which causes artificial diffusion as shown in Figure 3.15. When the error appears on the velocity field, we see too much viscosity, losing lots of interesting motions such as swirls. From the level set simulation, we see volume loss; the thin or sharp feature of the fluid gets vanished in the air. Also, unlike the particle-based methods that only require particle points where the fluid is, a grid-based simulation requires discretization of the entire domain, meaning that the empty region that fluid does not occupy also needs grid points.

To overcome the limits of the grid-based simulation, a wide range of studies have been conducted. Instead of the uniform Cartesian grids, adaptive data structures to put more grid points near the area of interest were introduced by using octrees [11,77,123], compressed-grids [53,57], or domain extension [126]. Methods to improve the accuracy of the solvers with same grid resolution have been studied as well [49,64,67,102]. Also, while the free-surface model does not capture the interaction between the liquid and the air, coupling the dynamics to simulate bubbles [28,50,110], multiple fluids [78], or with solid objects are also active research areas. Liquid and gas are not the only fluids that the grid-based framework can simulate. The grid-based framework can also handle fires [44,52,94] or explosions [94], too.

We have learned the pros and cons of both the particle-based and the grid-based methods. Obviously, one may wonder that why can't we mix the two? In the following chapter, we will cover how to hybridize two heterogeneous frameworks to leverage the strength of both particles and grids.

4

Hybrid Solvers

4.1 Why Hybrid?

As discussed earlier, conventional particle-based and grid-based approaches have their own pros and cons. The particle-based methods, such as SPH, conserve mass and momentum better than the grid-based methods in general. Also, the computation is relatively simpler and can interact with arbitrary geometry quite easily. On the contrary, the results are noisy sometimes, and the maximum time-step is often limited. The grid-based methods, however, tends to produce smoother results and the allowed time-step is relatively large. However, the numerical diffusion makes the fluid volume dissipate and introduces artificial viscosity. So it becomes quite natural that we would want to combine these two heterogeneous frameworks and come up with a hybrid framework. In this chapter, we are going to cover a number of hybrid methods to overcome the problems we have with the purely particle-based or grid-based approaches.

4.2 Particle-in-Cell Method

As the name suggests, particle-in-cell (PIC) method is a framework that tracks particles in grid cells [41,46,47]. So far, we have covered level set–based approach in Section 3.6. Both methods are purely based on grids, and therefore suffer from numerical diffusion which causes loss of details and volume. PIC method, on the contrary, tracks fluid volume in a Lagrangian manner so that it does not introduce interpolation error from the semi-Lagrangian method. It may sound similar to SPH from Section 2.3, but the key difference is that SPH considers per-particle interaction whereas PIC only uses particles to mark grid cells whether it is occupied or not, so that the particle interaction within a grid cell is ignored. This may result in clustered particles since per-particle collisions are not resolved. But at the same time, computing pressure to make the fluid incompressible with grid will let PIC avoid oscillations or compressions that can lead to numerical instability.

Figure 4.1 shows the overview of the PIC algorithm from the higher level. Starting from the particles, the solver transfers the velocities from particles

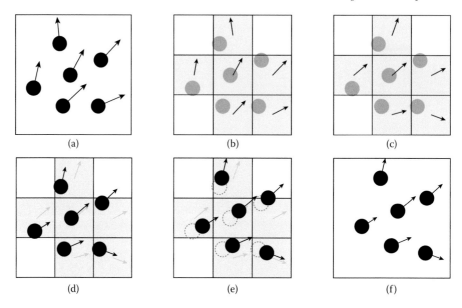

(a) (b) (c)

(d) (e) (f)

FIGURE 4.1
Overview of the PIC method. A PIC-step starts with particles (a). The velocity at each particle is then transferred to grids (b), computes nonadvection forces (c), transfers the velocity back to the particles (d), then moves the particles (e), and then the next PIC-step is performed to the final state (f).

to grids using linear interpolation weighting and marks the grid cells that are occupied by the particles. We then compute nonadvection steps from the grid-based solver, including gravity, viscosity, and pressure. Once the grid-based steps are completed, the velocities are transferred back to the particles. Finally, we update the position of the particles by following the underlying flow from the grid. A physics solver class that encapsulates the process is shown below.

```
1   class PicSolver3 : public GridFluidSolver3 {
2   public:
3       PicSolver3();
4
5       virtual ~PicSolver3();
6
7       ScalarGrid3Ptr signedDistanceField() const;
8
9       const ParticleSystemData3Ptr& particleSystemData() const;
10
11  protected:
12      void onBeginAdvanceTimeStep(double timeIntervalInSeconds) override;
```

```
13
14      void computeAdvection(double timeIntervalInSeconds) override;
15
16      ...
17
18      virtual void transferFromParticlesToGrids();
19
20      virtual void transferFromGridsToParticles();
21
22      virtual void moveParticles(double timeIntervalInSeconds);
23
24   private:
25      ...
26
27      void extrapolateVelocityToAir();
28
29      void buildMarkers();
30   };
31
32   ...
33
34   void PicSolver3::onBeginAdvanceTimeStep(double timeIntervalInSeconds) {
35      transferFromParticlesToGrids();
36      buildMarkers();
37      extrapolateVelocityToAir();
38      applyBoundaryCondition();
39   }
40
41   void PicSolver3::computeAdvection(double timeIntervalInSeconds) {
42      extrapolateVelocityToAir();
43      applyBoundaryCondition();
44      transferFromGridsToParticles();
45      moveParticles(timeIntervalInSeconds);
46   }
```

As shown in the overview figure, the solver transfers particle velocity, marks grids where particles are occupying, extends the velocity to the air region, and applies the boundary condition in the preprocessing step onBeginAdvanceTimeStep. You may have noticed that this new solver simulates free-surface flow in Section 3.6 from the velocity extrapolation part. Since one of the advantages of using particles is mass conservation, we will utilize it to simulate dissipation-free liquid animation.

The class also overrides the advection step, computeAdvection, with particle update. The routine is called after the nonadvection steps. Thus, it first starts with extending the velocity to the air region again, followed by constraining the velocity with the boundary condition. Then, we transfer the velocity from grids to particles and move particles.

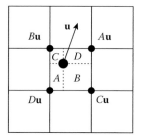

FIGURE 4.2
For a given particle with velocity **u**, the value is distributed to the nearby grid-points with area-based weights A, B, C, and D.

From the code, the PIC-specific part would be the `transfer...` function calls. Let's find out the details of each function.

4.2.1 Particle-to-Grid Transfer

First, consider the particle-to-grid transfer. Figure 4.2 illustrates the simplified 2D example to show how the particle's velocity is distributed to the nearby grid points. The weights, A, B, C, and D, are determined by the area (volume in 3D) within the grid cell. The sum of all the weights is 1. These weights are the same weights we saw from the bilinear interpolation (trilinear in 3D) in Section 1.3.6, but in this case, we perform distribution instead of interpolation.

The actual implementation can be written as follows:

```
1   void PicSolver3::transferFromParticlesToGrids() {
2       ...
3
4       // Clear velocity to zero
5       flow->fill(Vector3D());
6
7       ...
8
9       // Weighted-average velocity
10      for (size_t i = 0; i < numberOfParticles; ++i) {
11          std::array<Point3UI, 8> indices;
12          std::array<double, 8> weights;
13
14          uSampler.getCoordinatesAndWeights(
15              positions[i], &indices, &weights);
16          for (int j = 0; j < 8; ++j) {
17              u(indices[j]) += velocities[i].x * weights[j];
18              uWeight(indices[j]) += weights[j];
19          }
20
```

```
21        // Similar process for v and w
22    }
23
24    uWeight.forEachIndex([&](size_t i, size_t j) {
25        if (uWeight(i, j) > 0.0) {
26            u(i, j) /= uWeight(i, j);
27            _uMarkers(i, j) = 1;
28        }
29    });
30
31    // Similar process for v and w
32 }
```

The function first clears the velocity grid field to zero. Then, for each particle, the weights are accumulated to the nearby grid points. The code uses a utility function `getCoordinatesAndWeights` which can be found in `LinearArraySampler3` class in `include/jet/array_samplers3.h`. Now, since we are using a face-centered grid for storing velocity, we process the accumulation for each u, v, and w. After finishing the accumulation, the weight is normalized. Also, we mark the grid points with any nonzero weight. The marked grid cells are colored gray in Figure 4.1. When determining whether the grid cell is inside the liquid or the air, these markers will be used.

4.2.2 Grid-to-Particle Transfer

After computing gravity, viscosity, and pressure, we transfer the velocity back to the particles. This process is quite simple; It's just a linear interpolation. See the code below.

```
1 void PicSolver3::transferFromGridsToParticles() {
2    ...
3
4    parallelFor(kZeroSize, numberOfParticles, [&](size_t i) {
5        velocities[i] = flow->sample(positions[i]);
6    });
7 }
```

Straightforward isn't it? Let's move on to the next topic.

4.2.3 Moving Particles

To update particles' positions, we perform a similar process in the semi-Lagrangian method (Section 3.4.2) but in the opposite direction. For each particle, we compute its new location using the mid-point rule. The intermediate velocity is determined by evaluating the grid's velocity at a given location. We can also take the substepping if the time-step is too large (thus, CFL number is high) [127]. The corresponding code is shown below.

```
1   void PicSolver2::moveParticles(double timeIntervalInSeconds) {
2       ...
3
4       parallelFor(kZeroSize, numberOfParticles, [&](size_t i) {
5           Vector2D pt0 = positions[i];
6           Vector2D pt1 = pt0;
7
8           // Adaptive time-stepping
9           unsigned int numSubSteps
10              = static_cast<unsigned int>(std::max(maxCfl(), 1.0));
11          double dt = timeIntervalInSeconds / numSubSteps;
12          for (unsigned int t = 0; t < numSubSteps; ++t) {
13              Vector2D vel0 = flow->sample(pt0);
14
15              // Mid-point rule
16              Vector2D midPt = pt0 + 0.5 * dt * vel0;
17              Vector2D midVel = flow->sample(midPt);
18              pt1 = pt0 + dt * midVel;
19
20              pt0 = pt1;
21          }
22
23          // Handle collision
24      });
25  }
```

As you can see, the number of substeps is determined by maximum CFL number. Again, the CFL number represents the maximum number of grid cells the information can propagate. Thus, subdividing the time-step with the max CFL number means we want the particles to travel no more than one grid cell per iteration. Just like the back-tracing from semi-Lagrangian, this will let the solver can handle rotating flow better than the version without substepping.

4.2.4   Results

The example simulation results are shown in Figure 4.3 that are generated with the same dam-breaking experiment configuration of the Predictive-Corrective Incompressible SPH (PCISPH) example (see Figure 2.13). Note that the thin water structure is well-captured during the simulations. This is one of the strengths of the methods using particles. But at the same time, the simulation looks relatively viscous because of the interpolation-based transfers between the grid and particles which introduce numerical dissipation. From the following section, we will see how we can reduce such an artificial damping using a method called FLIP.

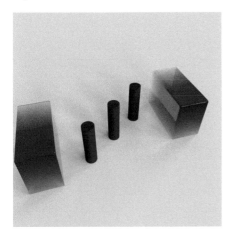

FIGURE 4.3
Sample simulation results from the PIC solver. The water slides interact with solid obstacles and produce splashes. The simulation is performed using 875k particles and $150 \times 100 \times 75$ resolution grid.

4.3 Fluid-Implicit-Particle Method

The main source of the artificial viscosity from the PIC method is in the back and forth interpolation between grid and particles. This seems inevitable because of the nature of the hybrid methods—mixing up heterogeneous discretization frameworks. We can think of introducing the higher-order interpolation methods such as Catmull–Rom spline (Section 3.4.2.3), but still the performance cannot exceed that of the purely grid-based methods. Although the PIC was able to improve the mass conservation problem of the grid,

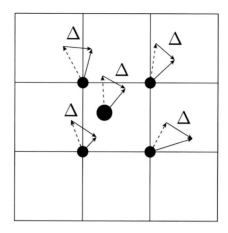

FIGURE 4.4
When transferring velocity from grid to particle, the FLIP method interpolates
only the updated deltas instead of the full velocity.

can't we also adopt the low-dissipation flow from the particle-based methods?
Fortunately, there is a solution.

First introduced to the computational physics world by Brackbill et al. [20]
and adopted to the graphics community by Zhu and Bridson [127], fluid-
implicit-particle (FLIP) method has much less velocity dissipation than the
PIC method. The FLIP method is an extension to the PIC, and in fact, just
adding several lines of code will turn the PIC solver into the FLIP simulator.

When converting velocity from a grid, the PIC simply performs interpolation. Note that the idea of PIC is to delegate the nonadvection (gravity,
viscosity, and pressure) computation from particle to grid. Thus, if we transfer
the delta velocity between, before, and after the nonadvection steps to the particles, we can still achieve the goal. In this case, we don't need to interpolate
the full velocity field, but just the delta velocity which has much smaller magnitude than the actual vector field. Therefore, transferring the delta would
introduce less interpolation error, which means less velocity dissipation. This
is the key idea of the FLIP method which is shown in Figure 4.4.

As mentioned, the implementation of FLIP is extremely simple. Please
take a look at the code below.

```
1   class FlipSolver3 : public PicSolver2 {
2   public:
3       FlipSolver3();
4
5       virtual ~FlipSolver3();
6
7   protected:
8       void transferFromParticlesToGrids() override;
```

```
9
10      void transferFromGridsToParticles() override;
11
12    private:
13      FaceCenteredGrid3 _delta;
14    };
```

The new class, `FlipSolver3`, extends `PicSolver3` which we built from the previous section. There are only two new functions to customize the velocity transfer and one member data to store the delta velocity. The implementation of each function is shown below.

```
1   void FlipSolver3::transferFromParticlesToGrids() {
2       PicSolver3::transferFromParticlesToGrids();
3
4       // Store snapshot
5       _delta.set(*gridSystemData()->velocity());
6   }
7
8   void FlipSolver3::transferFromGridsToParticles() {
9       auto flow = gridSystemData()->velocity();
10      auto positions = particleSystemData()->positions();
11      auto velocities = particleSystemData()->velocities();
12      size_t numberOfParticles = particleSystemData()->numberOfParticles();
13
14      // Compute delta
15      flow->parallelForEachU([&](size_t i, size_t j, size_t k) {
16          _delta.u(i, j, k) = flow->u(i, j, k) - _delta.u(i, j, k);
17      });
18
19      ...
20
21      // Transfer delta to the particles
22      parallelFor(kZeroSize, numberOfParticles, [&](size_t i) {
23          velocities[i] += _delta.sample(positions[i]);
24      });
25  }
```

From `transferFromParticlesToGrids`, it takes the snapshot of the velocity on grids after the particles-to-grids transfer. Then, from `transferFromGridsToParticles`, the delta velocity is computed and applied to the particles.

4.3.1 Results

Figure 4.5 shows the examples from the FLIP solver. Under the same configuration, the results from FLIP shows less velocity dissipation compared with the PIC results (Figure 4.3). Again, the example images were rendered using Mitsuba renderer [59].

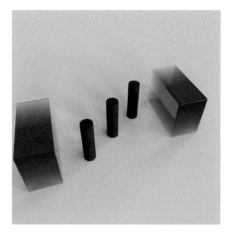

FIGURE 4.5
Sample simulation results from the FLIP solver. The water slides interact
with solid obstacles and produce bigger splashes than the result from the PIC
solver. The simulation is performed using 875k particles and $150 \times 100 \times 75$
resolution grid.

Due to its stable, but less-dissipative solution, the FLIP method is one of
the most popular fluid solvers in the commercial software packages, such as
RealFlow [5], Houdini [2], and Naiad [17].

4.4   Other Methods

So far, we have covered PIC-style methods. Although not currently implemented in our codebase, the rest of the chapter will briefly cover two notable
hybrid methods—particle level set and vortex particle method.

4.4.1 Particle Level Set Method

While the PIC and FLIP methods focus on velocity transfers, the particle level set method concentrates on the geometry fixes. As discussed in Chapter 3, the liquid simulator using level set suffers from the mass dissipation problem mainly due to the grid-based advection and reinitialization. The particle level set method solves the problem by fixing the level set solution using particles with signed distance. If the particles are on the other side of the interface after advection or reinitialization, there could have been numerical diffusion. In such a case, the signed-distance field is fixed geometrically by the particles, assuming that the particles are spheres. The idea was first proposed by Enright et al. [36,37] to resolve highly detailed geometric features using particle-grid hybrid level set even under severe distortions. Figure 4.6 shows one of the example simulations using particle level set method. Note that the thin structure of the sprays is well preserved.

The "escaped" particles that are on the other side of the interface can also be utilized to create secondary spray or foams. Naturally, we can apply particle-based methods, such as simple free-flight model or even full-SPH, to solve those sprays as shown in many studies [79,110]. Similarly, a number of studies on simulating bubbly flows by simulating escaped *air* particles are also introduced [51,69].

While the particle level set method focuses on preserving the volume, the vortex particle method tries to keep the vorticity of the velocity field. Let's find out what is the basic idea behind the method.

4.4.2 Vortex Particle Method

One of the properties that make fluid flows look dynamic is the vorticity. It is evaluated by the curl operator (Section 3.3) applied to the velocity field, and it represents the rotational flow of the fluid. Although such vorticity makes

FIGURE 4.6
Example of a simulation using the particle level set method from Kim et al. [68]. The emitters are injecting thin liquid sprays into the tank.

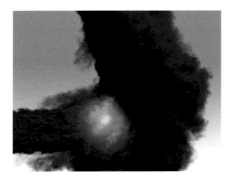 

FIGURE 4.7
Examples using the vortex particle method. (From D. Kim, S.W. Lee, O.-Y. Song, and H.-S. Ko. Baroclinic turbulence with varying density and temperature. *IEEE Transactions on Visualization and Computer Graphics*, 18(9): 1488–1495, © (2012) IEEE.)

realistic turbulence-like animation, it is often lost when solving the advection step due to the numerical dissipation. Thus, many works in the literature discuss various kinds of approaches to preserve or revive the vorticities [42], and one such method is called the vortex particle method [66,97,103,121]. Figure 4.7 shows some of the examples from the vortex particle simulation.

Similar to other hybrid methods that let the particles solve the advection problem by carrying specific physical quantities, the vortex particle method, as the name suggests, lets the particles transfer the vorticities. After moving the particles like PIC or FLIP, the velocity integrated from the vorticity is accumulated to the nearby grid points. More intuitively, it can be viewed as the particle stirs the flow (add more vorticity) where it lands, based on the magnitude and rotational axis that are carried by the particles.

4.5 Discussion and Further Reading

In this chapter, we covered PIC and FLIP algorithms which combine both particles and grids. The PIC method solves the advection problem using particles, and other forces, such as gravity, viscosity, and pressure, are computed using grids. This approach has an advantage in preserving mass or volume but introduces even more artificial viscosity into the system. The improved PIC method, FLIP, solves the numerical diffusion by transferring the delta-velocity between the particles and grids, instead of the full velocity field.

Although hybrid methods resolve some artifacts from particles or grids, we cannot say the hybrid is "better" than the purely Lagrangian-based or Eulerian-based approaches. Since the PIC-type methods use particles to represent fluid volume, they are not free from the blobby surface that other particle-based methods have. Also, the methods still require background grids, meaning the computational domain and number of the discretization points increases as the particles spread out in space. Thus, the hybrid methods do inherit some of the disadvantages from both particles and grids.

Depending on the targeting fluid phenomena, the simulation method should be carefully selected. For instance, SPH or FLIP methods are preferred when simulating sprays or splashes in general. For smoke or fire simulation, grid-based methods which can generate smooth results would be the better choice. For animating a mid- to large-scale body of water, the level set method will create realistic waves. In the case of a highly viscous flow, such as muds or even sands, PIC method can efficiently generate the animation [127].

There are many other interesting topics this book couldn't cover. For instance, simulating liquid surface with explicit triangular mesh [120], soap bubble films [33,63], or simulating oceanic scale of fluid dynamics using height field [115] are worth investigating further. To learn more about more areas and to follow the state-of-the-art research on fluid animation, check out the presentations and papers from computer graphics conferences, such as ACM SIGGRAPH, Eurographics, or Symposium on Computer Animation. The course notes from many schools and conferences are great materials, too. Bridson's book on fluid simulation [21] also provides an insightful explanation of computational fluid dynamics for computer graphics applications.

A

More on Basics

A.1 CG and PCG Implementation

As described in Shewchuk 1994 [107], the PCG algorithm can be written as follows:

```
 1  void pcg(A, x, b) {
 2      Build preconditioner M from A
 3
 4      Compute r = b − Ax
 5
 6      Solve d = M⁻¹r
 7
 8      Solve σⁿᵉʷ = r · d
 9
10      while (σⁿᵉʷ > tolerance² && i < maxIter) {
11          q = Ad
12
13          α = σⁿᵉʷ/d · q
14
15          x = x + αd
16
17          if (i % 50 == 0) {
18              r = b − Ax
19          } else {
20              r = r − αq
21          }
22
23          s = M⁻¹r
24
25          σᵒˡᵈ = σⁿᵉʷ
26
27          σⁿᵉʷ = r · s
28
29          β = σⁿᵉʷ/σᵒˡᵈ
30
31          d = s + βd
32      }
33  }
```

To implement the algorithm above, we need two additional modules—the linear algebra routines and the preconditioner. The linear algebra routine module provides basic matrix and vector operations such as set, copy, multiplication, dot product, and norms. Consider the following interface:

```
template <typename S, typename V, typename M>
struct Blas {
    typedef S ScalarType;
    typedef V VectorType;
    typedef M MatrixType;

    // Sets the given scalar value to the output vector.
    static void set(ScalarType s, VectorType* result);

    // Sets the given vector to the output vector.
    static void set(const VectorType& v, VectorType* result);

    // Sets the given scalar value to the output matrix.
    static void set(ScalarType s, MatrixType* result);

    // Sets the given matrix to the output matrix.
    static void set(const MatrixType& m, MatrixType* result);

    // Performs dot product.
    static ScalarType dot(const VectorType& a, const VectorType& b);

    // Calculates a*x + y.
    static void axpy(
        ScalarType a,
        const VectorType& x,
        const VectorType& y,
        VectorType* result);

    // Performs matrix-vector multiplication.
    static void mvm(
        const MatrixType& m,
        const VectorType& v,
        VectorType* result);

    // Calculates b - A*x.
    static void residual(
        const MatrixType& a,
        const VectorType& x,
        const VectorType& b,
        VectorType* result);

    // Returns the length of the vector.
    static ScalarType l2Norm(const VectorType& v);
```

```
45      // Returns the absolute maximum value among the vector elements.
46      static ScalarType lInfNorm(const VectorType& v);
47    };
```

The code above lists the linear algebra routines. Name of the struct, `Blas`, comes from BLAS (Basic Linear Algebra Subprograms) [75] but much simplified.

Then, a preconditioner object is used to compute the preconditioning matrix from a system matrix when solving CG. Consider the following code:

```
1    template <typename BlasType>
2    struct NullCgPreconditioner final {
3        void build(const typename BlasType::MatrixType&) {}
4
5        void solve(
6            const typename BlasType::VectorType& b,
7            typename BlasType::VectorType* x) {
8            BlasType::set(b, x);
9        }
10   };
```

The struct above builds a null preconditioner, hence $\mathbf{M} = \mathbf{I}$. This preconditioner does nothing when the `build` function is called. The function `solve` computes $x = \mathbf{M}^{-1}\mathbf{b}$, and in this particular case, it simply copies b to x.

Using all these infrastructures—the linear algebra routines and preconditioner—we can implement the CG as shown here.

```
1    template <typename BlasType>
2    void cg(
3        const typename BlasType::MatrixType& A,
4        const typename BlasType::VectorType& b,
5        unsigned int maxNumberOfIterations,
6        double tolerance,
7        typename BlasType::VectorType* x,
8        typename BlasType::VectorType* r,
9        typename BlasType::VectorType* d,
10       typename BlasType::VectorType* q,
11       typename BlasType::VectorType* s,
12       unsigned int* lastNumberOfIterations,
13       double* lastResidual) {
14       typedef NullCgPreconditioner<BlasType> PrecondType;
15       PrecondType precond;
16       pcg<BlasType, PrecondType>(
17           A,
18           b,
19           maxNumberOfIterations,
20           tolerance,
21           &precond,
```

```
22            x,
23            r,
24            d,
25            q,
26            s,
27            lastNumberOfIterations,
28            lastResidual);
29    }
```

Note that the function `cg` is calling `pcg` with a null preconditioner. Based on the algorithm shown at the beginning of this section, the function `pcg` can be written as follows:

```
1    template <
2        typename BlasType,
3        typename PrecondType>
4    void pcg(
5        const typename BlasType::MatrixType& A,
6        const typename BlasType::VectorType& b,
7        unsigned int maxNumberOfIterations,
8        double tolerance,
9        PrecondType* M,
10       typename BlasType::VectorType* x,
11       typename BlasType::VectorType* r,
12       typename BlasType::VectorType* d,
13       typename BlasType::VectorType* q,
14       typename BlasType::VectorType* s,
15       unsigned int* lastNumberOfIterations,
16       double* lastResidual) {
17       BlasType::set(0, r);
18       BlasType::set(0, d);
19       BlasType::set(0, q);
20       BlasType::set(0, s);
21
22       M->build(A);
23
24       BlasType::residual(A, *x, b, r);
25
26       M->solve(*r, d);
27
28       double sigmaNew = BlasType::dot(*r, *d);
29       double sigma0 = sigmaNew;
30
31       unsigned int iter = 0;
32       while (sigmaNew > square(tolerance) * sigma0
33               && iter < maxNumberOfIterations) {
34           BlasType::mvm(A, *d, q);
35
36           double alpha = sigmaNew / BlasType::dot(*d, *q);
```

```
37
38        BlasType::axpy(alpha, *d, *x, x);
39
40        if (iter % 50 == 0 && iter > 0) {
41            BlasType::residual(A, *x, b, r);
42        } else {
43            BlasType::axpy(-alpha, *q, *r, r);
44        }
45
46        M->solve(*r, s);
47
48        double sigmaOld = sigmaNew;
49
50        sigmaNew = BlasType::dot(*r, *s);
51
52        double beta = sigmaNew / sigmaOld;
53
54        BlasType::axpy(beta, *d, *s, d);
55
56        ++iter;
57    }
58
59    *lastNumberOfIterations = iter;
60    *lastResidual = sigmaNew;
61 }
```

A.2   Adaptive Time Stepping

In Section 1.6, we discussed how the PhysicsAnimation class should call onAdvanceTimeStep during an upate cycle. The class was assuming that the time-step is identical to the frame time interval, but often this can introduce large numerical errors such that the simulation results are far from the real physical phenomena. Thus, although the commonly used frame rates are $1/24$, $1/30$, or $1/60$, we often want even smaller time intervals. For example, if some objects are moving too fast such that 30 or 60 FPS is still too large to capture finer details, we may want to divide a frame into smaller subframes. We can either fix the amount of subdivision of time interval or adaptively refine the time-steps based on the current simulation state. If it is too obvious that the simulation we are running will require small time-steps for an entire animation, then fixed time-stepping would be desirable. But if the simulation can handle large time-steps, but only requires smaller steps under special circumstances, the adaptive approach will save lots of computational costs. Such substeppings can be implemented within the function advanceTimeStep in PhysicsAnimaion class, and higher level implementation is shown below.

```
1   void PhysicsAnimation::advanceTimeStep(double timeIntervalInSeconds) {
2       if (_isUsingFixedSubTimeSteps) {
3           // Perform fixed time-stepping
4           ...
5       } else {
6           // Perform adaptive time-stepping
7           ...
8       }
9   }
```

Depending on the member variable _isUsingFixedSubTimeSteps, this code will either uniformly divide the given time-interval into multiple fixed smaller time-steps or perform adaptive sampling. Starting with the simpler version, the fixed time-stepping, it can be written as:

```
1   void PhysicsAnimation::advanceTimeStep(double timeIntervalInSeconds) {
2       if (_isUsingFixedSubTimeSteps) {
3           // Perform fixed time-stepping
4           const double actualTimeInterval
5               = timeIntervalInSeconds
6               / static_cast<double>(_numberOfFixedSubTimeSteps);
7           for (unsigned int i = 0; i < _numberOfFixedSubTimeSteps; ++i) {
8               onAdvanceTimeStep(actualTimeInterval);
9           }
10      } else {
11          // Perform adaptive time-stepping
12          ...
13      }
14  }
```

This is quite straightforward—just divide the given time interval into smaller sub-intervals, and advance multiple times. The adaptive time-stepping is slightly more complicated, though. If we go straight to the code, we can see the following:

```
1   void PhysicsAnimation::advanceTimeStep(double timeIntervalInSeconds) {
2       if (_isUsingFixedSubTimeSteps) {
3           // Perform fixed time-stepping
4           ...
5       } else {
6           // Perform adaptive time-stepping
7
8           double remainingTime = timeIntervalInSeconds;
9           while (remainingTime > kEpsilonD) {
10              unsigned int numSteps = numberOfSubTimeSteps(remainingTime);
11              double actualTimeInterval
12                  = remainingTime / static_cast<double>(numSteps);
13
```

```
14          onAdvanceTimeStep(actualTimeInterval);
15
16          remainingTime -= actualTimeInterval;
17        }
18      }
19  }
```

The code starts with the entire time interval for a given frame and then measures how much sub-steps are required for that time interval. The measurement is done by `numberOfSubTimeSteps` which is a virtual function. The subclasses that inherit the `PhysicsAnimation` class can override the function and implement its model-specific logic. Once the number of substeps is determined, the code advances a single substep and subtracts the subtime interval from the full-time interval to get the remaining time duration. Then, we repeat this process until the remaining time approaches zero.

B

More on Particles

B.1 SPH Kernel Functions

The volume integral of any valid kernel function should satisfy

$$\int W(r) = 1 \tag{B.1}$$

For example, the standard 3D SPH kernel function is

$$W_{std}(r) = \frac{315}{64\pi h^3} \begin{cases} (1 - \frac{r^2}{h^2})^3 & 0 \le r \le h \\ 0 & otherwise \end{cases} \tag{B.2}$$

The volume integral in spherical coordinates can be written as:

$$\iiint_V W(r) r^2 \sin\theta dr d\theta d\phi \tag{B.3}$$

After plugging in the standard SPH kernel function, the equation becomes:

$$\iiint_V \frac{315}{64\pi h^3} (1 - \frac{r^2}{h^2})^3 r^2 \sin\theta dr d\theta d\phi \tag{B.4}$$

Evaluating the above equation leads to 1. Similarly, a 2D area integral in polar coordinates can be written as:

$$\iint_A W(r) r\theta dr d\theta \tag{B.5}$$

Thus, the standard 2D SPH kernel function can be derived from the integral above, which is:

$$W_{std}(r) = \frac{4}{\pi h^2} \begin{cases} (1 - \frac{r^2}{h^2})^3 & 0 \le r \le h \\ 0 & otherwise \end{cases} \tag{B.6}$$

Similarly, the spiky 3D SPH kernel function is

$$W_{spiky}(r) = \frac{15}{\pi h^3} \begin{cases} (1 - \frac{r}{h})^3 & 0 \le r \le h \\ 0 & otherwise \end{cases} \tag{B.7}$$

and its 2D version is

$$W_{spiky}(r) = \frac{10}{\pi h^2} \begin{cases} (1 - \frac{r}{h})^3 & 0 \le r \le h \\ 0 & otherwise \end{cases} \tag{B.8}$$

B.2 PCISPH Derivation

In a predictive–corrective step from PCISPH, the primary goal is to calculate the correction pressure from the predicted position and the resulting density error. The following derivation is from Solenthaler and Pajarola 2007 [109].

First, let's try to calculate the density change when there's a small perturbation in particles' positions. Assume that after Δt, the density can be approximated by

$$\begin{aligned} \rho_i(t + \Delta t) &= m \sum_j W\left(\mathbf{x}_i(t + \Delta t) - \mathbf{x}_j(t + \Delta t)\right) \\ &= m \sum_j W\left(\mathbf{x}_i(t) + \Delta x_i(t) - \mathbf{x}_j(t) - \Delta \mathbf{x}_j(t)\right) \\ &= m \sum_j W\left(\mathbf{r}_{ij}(t) + \Delta \mathbf{r}_{ij}(t)\right) \\ &\simeq m \sum_j W\left(\mathbf{r}_{ij}(t)\right) + \nabla W\left(\mathbf{r}_{ij}(t)\right) \cdot \Delta \mathbf{r}_{ij}(t) \\ &= \rho_i(t) + \Delta \rho_i(t) \end{aligned} \tag{B.9}$$

where $\mathbf{r}_{ij} = \mathbf{x}_i - \mathbf{x}_j$. This leads to

$$\begin{aligned} \Delta \rho_i(t) &= m \sum_j \nabla W\left(\mathbf{r}_{ij}(t)\right) \cdot \Delta \mathbf{r}_{ij}(t) \\ &= m \left(\sum_j \nabla W_{ij} \Delta \mathbf{x}_i(t) - \sum_j \nabla W_{ij} \Delta \mathbf{x}_j(t) \right) \\ &= m \left(\Delta \mathbf{x}_i(t) \sum_j \nabla W_{ij} - \sum_j \nabla W_{ij} \Delta \mathbf{x}_j(t) \right) \end{aligned} \tag{B.10}$$

Now, assuming that $\tilde{p}$ is the correction pressure, let's see what is the resulting density change due to $\tilde{p}$. The original paper from Solenthaler and Pajarola [109] uses a leap-frog time integration to compute the position change due to the pressure gradient force:

$$\Delta \mathbf{x}_i = \Delta t^2 \frac{\mathbf{F}_i^p}{m} \tag{B.11}$$

where $\mathbf{F}_i^p$ (or $\mathbf{F}_{j\to i}^p$) is the sum of the pressure forces from all the neighboring particles j. Assuming that the nearby pressure is similar, and the density is close to the target density ρ_0, we get:

$$\mathbf{F}_i^p = \mathbf{F}_{j\to i}^p = -m^2 \sum_j \left(\frac{\tilde{p}_i}{\rho_i^2} + \frac{\tilde{p}_j}{\rho_j^2}\right) \nabla W_{ij}$$

$$\simeq -m^2 \left(\frac{\tilde{p}_i}{\rho_0^2} + \frac{\tilde{p}_i}{\rho_0^2}\right) \sum_j \nabla W_{ij}$$

$$= -m^2 \frac{2\tilde{p}_i}{\rho_0^2} \sum_j \nabla W_{ij} \tag{B.12}$$

Therefore, we can compute the position change of a particle i due to the pressure change:

$$\Delta \mathbf{x}_i = -\Delta t^2 m \frac{2\tilde{p}_i}{\rho_0^2} \sum_j \nabla W_{ij} \tag{B.13}$$

The pressure force contribution of a particle j to the particle i is equal to the force that particle i contributes to a particle j. Hence, we get the following:

$$\Delta \mathbf{x}_j = -\Delta t^2 m \frac{2\tilde{p}_i}{\rho_0^2} \nabla W_{ij} \tag{B.14}$$

Substituting Δx_i and Δx_j from Equation B.10, we get:

$$\Delta \rho_i(t) = m \left(\Delta \mathbf{x}_i(t) \sum_j \nabla W_{ij} - \sum_j \nabla W_{ij} \Delta \mathbf{x}_j(t) \right)$$

$$= \Delta t^2 m^2 \frac{2\tilde{p}_i}{\rho_0^2} \left(-\sum_j \nabla W_{ij} \cdot \sum_j \nabla W_{ij} - \sum_j (\nabla W_{ij} \cdot \nabla W_{ij}) \right) \tag{B.15}$$

Therefore, a density change $\Delta \rho$ maps to the pressure change $\tilde{p}$:

$$\tilde{p}_i = \frac{\Delta \rho_i(t)}{\beta(-\sum_j \nabla W_{ij} \cdot \sum_j \nabla W_{ij} - \sum_j (\nabla W_{ij} \cdot \nabla W_{ij}))} \tag{B.16}$$

where

$$\beta = \Delta t^2 m^2 \frac{2}{\rho_0^2} \tag{B.17}$$

So, if there is a density error ρ_{err}^* from the predicted position, we can compute the pressure to cancel out the error by:

$$\tilde{p}_i = \frac{-\rho_{err,i}^*}{\beta(-\sum_j \nabla W_{ij} \cdot \sum_j \nabla W_{ij} - \sum_j (\nabla W_{ij} \cdot \nabla W_{ij}))} \tag{B.18}$$

By simplifying the equation, we get:

$$\tilde{p}_i = \delta \rho^*_{err,i} \qquad (B.19)$$

where

$$\delta = \frac{-1}{\beta(-\sum_j \nabla W_{ij} \cdot \sum_j \nabla W_{ij} - \sum_j (\nabla W_{ij} \cdot \nabla W_{ij}))} \qquad (B.20)$$

This is the scalar `delta` from the code in Section 2.4. We can precompute this `delta` (or δ) by:

```
1   double PciSphSolver3::computeDelta(double timeStepInSeconds) {
2       auto particles = sphSystemData();
3       const double kernelRadius = particles->kernelRadius();
4
5       Array1<Vector3D> points;
6       BccLatticePointsGenerator pointsGenerator;
7       Vector3D origin;
8       BoundingBox3D sampleBound(origin, origin);
9       sampleBound.expand(1.5 * kernelRadius);
10
11      pointsGenerator.generate(
12          sampleBound, particles->targetSpacing(), &points);
13
14      SphSpikyKernel3 kernel(kernelRadius);
15
16      double denom = 0;
17      Vector3D denom1;
18      double denom2 = 0;
19
20      for (size_t i = 0; i < points.size(); ++i) {
21          const Vector3D& point = points[i];
22          double distanceSquared = point.lengthSquared();
23
24          if (distanceSquared < kernelRadius * kernelRadius) {
25              double distance = std::sqrt(distanceSquared);
26              Vector3D direction =
27                  (distance > 0.0) ? point / distance : Vector3D();
28
29              // grad(Wij)
30              Vector3D gradWij = kernel.gradient(distance, direction);
31              denom1 += gradWij;
32              denom2 += gradWij.dot(gradWij);
33          }
34      }
35
36      denom += -denom1.dot(denom1) - denom2;
37
38      return (std::fabs(denom) > 0.0) ?
```

```
39          -1 / (computeBeta(timeStepInSeconds) * denom) : 0;
40   }
41
42   double PciSphSolver3::computeBeta(double timeStepInSeconds) {
43       auto particles = sphSystemData();
44       return 2.0 * square(particles->mass() * timeStepInSeconds
45           / particles->targetDensity());
46   }
```

The code above generates uniformly distributed points in a small bounding box and computes δ by iterating all the particles from the center of the bounding box. The instance of a class `BccLatticePointsGenerator` generates points in the body-centered cubic pattern. This pattern has one point in the center of the unit cube and eight corner points.

C

More on Grids

C.1 Vector and Matrix for Grids

As discussed in Sections 3.4.4 and 3.4.5, the grid-based solver requires a linear system and its solver to compute stable diffusion and pressure Poisson equations. To form a linear system, we need vector and matrix data structures for grids. Especially, the matrix should be a sparse matrix (Section 1.3.3).

Constructing a vector for grids is simple; as mentioned in Section 3.4.4, a grid point (i, j, k) maps to $i + width \cdot (j + height \cdot k)$th element of vector. Hence, we define a type for the vector as follows:

```
1   typedef Array3<double> FdmVector3;
```

The prefix `Fdm` means it is the vector for FDM (finite difference method) calculation. The matrix definition is a bit more complicated but we use the same mapping; a grid point (i, j, k) maps to $i + width \cdot (j + height \cdot k)$th row/column of the matrix. Since this is a matrix for FDM applications, and most of the FDM in this book requires only immediate neighbors (such as the central differencing), we will assume that a row of the matrix will have at most seven columns (center, left, right, down, up, back, and front) in 3D and five columns in 2D. Also, another assumption we will make in this book and the codebase is that the matrix is symmetric ($A_{ij} = A_{ji}$). Hence, we can store only four columns in a row (center, right, up, and front) and other three can be accessed from the neighboring grid points. Figure C.1 shows how the matrix is constructed. A row is stored at a grid point, and each row stores the columns that correspond to its neighbors. The following code implements the data structure:

```
1   struct FdmMatrixRow3 {
2       double center = 0.0;
3       double right = 0.0;
4       double up = 0.0;
5       double front = 0.0;
6   };
7
8   typedef Array3<FdmMatrixRow3> FdmMatrix3;
```

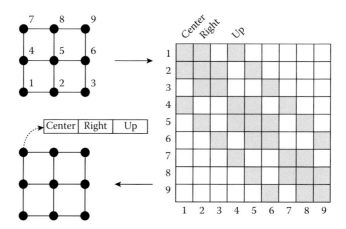

FIGURE C.1

A 3×3 2D grid with 1-ring neighbor finite differencing builds the matrix shown on the right. The sparse matrix can be stored in a grid format as shown on the lower left.

Using `FdmVector3` and `FdmMatrix3`, we can perform matrix–vector multiplication as follows:

```
void FdmBlas3::mvm(
    const FdmMatrix3& m,
    const FdmVector3& v,
    FdmVector3* result) {
    Size3 size = m.size();

    m.parallelForEachIndex([&](size_t i, size_t j, size_t k) {
        (*result)(i, j, k)
            = m(i, j, k).center * v(i, j, k)
            + ((i > 0) ? m(i - 1, j, k).right * v(i - 1, j, k) : 0.0)
            + ((i + 1 < size.x) ? m(i, j, k).right * v(i + 1, j, k) : 0.0)
            + ((j > 0) ? m(i, j - 1, k).up * v(i, j - 1, k) : 0.0)
            + ((j + 1 < size.y) ? m(i, j, k).up * v(i, j + 1, k) : 0.0)
            + ((k > 0) ? m(i, j, k - 1).front * v(i, j, k - 1) : 0.0)
            + ((k + 1 < size.z) ? m(i, j, k).front * v(i, j, k + 1) : 0.0);
    });
}
```

Note that the code is accessing the column that corresponds to the left neighbor $(i-1, j, k)$ by looking up the other row's `right` column, `m(i - 1, j, k).right`. Same applies for the down-neighbors and back-neighbors that we didn't store explicitly. Type `FdmBlas3` is a wrapper class that provides basic linear algebra operations like matrix–vector multiplication (see `Blas` from

Appendix A.1). Below is the core functions that `FdmBlas3` provides:

```cpp
struct FdmBlas3 {
    typedef double ScalarType;
    typedef FdmVector3 VectorType;
    typedef FdmMatrix3 MatrixType;

    // Sets the given scalar value to the output vector.
    static void set(double s, FdmVector3* result);

    // Sets the given vector to the output vector.
    static void set(const FdmVector3& v, FdmVector3* result);

    // Sets the given scalar value to the output matrix.
    static void set(double s, FdmMatrix3* result);

    // Sets the given matrix to the output matrix.
    static void set(const FdmMatrix3& m, FdmMatrix3* result);

    // Performs dot product.
    static double dot(const FdmVector3& a, const FdmVector3& b);

    // Calculates a*x + y.
    static void axpy(
        double a,
        const FdmVector3& x,
        const FdmVector3& y,
        FdmVector3* result);

    // Performs matrix-vector multiplication.
    static void mvm(
        const FdmMatrix3& m, const FdmVector3& v, FdmVector3* result);

    // Calculates b - A*x.
    static void residual(
        const FdmMatrix3& a,
        const FdmVector3& x,
        const FdmVector3& b,
        FdmVector3* result);

    // Returns the length of the vector.
    static double l2Norm(const FdmVector3& v);

    // Returns the absolute maximum value among the vector elements.
    static double lInfNorm(const FdmVector3& v);
};
```

When solving a linear system, it is common that the matrix $\mathbf{A}$, vector $\mathbf{x}$ and $\mathbf{b}$ from $\mathbf{A}\mathbf{x} = \mathbf{b}$ are all required at the same time. So we define a simple bundle class as follows:

```
1  struct FdmLinearSystem3 {
2      FdmMatrix3 A;
3      FdmVector3 x, b;
4  };
```

C.2   Iterative System Solver

In Section 1.3.4, we discussed about a number of linear system solvers. Let's find out how the methods can be implemented using `FdmVector3` and `FdmMatrix3`.

C.2.1   Jacobi Method

As shown in Section 1.3.4.2, the Jacobi method iterates the following step:

$$\mathbf{x}^{k+1} = \mathbf{D}^{-1}(\mathbf{b} - \mathbf{R}\mathbf{x}^k) \tag{C.1}$$

Using the FDM-optimized vector and matrix data structures, we can implement the equation above as follows:

```
1  void FdmJacobiSolver3::relax(
2      FdmLinearSystem3* system, FdmVector3* xTemp) {
3      Size3 size = system->x.size();
4      FdmMatrix3& A = system->A;
5      FdmVector3& x = system->x;
6      FdmVector3& b = system->b;
7
8      A.parallelForEachIndex([&](size_t i, size_t j, size_t k) {
9          double r
10             = ((i > 0) ? A(i - 1, j, k).right * x(i - 1, j, k) : 0.0)
11             + ((i + 1 < size.x) ? A(i, j, k).right * x(i + 1, j, k) : 0.0)
12             + ((j > 0) ? A(i, j - 1, k).up * x(i, j - 1, k) : 0.0)
13             + ((j + 1 < size.y) ? A(i, j, k).up * x(i, j + 1, k) : 0.0)
14             + ((k > 0) ? A(i, j, k - 1).front * x(i, j, k - 1) : 0.0)
15             + ((k + 1 < size.z) ? A(i, j, k).front * x(i, j, k + 1) : 0.0);
16
17         (*xTemp)(i, j, k) = (b(i, j, k) - r) / A(i, j, k).center;
18     });
19 }
```

To repeat the iteration above, we can write:

```
1   class FdmLinearSystemSolver3 {
2    public:
3       virtual bool solve(FdmLinearSystem3* system) = 0;
4   };
5
6   class FdmJacobiSolver3 final : public FdmLinearSystemSolver3 {
7    public:
8       ...
9
10      bool solve(FdmLinearSystem3* system) override;
11
12      ...
13
14   private:
15      unsigned int _maxNumberOfIterations;
16      unsigned int _lastNumberOfIterations;
17      unsigned int _residualCheckInterval;
18      double _tolerance;
19      double _lastResidual;
20
21      FdmVector3 _xTemp;
22      FdmVector3 _residual;
23
24      void relax(FdmLinearSystem3* system, FdmVector3* xTemp);
25   };
26
27   bool FdmJacobiSolver3::solve(FdmLinearSystem3* system) {
28      _xTemp.resize(system->x.size());
29      _residual.resize(system->x.size());
30
31      for (unsigned int iter = 0; iter < _maxNumberOfIterations; ++iter) {
32          relax(system, &_xTemp);
33
34          _xTemp.swap(system->x);
35
36          if (iter != 0 && iter % _residualCheckInterval == 0) {
37              FdmBlas3::residual(
38                  system->A, system->x, system->b, &_residual);
39
40              if (FdmBlas3::l2Norm(_residual) < _tolerance) {
41                  break;
42              }
43          }
44      }
45
46      FdmBlas3::residual(system->A, system->x, system->b, &_residual);
```

```
47        _lastResidual = FdmBlas3::l2Norm(_residual);

48

49        return _lastResidual < _tolerance;
50    }
```

Here, the class `FdmJacobiSolver3` inherits from the abstract base class `FdmLinearSystemSolver3` which represents a linear system solver interface. Within the `solve` function (which solves the given linear system), the code calls the `relax` function we defined previously, and then sees if the iteration can be terminated by evaluating the residual and its L2-norm. The residual is defined as:

$$\mathbf{r} = \mathbf{b} - \mathbf{Ax} \tag{C.2}$$

and the L2-norm is the vector's length. Therefore, if the length of the residual vector is small enough, the iteration will be terminated.

C.2.2 Gauss–Seidel Method

The iteration equation for the Gauss–Seidel method can be written as follows:

$$x_i^{k+1} = \frac{1}{a_{ii}} \left(b_i - \sum_{j>i} a_{ij} x_j^{k+1} - \sum_{j>i} a_{ij} x_j^k \right) \tag{C.3}$$

The corresponding implementation is very similar to the Jacobi method, which is:

```
1     void FdmGaussSeidelSolver3::relax(FdmLinearSystem3* system) {
2         Size3 size = system->x.size();
3         FdmMatrix3& A = system->A;
4         FdmVector3& x = system->x;
5         FdmVector3& b = system->b;
6
7         A.forEachIndex([&](size_t i, size_t j, size_t k) {
8             double r
9                 = ((i > 0) ? A(i - 1, j, k).right * x(i - 1, j, k) : 0.0)
10                + ((i + 1 < size.x) ? A(i, j, k).right * x(i + 1, j, k) : 0.0)
11                + ((j > 0) ? A(i, j - 1, k).up * x(i, j - 1, k) : 0.0)
12                + ((j + 1 < size.y) ? A(i, j, k).up * x(i, j + 1, k) : 0.0)
13                + ((k > 0) ? A(i, j, k - 1).front * x(i, j, k - 1) : 0.0)
14                + ((k + 1 < size.z) ? A(i, j, k).front * x(i, j, k + 1) : 0.0);
15
16            x(i, j, k) = (b(i, j, k) - r) / A(i, j, k).center;
17         });
18    }
```

Note that the loop `forEach` is a serial process because the code depends on the other grid points.

C.2.3 Conjugate Gradient Method

As described in Appendix A.1, we can implement the grid-based CG solver by plugging-in the linear algebra routine, `FdmBlas3`, to the CG solver. Consider the following code:

```
1   bool FdmCgSolver3::solve(FdmLinearSystem3* system) {
2       FdmMatrix3& matrix = system->A;
3       FdmVector3& solution = system->x;
4       FdmVector3& rhs = system->b;
5
6       Size3 size = matrix.size();
7       _r.resize(size);
8       _d.resize(size);
9       _q.resize(size);
10      _s.resize(size);
11
12      system->x.set(0.0);
13      _r.set(0.0);
14      _d.set(0.0);
15      _q.set(0.0);
16      _s.set(0.0);
17
18      cg<FdmBlas3>(
19          matrix,
20          rhs,
21          _maxNumberOfIterations,
22          _tolerance,
23          &solution,
24          &_r,
25          &_d,
26          &_q,
27          &_s,
28          &_lastNumberOfIterations,
29          &_lastResidual);
30
31      return _lastResidual <= _tolerance
32          || _lastNumberOfIterations < _maxNumberOfIterations;
33  }
```

Now, extending the code to the PCG solver can be done by implementing the preconditioner as follows:

```
1   class FdmIccgSolver3 final : public FdmLinearSystemSolver3 {
2    public:
3       ...
4
5       bool solve(FdmLinearSystem3* system) override;
6
```

```
 7        ...
 8
 9    private:
10        struct Preconditioner final {
11            ConstArrayAccessor3<FdmMatrixRow3> A;
12            FdmVector3 d;
13            FdmVector3 y;
14
15            void build(const FdmMatrix3& matrix);
16
17            void solve(
18                const FdmVector3& b,
19                FdmVector3* x);
20        };
21
22        ...
23    };
24
25    bool FdmIccgSolver3::solve(FdmLinearSystem3* system) {
26        FdmMatrix3& matrix = system->A;
27        FdmVector3& solution = system->x;
28        FdmVector3& rhs = system->b;
29
30        Size3 size = matrix.size();
31        _r.resize(size);
32        _d.resize(size);
33        _q.resize(size);
34        _s.resize(size);
35
36        system->x.set(0.0);
37        _r.set(0.0);
38        _d.set(0.0);
39        _q.set(0.0);
40        _s.set(0.0);
41
42        _precond.build(matrix);
43
44        pcg<FdmBlas3, Preconditioner>(
45            matrix,
46            rhs,
47            _maxNumberOfIterations,
48            _tolerance,
49            &_precond,
50            &solution,
51            &_r,
52            &_d,
53            &_q,
54            &_s,
55            &_lastNumberOfIterations,
```

```
56              &_lastResidual);
57
58        return _lastResidual <= _tolerance
59              || _lastNumberOfIterations < _maxNumberOfIterations;
60    }
```

The codebase implements modified incomplete Cholesky decomposition [24] for the preconditioner Preconditioner as shown below.

```
1    void FdmIccgSolver3::Preconditioner::build(const FdmMatrix3& matrix) {
2        Size3 size = matrix.size();
3        A = matrix.constAccessor();
4
5        d.resize(size, 0.0);
6        y.resize(size, 0.0);
7
8        matrix.forEachIndex([&](size_t i, size_t j, size_t k) {
9            double denom
10               = matrix(i, j, k).center
11               - ((i > 0) ?
12                   square(matrix(i - 1, j, k).right) * d(i - 1, j, k) : 0.0)
13               - ((j > 0) ?
14                   square(matrix(i, j - 1, k).up)    * d(i, j - 1, k) : 0.0)
15               - ((k > 0) ?
16                   square(matrix(i, j, k - 1).front) * d(i, j, k - 1) : 0.0);
17
18           if (std::fabs(denom) > 0.0) {
19               d(i, j, k) = 1.0 / denom;
20           } else {
21               d(i, j, k) = 0.0;
22           }
23       });
24   }
25
26   void FdmIccgSolver3::Preconditioner::solve(
27       const FdmVector3& b,
28       FdmVector3* x) {
29       ssize_t sx = static_cast<ssize_t>(size.x);
30       ssize_t sy = static_cast<ssize_t>(size.y);
31       ssize_t sz = static_cast<ssize_t>(size.z);
32
33       b.forEachIndex([&](size_t i, size_t j, size_t k) {
34           y(i, j, k)
35               = (b(i, j, k)
36               - ((i > 0) ? A(i - 1, j, k).right * y(i - 1, j, k) : 0.0)
37               - ((j > 0) ? A(i, j - 1, k).up    * y(i, j - 1, k) : 0.0)
38               - ((k > 0) ? A(i, j, k - 1).front * y(i, j, k - 1) : 0.0))
39               * d(i, j, k);
40       });
```

```
41
42     for (ssize_t k = sz - 1; k >= 0; --k) {
43         for (ssize_t j = sy - 1; j >= 0; --j) {
44             for (ssize_t i = sx - 1; i >= 0; --i) {
45                 (*x)(i, j, k)
46                     = (y(i, j, k)
47                     - ((i + 1 < sx) ?
48                         A(i, j, k).right * (*x)(i + 1, j, k) : 0.0)
49                     - ((j + 1 < sy) ?
50                         A(i, j, k).up   * (*x)(i, j + 1, k) : 0.0)
51                     - ((k + 1 < sz) ?
52                         A(i, j, k).front * (*x)(i, j, k + 1) : 0.0))
53                     * d(i, j, k);
54             }
55         }
56     }
57 }
```

References

[1] ASCII art. Available at https://en.wikipedia.org/wiki/ASCII_art. Accessed on August 30, 2016.

[2] Houdini 14.0 documentation. Available at http://www.sidefx.com/docs/houdini14.0/. Accessed on August 30, 2016.

[3] RealFlow 2015 documentation. Available at http://support.nextlimit.com/display/rf2015docs/RealFlow+2015+Documentation. Accessed on August 30, 2016.

[4] RealFlow 2015 documentation – dyverso fluids (DY). Available at http://support.nextlimit.com/pages/viewpage.action?pageId=38111978. Accessed on August 30, 2016.

[5] RealFlow 2015 documentation – hybrido fluids (HyFLIP). Available at http://support.nextlimit.com/pages/viewpage.action?pageId=38111289. Accessed on August 30, 2016.

[6] The Stanford 3D scanning repository. Available at http://graphics.stanford.edu/data/3Dscanrep/. Accessed on August 30, 2016.

[7] B. Adams and M. Wicke. Meshless approximation methods and applications in physics based modeling and animation. In *Eurographics 2009 Tutorials*, pages 213–239, 2009.

[8] J. A. Bærentzen and H. Aanæs. Generating signed distance fields from triangle meshes. *Informatics and Mathematical Modeling, Technical University of Denmark, DTU*, 20, 2002.

[9] D. Baraff and A. Witkin. Large steps in cloth simulation. In *Proceedings of the 25th Annual Conference on Computer Graphics and Interactive Techniques*, SIGGRAPH '98, pages 43–54, 1998.

[10] D. Baraff and A. Witkin. *Physically based modeling*. Online SIGGRAPH 2001 Course Notes, 2001.

[11] A. W. Bargteil, T. G. Goktekin, J. F. O'Brien, and J. A. Strain. A semi-Lagrangian contouring method for fluid simulation. *ACM Transactions on Graphics*, 25(1):19–38, 2006.

[12] A. W. Bargteil, C. Wojtan, J. K. Hodgins, and G. Turk. A finite element method for animating large viscoplastic flow. *ACM Transactions on Graphics (TOG)*, 26(3):16, 2007.

[13] C. Batty, F. Bertails, and R. Bridson. A fast variational framework for accurate solid-fluid coupling. *ACM Transactions on Graphics (TOG)*, 26(3):100, 2007.

[14] C. Batty, F. Bertails, and R. Bridson. A fast variational framework for accurate solid-fluid coupling – sample code. 2007. Available at http://www.cs.ubc.ca/labs/imager/tr/2007/Batty_VariationalFluids/. Accessed on August 30, 2016.

[15] M. Becker and M. Teschner. Weakly compressible SPH for free surface flows. In *Proceedings of the 2007 ACM SIGGRAPH/Eurographics Symposium on Computer Animation*, pages 209–217, Eurographics Association, 2007.

[16] P. Besl. *A case study comparing AoS (arrays of structures) and SoA (structures of arrays) data layouts for a compute-intensive loop run on Intel® Xeon® processors and Intel® Xeon Phi^{TM} product family coprocessors*. Technical report, Intel, 2013.

[17] D. Bodenstein. *Fluid simulations in an independent visual effects pipeline*. Ph.D. thesis, Drexel University, 2012.

[18] C. D. Boor. *A practical guide to splines*, volume 27. Springer-Verlag New York, 1978.

[19] P. Bourke. Interpolation methods. 1999. Available at http://paulbourke.net/miscellaneous/interpolation/. Accessed on August 30, 2016.

[20] J. U. Brackbill, D. B. Kothe, and H. M. Ruppel. FLIP: A low-dissipation, particle-in-cell method for fluid flow. *Computer Physics Communications*, 48(1):25–38, 1988.

[21] R. Bridson. *Fluid simulation for computer graphics*. A K Peters/CRC Press, Boca Raton, FL, 2015.

[22] R. Bridson and C. Batty. Computational physics in film. *Science*, 330(6012):1756–1757, 2010.

[23] R. Bridson, R. Fedkiw, and J. Anderson. Robust treatment of collisions, contact and friction for cloth animation. *ACM Transactions on Graphics (TOG)*, 21:594–603, 2002.

[24] R. Bridson and M. Müller-Fischer. Fluid simulation: Siggraph 2007 course notes. In *ACM SIGGRAPH 2007 Courses*, pages 1–81, ACM, 2007.

[25] R. Butt. *Introduction to numerical analysis using MATLAB®*. Jones & Bartlett Learning, 2009.

[26] V. Casulli and R. A. Walters. An unstructured grid, three-dimensional model based on the shallow water equations. *International Journal for Numerical Methods in Fluids*, 32(3):331–348, 2000.

[27] E. Catmull and R. Rom. A class of local interpolating splines. In R. Barnhill and R. Riesenfeld, editors, *Computer aided geometric design*, pages 317–326, Academic Press, Cambridge, MA, 1974.

[28] J. Cho and H.-S. Ko. Geometry-aware volume-of-fluid method. *Computer Graphics Forum*, 32:379–388, 2013.

[29] A. J. Chorin. Numerical solution of the Navier-Stokes equations. *Mathematics of Computation*, 22(104):745–762, 1968.

[30] T. J. Chung. *Computational fluid dynamics*. Cambridge University Press, 2nd edition, Cambridge, United Kingdom, 2014.

[31] Wikimedia Commons. *A Sunday on La Grande Jatte*, 1884.

[32] S. J. Cummins and M. Rudman. An SPH projection method. *Journal of Computational Physics*, 152(2):584–607, 1999.

[33] F. Da, C. Batty, C. Wojtan, and E. Grinspun. Double bubbles sans toil and trouble: Discrete circulation-preserving vortex sheets for soap films and foams. *ACM Transactions on Graphics (TOG)*, 34(4):149, 2015.

[34] M. Desbrun, and M-P. Gascuel. Smoothed particles: A new paradigm for animating highly deformable bodies. In *Computer Animation and Simulation'96*, pages 61–76. Springer Vienna, 1996.

[35] G. A. Dilts. Moving-least-squares-particle hydrodynamics—I. Consistency and stability. *International Journal for Numerical Methods in Engineering*, 44(8):1115–1155, 1999.

[36] D. Enright, R. Fedkiw, J. Ferziger, and I. Mitchell. A hybrid particle level set method for improved interface capturing. *Journal of Computational Physics*, 183(1):83–116, 2002.

[37] D. Enright, S. Marschner, and R. Fedkiw. Animation and rendering of complex water surfaces. *ACM Transactions on Graphics (TOG)*, 21(3):736–744, 2002.

[38] D. Enright, D. Nguyen, F. Gibou, and R. Fedkiw. Using the particle level set method and a second order accurate pressure boundary condition for free surface flows. In *ASME/JSME 2003 4th Joint Fluids Summer Engineering Conference*, pages 337–342, American Society of Mechanical Engineers, 2003.

[39] D. P. Enright. *Use of the particle level set method for enhanced resolution of free surface flows.* Ph.D. thesis, Stanford University, 2002.

[40] C. Ericson. *Real-time collision detection.* CRC Press, Boca Raton, FL, 2004.

[41] M. W. Evans, F. H. Harlow, and E. Bromberg. *The particle-in-cell method for hydrodynamic calculations.* Technical report, DTIC Document, 1957.

[42] R. Fedkiw, J. Stam, and H. W. Jensen. Visual simulation of smoke. In *Proceedings of the ACM SIGGRAPH 2001: Computer Graphics (Proc. ACM SIGGRAPH 2001)*, 35:15–22, 2001.

[43] R. P. Fedkiw, T. Aslam, B. Merriman, and S. Osher. A non-oscillatory eulerian approach to interfaces in multimaterial flows (the ghost fluid method). *Journal of Computational Physics*, 152(2):457–492, 1999.

[44] B. E. Feldman, J. F. O'Brien, and O. Arikan. Animating suspended particle explosions. *ACM Transactions on Graphics (TOG)*, 22:708–715, 2003.

[45] P. Goswami and C. Batty. Regional time stepping for SPH. In E. Galin and M. Wand, editors, *Eurographics 2014—Short papers*. The Eurographics Association, Strasbourg, France, pages 45–48, 2014. doi: 10.2312/egsh.20141011.

[46] F. H. Harlow. Fluid dynamics in group T-3 Los Alamos national laboratory. *Journal of Computational Physics*, 195(2):414–433, 2004.

[47] F. H. Harlow. *A machine calculation method for hydrodynamic problems.* Los Alamos Scientific Laboratory report LAMS-1956, 1955.

[48] F. H. Harlow, J. E. Welch. Numerical calculation of time-dependent viscous incompressible flow of fluid with free surface. *Physics of Fluids*, 8(12):2182, 1965.

[49] N. Heo and H.-S. Ko. Detail-preserving fully-eulerian interface tracking framework. *ACM Transactions on Graphics (TOG)*, 29(6):176, 2010.

[50] J.-M. Hong and C.-H. Kim. Discontinuous fluids. *ACM Transactions on Graphics (TOG)*, 24(3):915–920, 2005.

[51] J.-M. Hong, H.-Y. Lee, J.-C. Yoon, and C.-H. Kim. Bubbles alive. *ACM Transactions on Graphics (TOG)*, 27(3):48, 2008.

[52] J.-M. Hong, T. Shinar, and R. Fedkiw. Wrinkled flames and cellular patterns. *ACM Transactions on Graphics (TOG)*, 26:47, 2007.

[53] B. Houston, M. B. Nielsen, C. Batty, O. Nilsson, and K. Museth. Hierarchical RLE level set: A compact and versatile deformable surface representation. *ACM Transactions on Graphics (TOG)*, 25(1):151–175, 2006.

[54] J. Hunter. Matplotlib: A 2D graphics environment. *Computing in Science & Engineering*, 9:90, 2007.

[55] M. Ihmsen, N. Akinci, M. Becker, and M. Teschner. A parallel SPH implementation on multi-core CPUs. *Computer Graphics Forum*, 30(1):99–112, 2011.

[56] M. Ihmsen, J. Orthmann, B. Solenthaler, A. Kolb, and M. Teschner. SPH Fluids in Computer Graphics. *Eurographics 2014 – State of the Art Reports*, pages 21–42, 2014.

[57] G. Irving, E. Guendelman, F. Losasso, and R. Fedkiw. Efficient simulation of large bodies of water by coupling two and three dimensional techniques. *ACM Transactions on Graphics (TOG)*, 25:805–811, 2006.

[58] A. M. Jaffe. The millennium grand challenge in mathematics. *Notices of the AMS*, 53(6), 2006.

[59] W. Jakob. Mitsuba renderer. 2010. Available at http://www.mitsuba-renderer.org. Accessed on August 30, 2016.

[60] S. G. Jonathan, M. Cohen, and S. Tariq. Interactive fluid-particle simulation using translating eulerian grids. In *Interactive 3D graphics and games (I3D)*, ACM, pages 15–22, 2010.

[61] K. Käfer. Drawing text with signed distance fields in mapbox gl. 2014. https://www.mapbox.com/blog/text-signed-distance-fields/. Accessed on August 30, 2016.

[62] M. Kang, R. P. Fedkiw, and X.-D. Liu. A boundary condition capturing method for multiphase incompressible flow. *Journal of Scientific Computing*, 15(3):323–360, 2000.

[63] B. Kim, Y. Liu, I. Llamas, X. Jiao, and J. Rossignac. Simulation of bubbles in foam with the volume control method. *ACM Transactions on Graphics (TOG)*, 26:98, 2007.

[64] B. Kim, Y. Liu, I. Llamas, and J. Rossignac. FlowFixer: Using BFECC for fluid simulation. In *Eurographics Workshop on Natural Phenomena 2005*, Dublin, Ireland, 2005.

[65] D. Kim and H.-S. Ko. Eulerian motion blur. In *Eurographics Workshop on Natural Phenomena*, Crete, Greece, 2007.

[66] D. Kim, S. W. Lee, O.-Y. Song, and H.-S. Ko. Baroclinic turbulence with varying density and temperature. *IEEE Transactions on Visualization and Computer Graphics*, 18(9):1488–1495, 2012.

[67] D. Kim, O.-Y. Song, and H.-S. Ko. A semi-Lagrangian CIP fluid solver without dimensional splitting. *Computer Graphics Forum*, 27(2):467–475, 2008.

[68] D. Kim, O.-Y. Song, and H.-S. Ko. Stretching and wiggling liquids. *ACM Transactions on Graphics*, 28(5):120, 2009.

[69] D. Kim, O.-Y. Song, and H.-S. Ko. A practical simulation of dispersed bubble flow. *ACM Transactions on Graphics*, 29:70, 2010.

[70] J. Kim and P. Moin. Application of a fractional-step method to incompressible Navier-Stokes equations. *Journal of Computational Physics*, 59(2):308–323, 1985.

[71] T. Kim, N. Thürey, D. James, and M. Gross. Wavelet turbulence for fluid simulation. *ACM Transactions on Graphics*, 27(3):1–6, 2008.

[72] P. N. Klein. *Coding the matrix: Linear algebra through applications to computer science*. Newtonian Press, Newton, MA, 2013.

[73] S. Knight, C. Austin, C. Crain, S. Leblanc, and A. Roach. SCons: A software construction tool, 2011. Available at http://www.scons.org/. Accessed on August 30, 2016.

[74] A. Knoll. A survey of implicit surface rendering methods, and a proposal for a common sampling framework. *Visualization of Large and Unstructured Data Sets*, S-7:164–177, 2007.

[75] C. L. Lawson, R. J. Hanson, D. R. Kincaid, and F. T. Krogh. Basic linear algebra subprograms for Fortran usage. *ACM Transactions on Mathematical Software (TOMS)*, 5(3):308–323, 1979.

[76] W. E. Lorensen and H. E. Cline. Marching cubes: A high resolution 3D surface construction algorithm. *ACM SIGGRAPH Computer Graphics*, 21(4):163–169, 1987.

[77] F. Losasso, F. Gibou, and R. Fedkiw. Simulating water and smoke with an octree data structure. *ACM Transactions on Graphics*, 23:457–462, 2004.

[78] F. Losasso, T. Shinar, A. Selle, and R. Fedkiw. Multiple interacting liquids. *ACM Transactions on Graphics*, 25:812–819, 2006.

[79] F. Losasso, J. O. Talton, N. Kwatra, and R. Fedkiw. Two-way coupled SPH and particle level set fluid simulation. *IEEE Transactions on Visualization and Computer Graphics*, 14(4):797–804, 2008.

[80] M. Macklin and M. Müller. Position based fluids. *ACM Transactions on Graphics*, 32(4):104, 2013.

[81] S. Marschner and P. Shirley. *Fundamentals of Computer Graphics*. 4th edition, A K Peters, CRC Press, Boca Raton, FL, 2015.

[82] P. C. Matthews. *Vector calculus*. Springer, London, United Kingdom, 2000.

[83] S. McKee, M. Tomé, V. Ferreira, J. Cuminato, A. Castelo, F. Sousa, and N. Mangiavacchi. The mac method. *Computers & Fluids*, 37(8):907–930, 2008.

[84] S. Meyers. *Effective modern C++*. O'Reilly Media, Sebastopol, CA, 2014.

[85] J. Monaghan and A. Kocharyan. SPH simulation of multi-phase flow. *Computer Physics Communications*, 87(1):225–235, 1995.

[86] J. J. Monaghan. Smoothed particle hydrodynamics. *Annual Review of Astronomy and Astrophysics*, 30:543–574, 1992.

[87] J. J. Monaghan. Simulating free surface flows with SPH. *Journal of Computational Physics*, 110(2):399–406, 1994.

[88] J. J. Monaghan. Smoothed particle hydrodynamics. *Reports on Progress in Physics*, 68(8):1703, 2005.

[89] M. Müller, D. Charypar, and M. Gross. Particle-based fluid simulation for interactive applications. In *Proceedings of the 2003 ACM SIGGRAPH/Eurographics Symposium on Computer Animation*, pages 154–159, 2003.

[90] M. Müller, B. Heidelberger, M. Hennix, and J. Ratcliff. Position based dynamics. *Journal of Visual Communication and Image Representation*, 18(2):109–118, 2007.

[91] M. Müller, S. Schirm, M. Teschner, B. Heidelberger, and M. Gross. Interaction of fluids with deformable solids. *Computer Animation and Virtual Worlds*, 15(3–4):159–171, 2004.

[92] M. Müller, B. Solenthaler, R. Keiser, and M. Gross. Particle-based fluid-fluid interaction. In *Proceedings of the 2005 ACM SIGGRAPH/Eurographics Symposium on Computer Animation*, pages 237–244. ACM, 2005.

[93] R. Narain, J. Sewall, M. Carlson, and M. C. Lin. Fast animation of turbulence using energy transport and procedural synthesis. *ACM Transactions on Graphics*, 27(5):1–8, 2008.

[94] D. Q. Nguyen, R. Fedkiw, and H. W. Jensen. Physically based modeling and animation of fire. *ACM Transactions on Graphics*, 21(3):721–728, 2002.

[95] S. Osher and R. Fedkiw. *The level set method and dynamic implicit surfaces*. Springer-Verlag, New York, 2002.

[96] S. Osher and J. A. Sethian. Fronts propagating with curvature-dependent speed: Algorithms based on Hamilton-Jacobi formulations. *Journal of Computational Physics*, 79(1):12–49, 1988.

[97] S. I. Park and M. J. Kim. Vortex fluid for gaseous phenomena. In *Proceedings of the 2005 ACM SIGGRAPH/Eurographics Symposium on Computer Animation*, pages 261–270, ACM, 2005.

[98] D. Peng, B. Merriman, S. Osher, H. Zhao, and M. Kang. A PDE-based fast local level set method. *Journal of Computational Physics*, 155(2):410–438, 1999.

[99] Y. Saad. *Sparskit: A basic tool kit for sparse matrix computations*. 1990.

[100] Y. Saad. *Iterative methods for sparse linear systems*. SIAM, Philadelphia, PA, 2003.

[101] H. M. Schey. *Div, Grad, Curl, and all that: An informal text on vector calculus*. W. W. Norton & Company, New York City, NY, 2004.

[102] A. Selle, R. Fedkiw, B. Kim, Y. Liu, and J. Rossignac. An unconditionally stable MacCormack method. *Journal of Computational Physics*, 35(2–3):350–371, 2008. doi: 10.1007/s10915-007-9166-4.

[103] A. Selle, N. Rasmussen, and R. Fedkiw. A vortex particle method for smoke, water and explosions. *ACM Transactions on Graphics*, 24:910–914, 2005.

[104] J. Sethian and P. Smereka. Level set methods for fluid interfaces. *Annual Review of Fluid Mechanics*, 35:341–372, 2003.

[105] J. A. Sethian. *Level set methods and fast marching methods: Evolving interfaces in computational geometry, fluid mechanics, computer vision, and materials science*, volume 3. Cambridge University Press, 1999.

[106] C. Shen, J. F. O'Brien, and J. R. Shewchuk. Interpolating and approximating implicit surfaces from polygon soup. In *Proceedings of ACM SIGGRAPH 2004*, pages 896–904, August 2004.

[107] J. R. Shewchuk. *An introduction to the conjugate gradient method without the agonizing pain*. 1994.

[108] C.-W. Shu. *Essentially non-oscillatory and weighted essentially non-oscillatory schemes for hyperbolic conservation laws.* Springer, Springer Berlin Heidelberg, 1998.

[109] B. Solenthaler and R. Pajarola. Predictive-corrective incompressible SPH. *ACM Transactions on Graphics*, 28(3):1–6, 2009.

[110] O.-Y. Song, H. Shin, and H.-S. Ko. Stable but non-dissipative water. *ACM Transactions on Graphics*, 24(1):81–97, 2005.

[111] M. Souli, A. Ouahsine, and L. Lewin. Ale formulation for fluid–structure interaction problems. *Computer Methods in Applied Mechanics and Engineering*, 190(5):659–675, 2000.

[112] J. Stam. Stable fluids. *Computer Graphics Proceedings of the ACM SIGGRAPH '99*, 33(Annual Conference Series):121–128, 1999.

[113] A. Staniforth and J. Côté. Semi-Lagrangian integration schemes for atmospheric models—A review. *Monthly Weather Review*, 119:2206–2223, 1991.

[114] B. Stroustrup. C++11—The new ISO C++ standard. 2015. Available at http://www.stroustrup.com/C++11FAQ.html. Accessed on August 30, 2016.

[115] J. Tessendorf. Simulating ocean water. *Simulating Nature: Realistic and Interactive Techniques, SIGGRAPH*, 1(2):5, 2001.

[116] J. F. Thompson. Grid generation techniques in computational fluid dynamics. *AIAA Journal*, 22(11):1505–1523, 1984.

[117] A. M. Turing. Rounding-off errors in matrix processes. *The Quarterly Journal of Mechanics and Applied Mathematics*, 1(1):287–308, 1948.

[118] S. Van Der Walt, S. C. Colbert, and G. Varoquaux. The numpy array: A structure for efficient numerical computation. *Computing in Science & Engineering*, 13(2):22–30, 2011.

[119] E. W. Weisstein. Coordinate system. Available at http://mathworld.wolfram.com/CoordinateSystem.html. Accessed on August 30, 2016.

[120] C. Wojtan, M. Müller-Fischer, and T. Brochu. Liquid simulation with mesh-based surface tracking. In *ACM SIGGRAPH 2011 Courses*, page 8, ACM, 2011.

[121] J.-C. Yoon, H. R. Kam, J.-M. Hong, S. J. Kang, and C.-H. Kim. Procedural synthesis using vortex particle method for fluid simulation. *Computer Graphics Forum*, 28(7):1853–1859, 2009.

[122] J. Yu and G. Turk. Reconstructing surfaces of particle-based fluids using anisotropic kernels. *ACM Transactions on Graphics*, 32(1):5, 2013.

[123] Y. Yu and L. Shi. Visual smoke simulation with adaptive octree refinement. In *Proceedings of IASTED International Conference on Computer Graphics and Imaging, Kauai, Hawaii, USA*, pages 13–19, 2004.

[124] H. Zhao. A fast sweeping method for eikonal equations. *Mathematics of Computation*, 74(250):603–627, 2005.

[125] H. Zhao. Parallel implementations of the fast sweeping method. *Journal of Computational Mathematics*, 25(4):421, 2007.

[126] B. Zhu, W. Lu, M. Cong, B. Kim, and R. Fedkiw. A new grid structure for domain extension. *ACM Transactions on Graphics*, 32(4):63, 2013.

[127] Y. Zhu and R. Bridson. Animating sand as a fluid. *ACM Transactions on Graphics*, 24(3):965–972, 2005.

Index